DATE DUE

AUG 1 7 2004	

GAYLORD · PRINTED IN U.S.A.

The Iranian Revolution Then and Now

Indicators of Regime Instability

Dariush Zahedi

Westview PRESS

A Member of the Perseus Books Group

To my mother and the memory of my father

Copyright © 2000 by Westview Press, A Member of the Perseus Books Group

First published in 2000 in the United States of America by Westview Press, 5500 Central Avenue, Boulder, Colorado 80301-2877, and in the United Kingdom by Westview Press, 12 Hid's Copse Road, Cumnor Hill, Oxford OX2 9JJ

Published in paperback 2001.

Find us on the World Wide Web at www.westviewpress.com

Cataloging-in-Publication Data on file with the Library of Congress
ISBN 0-8133-3871-9 (pbk)

The paper used in this publication meets the requirements of the American National Standard for Permanence of Paper for Printed Library Materials Z39.48-1984.

PERSEUS
POD
ON DEMAND   10   9   8   7   6   5   4   3   2   1

Contents

Acknowledgments

I would like to extend my profound gratitude to the following individuals for their unwavering support and wise guidance: Thomas Greene, Ahmad Ghoreishi, Laurie Brand, Joseph Nyomarkay, Roy Mottahedeh, Huchang Chehabi, Habib Ladjevardi, and George Lenczowski. The merits of this work, if indeed there are any, should be directly attributed to their counsel. I, however, am entirely responsible for its defects.

Dariush Zahedi

1

Introduction

If violence is the father of every great upheaval, its mother is illusion. The belief which is always reborn in every great and decisive historical struggle is that this is the last fight, that after this struggle all poverty, all suffering, all oppression will be a thing of the past.

—*Franz Borkenau, "State and Revolution in the Paris Commune, the Russian Civil War, and the Spanish Civil War"[1]*

One of the most important distinguishing features of the 1979 Iranian revolution was its comparatively enormous popular base. According to the estimations of analysts who were closely monitoring the Iranian political scene during the revolutionary process, about 8 million people, approximately one-fifth of the entire Iranian population at the time, demonstrated against the still-formidable regime of Mohammad Reza Shah Pahlavi on a religious holiday in December 1978 (Cottam, 1990, p. 3). However, soon after the triumph of the revolution, when it became evident that the forces associated with Ayatollah Ruhollah Khomeini had clearly gained ascendancy in the postrevolutionary power struggle, the grand coalition that had managed to topple the shah's regime began to crumble. As a result, active support for the new regime dwindled to a highly committed core base. Composed of a proportion of the clerical establishment, the urban poor, and the lower middle class, this support enabled the regime to consolidate its power.

What is noteworthy about the recent history of the Islamic Republic is the continued corrosion in both the scale and scope of social support for the regime. Iran at the end of the twentieth century is a land of dashed hopes. More than twenty years after its inception, the theocracy is in grave trouble. Disillusioned, disgruntled, and destitute, Iranians in increasing numbers, including those who at one point constituted the revolution's most ardent supporters, have come to assume negative attitudes toward the disappointing outcome of "the greatest populist revolution in human history" (Cottam, quoted in Laipson, Sick, and Cottam, 1995, p. 10).

In an interview with a German newspaper shortly before his death in January 1995, Mehdi Bazargan, Iran's first postrevolution prime minister, asserted that the theocracy had the support of less than 5 percent of the populace (Sanger, 1995). Similarly, a veteran Iran expert, citing anecdotal evidence, recently estimated that not more than 1.5 to 15 percent of the population can be regarded as supporters of the regime (Laipson, Sick, and Cottam, 1995, p. 10). In Iran's most recent presidential election held in May 1997, an astounding 70 percent of the country's electorate voted for Mohammad Khatami, a former culture minister who had been sacked from his position because of his tolerant views and liberal interpretation of Islam. Khatami, who was viewed suspiciously by many of the most powerful figures in the Islamic republic, achieved his landslide victory because of the fact that many of the theocracy's ruling clerics, including Ayatollah Seyyed Ali Khamenei, Iran's supreme leader, had made their support for his archrival abundantly clear. Khatami thus came to be widely regarded, in a manner that neither he nor those who anointed him had anticipated, as the antiestablishment candidate. Khatami's triumph, therefore, may be interpreted as a resounding protest vote against the prevailing order.

Both before and after his inauguration in August 1997, Khatami has consistently emphasized his desire to institutionalize the rule of law, curb the theocracy's irksome (social and private) restrictions, and promote the establishment of a vibrant civil society. He has even been able to take some, albeit tentative, steps toward the realization of his vision. His efforts, however, have been continually resisted, and in some instances reversed, by the president's powerful conservative rivals, who control most of the nation's levers of power. Underscoring their desire for meaningful change and liberalization, Iranians nonetheless continue to be overwhelmingly supportive of Khatami and his vision. Responding to an opinion poll conducted by the Islamic Republic's news agency (IRNA) on the first anniversary of Khatami's May 1997 landslide victory, a staggering 75 percent of the nation's populace once again expressed continued support for the president ("Reformists Score Points as Iran Marks Two Decades of Revolution," 1999). In February 1999, proreform candidates associated with President Khatami captured approximately 80 percent of the ballots cast in nationwide elections for municipal councils (a provision of the Constitution that had up to then not been implemented), with 24 million of the 39 eligible voters going to the polls (Abdo, 1999b, p. 9). In what was widely regarded as an expression of popular dismay toward the politically dominant conservative faction, which has doggedly resisted reforms, Abdullah Nouri emerged as the top winner in Tehran. Nouri served as Khatami's minister of interior until June 1998, when he was impeached by the conservative-dominated Parliament. The conservative members of Parliament disapproved strongly of Nouri's "liberal" interpretation of the Constitution as well as his proclivity to authorize proreform rallies. Subsequently, Nouri was physically assaulted by Hezbollahi zealots in September 1998, and he was imprisoned in November 1999 because the newspaper that he directed had published articles that many from the conservative establishment considered deleterious to the system ("Iran: Reforming Win," 1999, p. 42). In February 2000, more than 80 percent of Iran's young and politically awakened electorate went to the polls and provided the reformist camp associated with Khatami with the majority of the seats in Parliament. In explaining the delegitimization of the ongoing system, primary weight is generally accorded to the ruling clerics' gross ineptitude in managing the Iranian economy, their repressiveness, and the blatant abuse, on the part of many in their ranks, of their power and privileges.

The Disintegration of the Iranian Revolution

Initially, the revolutionaries pledged to reverse the course of dependent economic development—favoring economic growth and rewarding a few well-connected families—pursued by the Pahlavi regime. Instead, they promised to create an economically developed and independent Iran in which the fruits of economic growth and prosperity were to be combined with equity and social justice. Civil liberties as well as the right of citizens to petition their government through the formation of voluntary associations and political parties were to be assured. Above all, however, both government and society were to become morally uplifted through piety and strict compliance with the dictates of Islam.

Socioeconomic Crises

In fact, precisely the reverse has occurred. The revolutionaries have reneged on all of their promises. Economic independence and prosperity have proved elusive, as the faction-ridden clerics have been unable to agree on what constitutes a viable "Islamic" economic system. A bloated and corrupt public sector, a climate of political uncertainty, and an apparent lack of direction have undermined confidence. As a result, investors—domestic and foreign—have largely refrained from risking their money in the Iranian market. The decline in the price of oil and Iran's massive debt burden have further damaged the economy. In the last few years, there have been seven major spontaneous riots over spiraling prices and appalling living conditions.

Shortly after the revolution, in search of self-sufficiency, the Iranian government nationalized a vast proportion of Iran's large-scale industries, as well as banking and insurance. Some of these businesses were appropriated by the government itself, while others were entrusted to largely autonomous, parastate "foundations" (Karshenas and Pesaran, 1995). The foundations have since amassed great power, operating largely above the law. Enjoying extensive access to the cheapest exchange rates, they have been able to monopolize many industries. Their practices have had the effect of compromising efficiency, discouraging competition, and undermining confidence. They have also contributed to the mushrooming of bureaucracy.

The number of individuals currently employed by government and quasi-governmental sectors has nearly tripled since the shah's era (from 800,000 in

1977–1978 to 2 million in 1992–1993). "According to the Organization of Employment Affairs, the productive labor of each government employee is less than one hour per day" (Ehsani, 1994, p. 21). Jealous of its enormous power and prerogatives, the bureaucracy was instrumental in derailing President Ali Akbar Hashemi Rafsanjani's initiatives toward economic rationalization and privatization.

Iran's efforts to attract investments (themselves a tacit abandonment of Ayatollah Ruhollah Khomeini's goal of independence from the West) are also impeded by Iran's image abroad, which has been tarnished by the assassination of opposition figures overseas, Khomeini's religious decree in 1989 sanctioning the death of Salman Rushdie (the British author of *The Satanic Verses*), and Iran's rejection of the Arab-Israeli peace process (Ehsani, 1994, p. 18). Moreover, many investors are wary of committing resources to "an unstable country with a government that has been in an undeclared state of war with the world's premier power" (Shirley, 1993, p. 107). As a result, most of Iran's trading partners, including the United States prior to the initiation of President Clinton's unilateral trade embargo in 1995, have been prepared to trade with Iran only on the basis of cash or short-term credit, refraining from large-scale investment (barring the capital-intensive and relatively secure oil and gas sectors).

Underlying Iran's economic deterioration has been the country's exploding population. In the course of the last twenty years, Iran's population has nearly doubled, reaching 64 million people, some 30 million more than at the end of the shah's rule. Iran's population explosion was ignited immediately after the revolution by the clerical elites' reintroduction of child marriages and discouragement of contraception (Hoodfar, 1994; Zonis, 1993). During the Iran-Iraq war, Ayatollah Khomeini encouraged Iranians to beget as many children as possible. Iran's increased population, Khomeini reasoned, would strengthen the country, providing it with more soldiers to become martyrs in Iran's holy war against the infidel armies of Saddam Hussein as well as in its struggle against the "world-devouring" United States. Subsequently becoming aware of the potentially devastating political ramifications of a rapidly expanding population, the Iranian government "issued a national birth control policy, which Ayatollah Khomeini ratified shortly before his death in 1989" (Hoodfar, 1994, p. 12). Partly due to this policy, but due even more to declining standards of living, the population growth rate was reduced from 3.2 percent in the 1980s to 2.3 percent in the early 1990s (Ehsani, 1994, p. 19). (According to some commentators, by the mid-1990s, the growth rate dropped further, to 1.8 percent [Ehteshami, 1995, p. 115].)

Iran's population explosion, however, has already taken its toll, and it is likely to present the regime with even more devastating consequences in the future. Largely concentrated in the country's urban centers, a large proportion of Iran's expanding population has joined the ranks of the dispossessed. Shortages and the failure of the government to meet fundamental needs have, as noted, sparked several spontaneous uprisings. The unemployment rate for those aged fifteen to twenty-four is twice the national average, which currently hovers around 30 percent. According to one estimate, among those who are fortunate enough to work, underemployment has climbed to 75 percent, while inflation on basic items now fluctuates from 40 to 200 percent. The unemployment and underemployment figures are likely to deteriorate in the future, inasmuch as the economy, even were it to undergo a miraculous recovery, would be hard-pressed to accommodate the huge pool of individuals seeking gainful employment or higher education. At present, about one-half of Iran's population is under fifteen, and a colossal 70 percent is under thirty. Even today, less than one-tenth of those who want to attend university are able to do so.[2]

The mismanagement of the Iranian economy, the population explosion, and the enormous cost of the devastating Iran-Iraq war ($650 billion, according to a conservative estimate) have pauperized Iran's population (Amirahmadi, 1992, pp. 260–262). Average per capita income in Iran today is only one-fourth of what it was in 1979, the year in which the Islamic Republic was established. Foreign diplomats stationed in Tehran estimate that close to 60 percent of Iranians live below the poverty line. Rather than combining prosperity with social justice, the revolution has resulted in the maximization of wealth and power for the few. The latest figures put out by the regime itself indicate that the collective income of the wealthiest 10 percent of Iran's population is 27.3 times greater than that of the poorest 10 percent. These figures indicate that the income disparity between rich and poor in Iran is twice the average for underdeveloped nations.[3] This is an especially abysmal record for a regime whose "pivotal claim has been that it speaks for the 'powerless' or 'disinherited' of the whole world, not merely of Iran or even the Muslim world" (Ramazani, 1989, p. 166).

The impoverishment of the Iranian populace has been accelerated recently by the plummeting of Iran's oil revenues and, in turn, the ballooning of its debt. After the conclusion of its war with Iraq, which it nearly lost outright, Iran began to borrow heavily overseas in order to finance hitherto neglected infrastructure projects and to import customer goods. The consumer imports, designed to placate the public after the chronic shortages of the war, were financed by short-term letters of credit, which came due just as the nation's oil revenues fell off (*Economist*, July 26, 1994).

Iran's foreign debt was recently officially estimated to stand at $32 billion, most of which is owed to Japanese and European firms ("Country Report: Iran," 1995, p. 23). About $12 billion of this debt came due in 1995; Iran, lacking the resources to pay, was forced to refinance. However, U.S. pressure prevented Iran from arranging multilateral rescheduling through the Paris Club of Bankers. Consequently, Iran had to negotiate nineteen separate debt agreements (Waldman, 1995). This burden has had lamentable implications for Iran's fragile economy. Iran was obliged to repay $4.5 billion in 1996 (one-third of its projected oil revenue) and $7 billion in 1997 (one-half of its oil revenue).

Compounding Iran's numerous economic problems is the decline in the value of the dollar. Iran receives about 85 percent of its foreign-exchange earnings from its oil, which is sold in dollars.[4] However, the dollar has lost about 25 percent of its value since 1994. As a result of this drop, offset by only a small rise in oil prices in the same period, oil-producing nations are now losing 20 percent of potential revenue (*Middle East Economic Digest,* 1995, p. 16). This situation is especially burdensome for Iran, since most of its debt is owed to Germany and Japan, two nations whose currencies have appreciated the most against the dollar.

Meanwhile, Iran is obliged to spend at least $2 billion a year for the next five years to improve and expand its oil fields, 88 percent of which have already passed their peak (Ehsani, 1994, p. 21; *Iran Times,* May 26, 1995). Prerevolution-ary production was almost twice its present level. Back then, Iran's average daily oil production was 5.5 million barrels a day, 500,000 barrels of which were con-sumed domestically and the remainder exported. Today, the nation produces ap-proximately 3.5 million barrels of oil per day, of which roughly 1.5 million bar-rels are consumed domestically (Mossavar-Rahmani, 1999, p. 32). At the same time, Iran's per capita oil income (which composes 85 percent of the country's export earnings) has plummeted from $1,300 during the final years of the shah's rule to less than $200 today (Amirahmadi, 1999, p. 88). It is especially important for Iran to invest in its oil-extraction capacity and to reduce its domestic con-sumption, for at current levels, domestic requirements will leave nothing for ex-ports by the end of 2010 ("An Economy in Disarray," 1994, p. 29).

Political Oppression

The disappointment in the political realm has been just as devastating. Civil lib-erties have been trampled upon, and the murder of political dissidents both in-side and outside the country has continued ("The Connection: An Exclusive Look at How Iran Hunts Down Its Opponents Abroad," 1994). Strict official cen-sorship has been imposed on domestic publications, broadcasts, and movies, and effective measures have been introduced to encourage self-censorship. The initial constitutional right of free expression has been amended to require the media to "enjoin the good and forbid the evil." This vague law has been abused by the regime to arbitrarily intimidate, harass, or imprison those whose activities and pronouncements are deemed to be "un-Islamic." Since January 1995, numerous publications have been shut down by the government, while several others have been forced to cease operating because the subsidies for paper accorded to them have suddenly been revoked (Wright, 1996, p. 171).

The former director of the American CIA, John Deutsche, recently asserted that since 1989, the Iranian regime has "murdered at least 48 [of its] opponents abroad" ("Tehran May Become More Aggressive," 1996, p. 15). In December 1995, a United Nations panel voted to condemn Iran's human rights compliance. In condemning Iran, the UN resolution cited the following factors as particularly reprehensible: "the high number of executions, cases of torture and cruel, inhu-man or degrading treatment or punishment . . . lack of adequate protection for religious minorities . . . excessive force in suppressing demonstrations, restrictions on the freedom of expression, thought, opinion and the press and widespread discrimination against women" ("UN Panel Knocks Iran Human Rights," 1995, p. 15).

In a relevant report, the UN Human Rights Commission has estimated the number of Iran's political prisoners as standing at 19,000, suggesting that the Islamic Republic is one of the most repressive regimes in the world (Teimourian, 1994, p. 70).

Although the formation of political parties is sanctioned by the regime's constitution, political groupings perceived as being even vaguely noncompliant have effectively been banned or prevented from functioning effectively. In Iran's parliamentary elections held in March 1996, four in ten aspiring candidates were removed from the ballot by the Council of Guardians, which has arrogated onto itself the power to, among other things, evaluate the Islamic credentials of office seekers (Jehl, 1996). Relatedly, only four out of the 238 candidates who had expressed interest in standing for Iran's 1997 presidential election were allowed by the council to take part in the contest. Labor unions have also been severely curtailed and voluntary associations brought under close supervision.

Pervasive Corruption

What of the Islamic revolutionaries' promise to create a virtuous citizenry, morally uplifted through compliance with Islamic principles? Venality is universally believed to be far more widely dispersed in both the public and private sectors today than it was under the shah's regime. Because the deplorable condition of the Iranian economy has made it increasingly difficult for people to make ends meet, functionaries from middle- and lower-ranking echelons have more often come to emulate many of their masters, taking to bribery and influence peddling to augment their scant incomes. Little, it seems, can be accomplished in Iran without bribing a bureaucrat; conversely, much can be achieved when the correct amount is paid to an appropriate authority. "Even the Revolutionary Guards who run the morality-enforcing Komitehs can be bought" (Marlowe, 1995, p. 42). Although this is understandable (in some societies it is even customary and can serve as a stabilizing influence), the main corruption problem in the Islamic Republic is not the low-level, albeit widespread, bureaucratic bribery; the gravest damage is being done at the top, by the powerful and the esteemed.

In 1998, the son of General Mohsen Rezai, the longest-serving commander of Iran's Revolutionary Guard Corps (who retired—or was purportedly pressured to retire—shortly after President Khatami's inauguration in 1997 because he had publicly endorsed Khatami's conservative archrival, Nategh Nouri, in the presidential election), defected to the United States. Rezai's son justified his defection on the basis of his revulsion to the exceptionally high degree of venality under the Islamic regime. He even accused Iran's supreme leader, Seyyed Ali Khamenei, and the sons of former president Rafsanjani of amassing great fortunes through corrupt and illegitimate means ("General Rezai's Son Defects to the U.S.," 1998). Recently, even President Rafsanjani acknowledged that "a total of 106 cases of corruption were uncovered in the past six months [of 1993] including sums exceeding $1.5 billion in 13 government departments, nine state banks, two government-owned insurance companies, and seven universities and research centers" (Banuazizi, 1994).[5] Among these cases was the country's biggest corruption scandal since the Islamic revolution. This episode involved eight officials, including Morteza Rafighdoost, whose brother, Mohsen Rafighdoost, was the former leader of the Revolutionary Guards (IRGC) and the head of Iran's largest conglomerate, the Foundation of the Oppressed. The officials were tried for and found guilty of manipulating approximately $400 million in a state-owned bank and of stealing some $30 million. Rafighdoost's involvement verifies suspicions that corruption has become extremely widespread among the nation's ruling elite.

Such depravity on the part of the mullahs and their associates, whose piety and selfless devotion to Islam had generally been taken for granted, has severely undermined their once irreproachable authority. As Walter Laquer explained in regard to the former Soviet Union, "The fundamental problem is not so much corruption per se as the enormous disparity between the profession of honesty and social justice and the real state of affairs" (Laquer, 1994, p. 62). Disillusionment is particularly acute inasmuch as Khomeini's had been essentially a moral revolution, a return to Islamic ideals.

The Research Question: Is Iran Ripe for Another Revolution?

Iran's socioeconomic and moral crises have resulted in the progressive alienation of much of the nation's significant social forces from the theocratic regime: "The bottom line is that the vast majority of Iranians are much worse off after seventeen years of theocratic rule than they were during the Shah's era" (Wright, 1996, p. 164). The existential privations and deprivations confronting the Iranian populace today raise a puzzle worthy of exploration. What is the likelihood that the Iranian state apparatus will remain immune from the "mounting social, [political] and economic problems confronting [the country]?" (Dekmejian, 1995, p. 218). The puzzle is all the more intriguing in light of Iran's tumultuous history. In examining the patterns of Iran's social movements over the course of the last hundred years, John Foran (1994a) detected six rebellions or revolutionary attempts, including one successful revolution, two successful coups d'état, and two unsuccessful autonomy movements. It should be remembered that as recently as 1979, Iranians proved themselves capable of "demonstrating their performance-related grievances in the form of a revolution" (Haghayeghi, 1993, p. 50).

It should also be noted that some of the prevalent objective circumstances in prerevolutionary Iran were less conducive to a successful revolutionary transfer of power than Iran's present situation. Contrary to Theda Skocpol's (1979) prognostications, the Iranian revolution occurred in an affluent and powerful state that had undergone no significant financial or international crises (Keddie, 1995b). Up to the very end, the shah retained not only the support of the United States but also that of the Soviet Union and China. In contrast, Iran today is bereft of influential and reliable allies. It has also engaged in, and has nearly lost, a devastating eight-year war with Iraq. Although the shah's regime did experience a minor financial crunch in the three years prior to the revolution, the present regime has, as noted, been recently experiencing a far more severe economic downturn.

Moreover, there are some striking parallels between the dynamics presently operative in Iran and the processes that contributed to the demise of Communist regimes in Eastern Europe and the Soviet Union. Economic stagnation in the face of transparent duplicity by an entrenched priviligentsia combined "with a deterioration of international standing and the growing awareness among large sectors of the population of the sharp contradictions between the bases of legitimation and actual performance" (Eisenstadt, 1992, p. 22) are remarkably reminiscent of what transpired in Communist regimes.

This study, then, will endeavor to assess the Islamic Republic's potential for revolution by analyzing the country's present situation in light of conditions that help to bring about or deflect revolutionary transfers of power. The term "potential" is deliberately chosen to underscore Thomas H. Greene's point that "revolution requires categories that can be answered with 'more' or 'less' helping to clarify our research problems in terms of degree instead of clouding them with the illusion of finality" (1990, p. 15). The study will seek to accomplish its objective through an in-depth, theoretically informed, comparative analysis of present-day and prerevolutionary Iran. The theory, along with the hypotheses deduced from it, will be composed through a careful integration of the relevant aspects of the cultural, structural, leadership, and resource mobilization theories of revolution. What are deemed to be the theoretically significant implications of the vast literature on Iran's revolution will also be incorporated and applied to Iran's present situation. The analytical framework will serve to structure the analysis and determine which factors will form the basis of the comparison to be conducted.

There are numerous, at times contradictory, studies on the processes and particularly the various causes of the Iranian revolution. There are also many, though far less numerous, studies on the specific aspects of the outcome of the revolution. But I know of no other in-depth analysis that devises a conceptual scheme that draws on both types of studies to assess the likelihood of another regime change in Iran.

It is the contention of this study that the revolutionary obliteration of an existing regime generally results from the convergence of two sets of interrelated variables: the regime's internal defects and vulnerabilities and the coordinated actions of the social groups and individuals opposed to it. This study identifies two "ideal-typical" forms of revolutionary change (collapses and overthrows). In the past, some regimes have fallen with minimal coordinated, prolonged, and purposive popular endeavor (collapse). Others, however, although fragile, would not have been destroyed without the concerted pressures and demands placed upon them from within civil society (overthrow). The 1979 Iranian revolution clearly belongs to the latter case. Based on the analyses presented in this study, prospects for the overthrow of the Islamic Republic are currently low. I will argue that the differences between present-day and prerevolutionary Iran in terms of key political variables (namely, the nature of the regime and the opposition, the patterns of between-group and within-group support for and opposition to the regime, and the qualities of regime and antiregime leadership), which shall shortly be elaborated and thoroughly analyzed, are in large measure responsible for the prevalent low vulnerability of the regime to being overthrown.

However, chances for the obliteration or modification of the prevailing order, because of debilitating factional rivalries and confrontations, are moderate. And they are likely to increase if the prevailing intra-elite cleavages, which have become increasingly frequent and open, acquire greater depth and become more pronounced. The regime is then likely to tear itself apart from above, paving the way for uncoordinated popular uprisings, a possible military takeover, or even civil war. Under such circumstances, the repressive apparatus will come to play an inordinately important role. Whichever group or individual receives the backing of the armed forces would be able to exert dominion over the ship of state and direct it in accordance to its vision of the just order. Since "many of the phenomena to which the Iranian revolution is often attributed [exist] . . . in at least as strong a form" (Keddie, 1995a, p. 7) in present-day Iran, the comparative approach will sharpen our understanding of Iran's current revolutionary potential, and perhaps revolutionary potential in general, by bringing into focus the variations between the two eras.

Methodology: Juxtaposing and Comparing

Machiavelli believed that "he who diligently examines past events foresees future ones" and "can apply to them the remedies used by the ancients" (quoted in Skinner, 1992, p. 59). Accordingly, Machiavelli sets out in the *Discourses* to discover the causes behind the Roman republic's greatness so that they may be replicated in his own and future times. Machiavelli may be overstating the degree to which we can foresee future events. But a careful analysis of past events may help to narrow the range of possible events, enabling us to better anticipate the likelihood of future occurrences. Alexis de Tocqueville puts it best when he declares:

> [T]he human mind may succeed in tracing a wide circle, as it were, which includes the future; but within that circle chance [unforeseen and unpredictable factors, individual actions, and events] rules, and eludes all our foresight. In every picture of the

future there is a dim spot which the eye of the understanding cannot penetrate. (de Tocqueville, quoted in Zetterbaum, 1967, pp. 9–10)

To diminish the size of the dim spot surrounding the prospects for regime change in Iran, this study will utilize what John Stuart Mill (Skocpol and Somers, 1980) referred to as the method of difference.[6] Labeling it the comparative method, Arend Lijphart (1988), has recently provided the most systematic explanation of the dynamics of this method. According to Lijphart, focusing on comparable cases (meaning cases that are similar in a large number of important characteristics but dissimilar in regard to variables about which relations are hypothesized) affords the researcher the opportunity to achieve a significant degree of control by keeping the secondary variables, as much as possible, constant. In what follows, the preconditions of the successful Iranian revolution of 1979 will be compared to Iran's present condition, in which a revolutionary movement has not, as yet, arisen. The differences in the dispositions of selected variables will be judged to account for the present system's revolutionary potential. The greater the differences in the configuration of the variables, the lower the present system's revolutionary potential.

The longitudinal intra-unit comparison of present-day with prerevolutionary Iran enables us to come "as close to a controlled comparison" as possible (Skocpol, 1994c, p. 319). As H. Eulau has observed, "[I]f 'control' is the sine qua non of all scientific procedure, it would certainly seem easier to obtain in a single culture" (quoted in Lijphart, 1988, p. 62). Keeping the important cultural, linguistic, and religious variables constant would allow us to better examine the fluctuation in other variables (Dogan and Pelassy, 1990). In this regard, the comparative method is "just as essential in bringing out the unique as to establish the similar" (Rustow, 1970, p. 11).

Moreover, concentrating on two cases has the added advantage of making it possible for us to conduct a thorough and intensive examination of both cases. It also allows for "an agile weaving back and forth between the cases," helping to enhance our "insight into each concrete case through contrast" (Foran, 1995, 121).

Chapter 2 will, after conducting a critical evaluation of the concept and theories of revolution, attempt to synthesize a flexible, nontautological framework for explicating and assessing the likelihood of revolutions. Chapters 3–6 will compare present-day and prerevolutionary Iran on the basis of this framework. Chapters 3 and 4 will focus on the social underpinnings of the monarchy versus the theocracy, examining the patterns of social-group support for and discontentment with each regime. Chapter 5 will scrutinize and compare today's oppositional forces with those operating in the prerevolutionary era. The task will be to explain how and why the multiplicity of contradictory opposition groups, representing the nation's social classes, were able to coalesce then and to assess the prospects for their cohesion now. Chapter 6 will contrast the nature and leadership qualities of the present and previous regimes.

Chapter 7 will integrate and analyze the results of the comparisons conducted in the previous chapters. After explicating why the prevailing circumstances do not pose a threat to the continued existence of the Islamic regime, this chapter will suggest what changes in the configuration of variables considered salient in this framework are likely to result in the creation of a truly revolutionary situation in Iran.

Notes

1. Published in *Sociological Review* 29 (January 1937), quoted in Walt (1992), p. 340, n. 65.

2. Unemployment, inflation, and population figures in Wright (1996) appear on pp. 163–165; in Cordesman (1994), on p. 24. For university attendance, see Banuazizi (1994), p. 6.

3. For average per capita income in Marlowe (1995), see p. 43. The statistics put out by the regime on income disparity are cited in "Iran's Richest Are Still Richer Than Most Rich," *Iran Times*, March 1, 1996, p. 15. For the diplomats' estimate of Iran's poverty rate, see Wright (1996), p. 164.

4. Currently, Iran's "per capita oil income in real terms is about one-fourth of what it was in the two years before the Iranian revolution" (Sanger, 1995).

5. Banuazizi is quoting Al-Sharq al-wasat (London, January 8, 1994). One analyst, speaking only partly in jest, echoed the feelings of most Iranians when he recently observed that "now there [is] only one grand ayatollah in Iran, 'Ayatollah Dollar.'" Quoted (without attribution) in F. Halliday (1994).

6. For a summary of Mill's method of difference as well as his method of agreement, see Skocpol and Somers (1980), pp. 183–184.

2

The Problem of Revolution

It is the contention of this study that none of the approaches in the plethora of theoretical literature on revolutions and revolutionary movements is, by itself, sufficient to account for either the Iranian revolution of 1979 or the present regime's potential for revolution. Before enumerating the fundamental flaws and strengths of existing theories and attempting to synthesize yet another "eclectic" theoretical framework, it is appropriate to reflect on the nature, causes, and possible solubility of some of the most tenacious problems involved in theorizing about the complex concept of revolution. If, as this chapter will attempt to show, revolutions are not "singular phenomena for which it is possible to state a single invariant set of necessary conditions, sufficient conditions, and internal sequences" (Tilly, 1992, p. 1084), then we cannot reasonably hope to ever be able to generate a universally applicable theory of revolution. An awareness of the variety and variability of revolutions will also go a long way toward explaining why there are more theories of revolution than the cases they purport to explain.

Comprehending the difficulty of theorizing about a society's potential for revolution is bound to be a sobering experience. But such inquiry can also serve to illuminate research in political change by forcing us to concede that the acquisition of an invariant theoretical understanding about revolution is, in all likelihood, unattainable. To know thyself, according to Socrates, is the beginning of wisdom. Although directed toward individuals, this generalization can apply, with equal force, to different fields of inquiry, including the study of revolutionary potential. Fully cognizant of our insoluble limitations, we can, instead of expending effort in pursuit of an elusive objective, concentrate on remedying our surmountable weaknesses. Accordingly, this chapter will first present an examination of the difficulties inherent in theorizing about revolutions. It will then utilize this analysis as a point of departure for constructing a flexible framework that can serve as a tool for explaining and projecting revolutionary phenomena. A key distinguishing feature of this framework will be its attempt to incorporate the assertion that a multiplicity of differing preconditions can be associated with the development of revolutions within its purview.

What Is Revolution?

In his relatively recent book, *Revolution*, written for the purpose of summarizing and categorizing what he regards as the most important theories of revolution and civil violence, Michael Kimmel (1990) reviews more than thirty theories in detail and examines at least a dozen more in passing. Such regrettable overabundance of theoretical literature is itself a good indication of our minuscule comprehension of revolutionary phenomena. It is also a sad commentary on the field's capacity for theory development.

It is often argued that in addition to our inability to replicate and control for extraneous variables (Greene, 1990, pp. 8–10), we are in part hamstrung in our endeavor to theorize about revolution because revolutions, unlike the phenomena studied in the natural sciences, are defined not naturally, but subjectively (Taylor, 1984, p. 152). Bereft of objective existence, the term "revolution" is a mental construct (Calvert, 1990, p. 23). Consequently, it has come to mean different things to different people. According to Mohsen Milani (1994), one of the foremost scholars of the Iranian revolution, "[T]oday few other words in the lexicon of social sciences are more ubiquitously and loosely used than the term 'revolution,' a reflection of the preparadigmatic stage of the study of revolution" (Milani, 1994, p. 9). The implication, as Harry Eckstein (1992) explained in regard to political development, is that "if a concept is encumbered with many meanings, theories using it also will vary alarmingly because they are not about the same thing" (Eckstein, 1992, p. 230). Expressing a similar sentiment, Rod Aya has not so much emphasized the need for precise definitions, which "are neither right nor wrong" (Aya, 1984, p. 322) (meaning that they are only useful to the extent that they enhance our comprehension of the term), as he has lamented the failure to draw sharp and "adequate distinctions [between revolution and other types of regime change, which] . . . slow solving problems of explanation. Hence, though we need not define, we must often distinguish" (Aya, 1984, p. 323; see also Selbin, 1993, p. 5).

Taking issue with the above argument, I shall attempt to show that although there is no consensus among scholars on how the abstract concept of revolution ought to be defined, their definitions of revolution have far more in common than their interpretations of the factors that produce it. As will subsequently be seen, it is conceivable to propose a definition of revolution agreeable to both the less dogmatically inclined structuralists (who, according to their chief exponent Theda Skocpol, emphasize "objective relationships and conflicts among variously situated groups and nations, rather than interests, outlooks or ideologies" [Skocpol, 1979, p. 291]) and the "subjectivists" (who, while generally not discounting the importance of objective variables and the vulnerabilities of the state, view revolution as both voluntary and purposive). Most analysts are also careful to distinguish revolution from other processes through which regimes are challenged, altered, or modified. Consequently, our disagreements in defining revolution should not be granted undue emphasis in explaining our inability to adequately account for it.

Skocpol regards revolution as:

> a rapid, basic transformation of a society's state and class structures . . . accompanied and in part carried through by class based revolts from below. Social revolutions are set apart from other sorts of conflicts and transformation processes above all by the combination of two coincidences: . . . societal structural change with class upheaval, and the coincidence of political with social transformation. (Skocpol, 1979, p. 7)

For Samuel Huntington, revolution is:

> a rapid, fundamental and violent domestic change in the dominant values and myths of a society, in its political institutions, social structure, leadership and government activity and policies. Revolutions are thus to be distinguished from insurrections, rebellions, revolts, coups, and wars of independence. (Huntington, 1968, p. 264)

Ekkart Zimmerman emphasizes the necessity of viewing revolution as "an outcome and not a goal." According to Zimmerman, "[A] revolution is the successful overthrow of the prevailing elite(s) by a new elite(s) who after having taken over power (which usually involves the use of considerable violence and the mobilization of masses) fundamentally change the social structure and therewith also the structure of authority" (1983, p. 298).

Although a firm believer in the intentionality of revolution, Selbin derives significant inspiration from Skocpol (1979, 1994a–d), whom he credits for having "reintroduced the element of process, which is missing from the definition proposed by Huntington" (Selbin, 1993, p. 10). Nonetheless, he chides her for not having considered the role of people in the revolutionary process. Selbin defines revolution as "the successful overthrow of a ruling elite by a revolutionary vanguard that has mobilized broad popular support and undertaken the transformation of a society's political, economic, and social structure in a contemporaneous and mutually reinforcing fashion" (Selbin, 1993, p. 11).

Charles Tilly considers revolution "to be a forcible transfer of power over a state in the course of which at least two distinct blocs of contenders make incompatible claims to control the state, and some significant portion of the population subject to the State's jurisdiction acquiesces in the claims of each bloc" (Tilly, 1993, p. 8).

Writing in the *Penguin Dictionary of Politics*, Jack Robertson advances a highly purposive definition of revolution:

> A revolution . . . properly so called, is a violent and total change in a political system which not only vastly alters the distribution of power in the society, but results in

major changes in the whole social structure. . . . In political science the primary
meaning must be the deliberate, intentional, and probably violent overthrow of one
ruling class by another which leads the mobilized masses against the existing system.
(quoted in Calvert, 1990, p. 3)

Finally, adopting an excessively restrictive position, Hannah Arendt declares
that only if "the liberation from oppression aims at least at the constitution of
freedom, can we speak of revolution" (Arendt, 1979, p. 4).

What is presented above is admittedly only a small sample of the enormous
number of definitions advanced in order to clarify the meaning of revolution.
However, other definitions, whether proposed by specialists on countries in
which revolutions have taken place or by experts on the topic of revolution, are
by and large variations on the same themes. A careful examination of the above
definitions makes it clear that explicit or implicit in almost all of them is the notion that a truly revolutionary transfer of power entails at least three components. First is the breakdown and obliteration of the old regime. The second
component involves the creation, by at least an element of the triumphant contending group, of a new political, social, and economic order, distinctly different
from the old. Finally, the new order must be endowed with some capacity to consolidate and perpetuate itself for a period of time.

All of the definitions cited above regard popular participation and mobilization
as an essential element in either the destruction of the old order or the creation of
the new order, or both. All definitions except that of Tilly (1978, 1993), assert that
revolutionary change must entail fundamental alterations in the organization of
both the society and polity. All definitions also imply that a sharp distinction
should be made between revolution and other forms of regime change, such as
coups and wars of national liberation. Lastly, none of the above definitions and
"very few [others] . . . appear to agree with Hannah Arendt's argument that revolution should be applied to those relatively infrequent and modern movements
that have extended the scope of human freedom" (Greene, 1990, p. 13).

Revolution, as it shall be defined in this study, is the obliteration of an established political system, in part due to popular uprisings, and its replacement by a
system essentially different from the previous one. Revolution is a process, and it
entails fundamental political, socioeconomic, and ideological transformations.
This conceptualization builds directly upon the points of agreement of existing
definitions. It strives to be value neutral and does not endeavor to define revolution on the basis of the application of moral principles to its outcome. Instead of
collapse or overthrow, the term "obliteration" is deliberately chosen. This selection is designed to placate both those structuralists who maintain with the aboli-
tionist Wendell Phillips that "revolutions are not made; they come" (quoted in
Wickham-Crowley, 1991, p. 151)[1] and the highly heterogeneous group of "subjectivists" who "endorse (sometimes implicitly) the theoretical position that revolutions occur because of the revolutionary intent of revolutionary actors"

(Wickham-Crowley, 1991, pp. 151–152).[2] But much more important, it intends to underscore the point that the issue of whether revolutions are ultimately purposefully made by the conscious actions of revolutionary leaders and incited masses or whether they are the unplanned consequences of prevailing objective inter- and intranational relations should be treated as a proposition to be tested rather than an assumption to be made.

The Variety of Revolutions

What is at issue here (are revolutions made or do they come?) has been described by Mark Hagopian as perhaps the most "vexsome question in the study of revolution" (1975, p. 177). Similarly, Timothy Wickham-Crowley has referred to this puzzle as one of "the most important unresolved issues in the study of revolution" (1991, p. 151). Such somber comments should sensitize us to the gravity of the question under consideration. And given the complexity and diversity of revolutionary situations and outcomes, they should make us ponder to what extent we will be able to supply a straightforward answer to this perplexing question.

We may reasonably be tempted to infer that the present dispute primarily concerns the first aspect of revolution, that is, the downfall and destruction of the old regime, discussed above. After all, successful and sustainable efforts at reconstructing state and society require, at a minimum, centrally directed and coordinated endeavors. "Without the concerted effort to remake society, an insurrection remains no more than an unconstitutional transfer of power" (Colburn, 1994, p. 6). But Skocpol (1979), who, particularly in her pre-1980 writings, was the most notable social scientist to advocate an entirely involuntary interpretation of revolution, maintained that in the classical revolutions she analyzed (France, Russia, and China), both state breakdown and the transformation of society resulted from objectively determined spontaneous actions of strategically placed social classes. Here, Sidney Hook's (1965) critique of Trotsky's interpretation of the Russian revolution can apply, with equal force, to Skocpol's (1979) argument: "It is as if Trotsky, after [demonstrating] that under certain conditions of cumulative strain and wear an old man must die, were to point to the same conditions as proof that a new life must be born" (Hook, 1965, p. 114).[3] As Greene has noted, "[B]y itself, spontaneity is incapable of effecting revolution*ary* change. The study of spontaneity . . . helps to demonstrate the essential role of organization in the realization of revolutionary goals" (1990, p. 88).

Indeed, recognizing the limitations of Skocpol's (1979) explanatory scheme, Jack Goldstone, Skocpol's former pupil, has undertaken an elaborate attempt to rectify his teacher's overly mechanistic framework. While agreeing with Skocpol that only objective structures (social, political, and international) and material causes are responsible for the genesis of revolution and state breakdown, he rejects her analysis of revolutionary outcomes. Instead, he asserts that the ideological inclinations of revolutionary leaders play a determining role in both the postrevolutionary power struggle and the rearrangement of society (Goldstone, 1991, 1995a, 1995b).

Even if Skocpol's involuntary explanatory scheme is incapable of adequately accounting for all components of revolutionary change, it may be able to illuminate the demise of the regimes she chose to analyze in her renowned book, *States and Social Revolutions* (1979). Indeed, the fact that Trotsky, "despite his misgivings about unorganized revolutionary activity, . . . grudgingly admitted that the February Revolution [1917] was largely a spontaneous event" (Greene, 1990, p. 89) strengthens our resolve to ascertain the theoretical foundations and possible applicability of Skocpol's generalizations to other cases.

Following de Tocqueville, Skocpol adopts a top-down (rather than a bottom-up)[4] view of revolution, stressing that the dismantling of the old regime starts at the top with the decay of the state structure. But whereas de Tocqueville had ingeniously combined both objective and subjective factors, stressing that structural defects and vulnerabilities of the state can produce revolution only if they are perceived as such by the populace (de Tocqueville, 1955, pp. 176–177; Kurzman, 1996, p. 153), Skocpol (1979) focuses only upon objective variables. Her dogged insistence on concentrating solely on material factors is more reminiscent of Marx, although she cannot be considered a Marxist because she is not primarily preoccupied with class conflict. Indeed, in explaining the causes of revolution, she accords greater weight to political rather than economic variables. Although not an economic determinist, she can surely be classified as a state structuralist (Kimmel, 1990). Indeed, the framework she advances in *States and Social Revolutions* is arguably even more deterministic than that of Marx, who had (in one of his less deterministic utterances) acknowledged that "[m]en make their own history, but they do not make it just as they please" (Marx, 1978, p. 595). Yet for Skocpol, "those who make the revolution are conspicuous by their absence" (Selbin, 1993, p. 11). Her working assumption appears to be not only that "orientations [cannot] mediate between social settings and political behavior" (Eckstein, 1972, p. 20) but that structures and objective circumstances predetermine people's actions.

Rather than concentrate on individual or mass distresses and disenchantment, then, Skocpol (1979) focuses on the state as well as its connections with domestic social classes and other states in the competitive transnational political economy. "In the first place, an adequate understanding of social revolutions requires that the analyst take a nonvoluntarist, structural perspective on their causes and processes" (p. 14). Skocpol regards the state as a "structure with a logic and interest of its own" (p. 24), distinct from economically dominant classes. To preserve and enhance its capabilities vis-à-vis internal groups and external competitors, the state seeks to extract revenue from society.

According to Skocpol, revolutions take place "only in countries situated in disadvantaged positions within international arenas" (1979, p. 23). Within this context, she maintains that social revolutions occur as a result of the confluence of several factors. Engaged in military and economic competition with more powerful nations, the prerevolutionary state attempts to initiate reforms in order to overcome financial crises and improve its extraction of taxes and military capabilities. However, existing social structures dominated by the landed upper class, which also composes most of the military officer corps, inhibit the state from successfully implementing such reforms. This results in the progressive weakening of the state apparatus. The ensuing emasculation of coercive organs, which usually results in (and is compounded by) a defeat in war, provides the peasantry with an opportunity to engage in insurrection and destroy the property basis of the landed aristocracy. Despite her attempts to eschew subjective variables, Skocpol asserts that peasants, who are generally subject to maltreatment, "always have grounds for rebellion against landlords, state agents, and merchants who exploit them" (Skocpol, 1979, p. 115).

But the revolt of peasants is, as we have come to expect, also dependent upon structures. According to Skocpol, the presence of agrarian structures that are autonomous as local entities and inhabited by peasants endowed with a high level of solidarity result (in conjunction with the collapse of the state's coercive apparatus) in peasant uprisings. In addition, "Such conditions are usually attendant to rentier agrarian systems where local peasants work small plots of land and are free from strict supervision by the landed elite" (Berejikian, 1992, p. 648).

In Skocpol's (1979) scheme, the occurrence of all these factors in tandem are both necessary and sufficient to produce a revolution.[5] Turning to actual cases of revolution, we discover that the conceptual utility of Skocpol's analytical framework for explaining the demise of the regimes she chose to study in *States and Social Revolutions* is rather high. When Louis XVI reluctantly convened the Estates General for the first time since 1615 in 1789, avowedly revolutionary groups were conspicuously absent from the French political scene. The National Assembly, which eventually split into several competing revolutionary groups, was largely formed from the Third Estate.[6] When the Russian state collapsed in February 1917, largely because of ignominious defeats inflicted upon it by Germany in World War I and spontaneous bread riots in Petrograd, Lenin was still in Switzerland and the Bolshevik party was inactive and in hiding.[7] Similarly, "The Manchu Dynasty in China, after a long period of decay and the siphoning away of its imperial powers into the hands of provincial elites, finally fell in 1911. Mao Zedong was but a teenager then, and the Chinese Communist Party was not formed until 1921" (Wickham-Crowley, 1991, p. 152).

Consonant with Skocpol's (1979) theoretical scheme, in both prerevolutionary France and China, the partial overlap between the landed upper classes and the state apparatus prevented the state from initiating badly needed fiscal and military reforms. Had such reforms been successfully carried out in a timely fashion, they could have reorganized the state and averted its collapse. Similarly, Skocpol clearly demonstrates that in Russia, although the Tsarist state enjoyed greater autonomy from its upper classes, the national military-administrative breakdown came about not as a result of purposive popular endeavor but from defeat in war. Alternative actions taken by Louis XVI and Nicholas II could, conceivably, have altered the course of the revolutions in Russia and, particularly, France. More-over, the presence of Sun Yat-sen undoubtedly played an important role in the timing of the demise of the Manchu dynasty. Although Skocpol does not con-sider such factors, she nevertheless persuasively shows that the actions of these individuals were not instrumental in the breakdown and collapse of the regimes under study.

Regrettably, however, Skocpol's (1979) theoretical orientation cannot be gen-eralized beyond her cases, and its applicability to other revolutions is minuscule at best and irrelevant at worst. Indeed, subsèquent events have forced Skocpol to gradually distance herself from, and eventually recant, the assertion that no rev-olution is actually "made." Coinciding with the publication of her book in 1979, the Iranian revolution took place in an unweakened state that had undergone no international or financial crises and was almost entirely autonomous from its so-ciety. Furthermore, the peasantry was conspicuous in Iran's revolution by being entirely absent from the upheaval. As Nikki Keddie (1995a) has observed, what distinguished prerevolutionary Iran from other nations in the region, which did not undergo revolutions, was the highly pronounced disjunction between the shah's regime and Iran's social groups, the unique authority and resources of the Shia clergy in Iran, and the peculiarities of the shah's authoritarian yet indecisive (in sharp contrast to Khomeini's charismatic and resolute) leadership.[8]

According to Keddie:

[I]n the case of the Russian revolution and certain other revolutions, there were so many important contributing causes that even had certain causative factors been re-moved, a revolution would very likely have occurred. In the Iranian case, however, one can think of acts by the Shah that might have averted the revolution. (Keddie, 1995a, p. 8)

Thus, for Keddie, the Iranian revolution seems to underscore the point that "it is not the case that dramatic major events always have dramatic political or struc-tural causes; sometimes yes, sometimes no" (Keddie, 1995a, p. 8).[9]

We may amend Keddie's (1995a) statement by adding that although state vul-nerabilities and objective structural preconditions are necessary to bring about the destruction of the ongoing system, they are not usually sufficient. The specific actions and reactions of subjective actors (both the pro- and antiregime forces) who operate within and largely in response to the parameters and possibilities provided by the prevailing objective order, as well as the ideology they propagate and the cultural milieu in which they function, can often make a crucial differ-ence. Objective structures and weaknesses have to be seized and exploited by those who desire the revolutionary transformation of society.[10]

Social scientists, in their efforts to understand and explain the world, have tended to marginalize individuals or omit them altogether. Institutions and structures, al-

though they undeniably acquire a momentum, an existence that at times may appear
to be their own, are constructions, artifacts created and popularized by people. (Selbin 1993, p. 138)

In formulating her hypothesis, Skocpol (1979), it seems, relied solely on those
cases in which structural conditions were largely sufficient to account for the
state's breakdown.

Consequently, when the Iranian revolution occurred in 1979, Skocpol had to
admit that the revolution had "uniquely" been made. In her article on the Iranian revolution (Skocpol, 1994d), which first appeared in 1982,[11] Skocpol, who
had previously ascribed no explanatory value to cultural variables and the leadership and organization skills of opposition groups, emphasized the determining
influence of the ideology and organization of the Shia hierocracy in the Iranian
revolution. "In sum, Shi'a Islam was both organizationally and culturally crucial
to the *making* of the Iranian Revolution against the Shah" (Skocpol, 1994d, p.
249). Later, responding to William Sewell's scathing criticism of her neglect of
ideology in analyzing the unfolding of the French revolution, Skocpol departed
even further from her previous structural determinism. She admitted to having
"treated the issues [the impact of ideology and culture] too cursorily" (Skocpol,
1994a, p. 199) and maintained that they exert a "causally unique" influence on
each revolution."[12]

In her article on Iran, Skocpol also acknowledged that the peasantry can indeed be a passive social group and that international conflict and peasant insurrection were not essential to the revolutionary process. Nevertheless, she retained
her emphasis on structural variables, this time (borrowing from the economist
Hossein Mahdavy [1970]) stressing the "rentier" nature of the Iranian economy
as well as the absolutist nature of the polity as significant causes for the fragility
of the shah's regime. As Said Amir Arjomand (1988) has pointed out, however,
the Iranian economy had essentially been (and continues to be) rentier ("a state
based on rent in the form of oil revenue rather than taxation" [Arjomand, 1988,
p. 191]) since the reign of Reza Shah (1925–1941). Furthermore, what Iran received in the form of royalties from the Anglo-Iranian Oil Company during the
rule of Reza Shah was "minuscule compared to the oil revenue in the 1970s" (Arjomand, 1988, p. 191). Therefore, it is inappropriate to attach undue weight to
rentierism as a major cause of the revolution.

It is surprising that in dissecting the causes of the Iranian revolution, Skocpol
(1994d), while admitting some of the fundamental shortcomings of the theoretical framework she had formulated earlier, continued to maintain that the revolution was unique in that it was made. Even a cursory examination of previous
revolutions, however, reveals that internal regime frailties as well as socioeconomic, political, and international crises were generally insufficient, by themselves, to result in the breakdown, let alone the transformation, of societies and
polities. Prior to the destruction of the monarchy in Iran, there had clearly been

revolutions "unlike the pattern [Skocpol] (mostly) found, in which the sequence she observed [had] not been replicated . . . There [were] regimes that [had] clearly fallen (in large part) because of the conscious actions of the revolutionaries themselves" (Wickham-Crowley, 1991, p. 153).

Apart from Iran, we can, among other cases, point to the Mexican (1910), Bolivian (1952), Cuban (1959), and Nicaraguan (1979) regimes as having been overthrown because of the "pressures and demands placed upon [them] from within civil society" (Wickham-Crowley, 1991, p. 167). We can also point to the Bolshevik revolution of October 1917 and the Chinese Communist revolution of 1949. Indeed, in the case of China, Skocpol herself is ultimately forced to acknowledge that peasant insurrection did not result from autonomous collective action but was instead dependent upon the mobilization of the peasantry by Chairman Mao's Communist guerrillas. Interestingly, in analyzing the Mexican revolution, Ronald Waterbury (in Berejikian, 1992) has found that "during the period of virtual state collapse in the early 1900s Oaxacan peasants, who were structurally positioned to take advantage of decreased state sanctioning," did not engage in rebellion. Instead, they "opposed Zapatista leaders, who were ostensibly fighting to improve their condition. [But] Monelos, with its system of modern haciendas and almost complete local control over local peasant life, was visited with active and violent rebellion" (Berejikian, 1992, p. 649).

In the case of Russia, while Skocpol has persuasively demonstrated that the collapse of the Tsarist state in February did not result from the conscious actions of revolutionary forces, the same cannot be said of the fall of Kerensky and the triumph of the Bolsheviks. Indeed, even Trotsky, who was not given to exaggerating the role of individuals in history, strongly implies that without Lenin the October revolution would not have occurred. Coincidentally, the subsequent triumph of the Bolsheviks in the Russian Civil War can itself, in some measure, be attributed to Trotsky's own skillful leadership of the Red Army. Trotsky's primary concern is to demonstrate that the Bolshevik revolution was a historical necessity. Yet "all Trotsky [manages to show] is that the objective historical situation made a Bolshevik triumph possible." As to how this possibility was transformed into reality, "his answer rises out of every crucial page where he is discussing events and not defending a faith." The revolution took place "because of the leadership of Lenin . . . But this is immediately counteracted by subsequent passages in which Trotsky denies the legitimacy of the very question he has asked [whether the accidental presence of Lenin on the historical scene was crucial] and tried to answer" (Hook, 1965, p. 217).[13]

How, then, in light of the above analysis, are we to supply an answer to the question under consideration (Are revolutions made or do they come?). We may conclude that all revolutions, as Skocpol has now come to argue, "are ultimately 'made' by revolutionaries, but not . . . within political contexts they themselves have chosen, to paraphrase Karl Marx" (Goodwin and Skocpol, 1989, p. 495).

Revolutions are deliberate because their second component (the creation of a new order following the demise of the old) cannot emerge from "patterned relationships beyond the manipulative control of any single group or individual" (Skocpol, 1994c, p. 200), although such relationships can certainly impact the extent to which the new order can be realized and consolidated. As Montesquieu observed, "[A]t the birth of societies, it is the leaders of the Commonwealth who create the institutions, afterward it is the institutions that shape the leaders" (quoted in Dekmejian, 1987, p. 79).[14] A revolution, then, must, in the final analysis, be made by the willful actions of conscious individuals.

But what of the first aspect of revolution, the breakdown of the established system? Here, our analyses have illustrated that although objective conditions always exert a significant bearing on the demise of the old regimes, they can, at times, be so overbearing as to bring about the collapse of the state apparatus with minuscule or no purposive popular endeavor. This being the case, then our task becomes, in the words of Wickham-Crowley, to "specify the conditions under which revolutionaries bring down the old regimes versus those in which regimes collapse without [or with minimal] such intervention" (1991, p. 54).

Variability Among Revolutions

First, we should note that Wickham-Crowley's own response to the above question is woefully inadequate. Wickham-Crowley (1991) singles out Tilly's (1978) resource mobilization theory of revolution as a typical purposive theory and proceeds to develop his argument in order both to counter and to amend Tilly's propositions. Tilly had divided the revolutionary process into two stages, the revolutionary situation and the revolutionary outcome. According to Tilly, a revolutionary situation (a derivative of Trotsky's concept of dual power) comes about as a result of (1) the appearance of revolutionary challengers seeking to gain control of the state; (2) the expression of support for the challengers from a significant proportion of the populace; and (3) the inability or unwillingness of the incumbents to suppress the challengers or extinguish people's support for them, or both. The revolutionary outcome takes place when the insurgents manage to displace the power holders and achieve control over the state.

Wickham-Crowley chides Tilly for assuming that a revolutionary situation must always precede a revolutionary outcome. However, failing to recognize that Tilly's apparent theory is, in fact a definitional tautology, Wickham-Crowley asserts, also in the form of a tautology, that

> [t]he construction of dual power prior to revolution must be linked to those cases in which the masses are being mobilized to revolutionary activity, since it is the challengers for power who are the mobilizers. If this is true, then we might also postulate that where dual power exists prior to revolution, one is likely to find a state that has

not collapsed due to its own internal and international pressures, but in good part has fallen because of pressures and demands placed upon it from within civil society. (Wickham-Crowley, 1991, p. 167)

Wickham-Crowley's statements are true by definition, and they only serve to prompt us to seek a more meaningful answer to the intriguing puzzle he has himself detected. Moreover, his further elaboration that "agrarian protobureaucracies," especially "where there is a partial overlap in personnel and powers between the landed elite and the apparatus of the state" (Wickham-Crowley, 1991, p. 168) (as was the case in prerevolutionary France and China), are highly vulnerable to administrative and military collapse does not go beyond Skocpol (1979) and is not relevant to the modern world. The conditions associated with the administrative breakdown of the former Soviet Union and the collapse of communism in Eastern Europe, for example, bear no resemblance to those cited by Skocpol (1979) and embraced by Wickham-Crowley (1991).

Wickham-Crowley is correct to point out that revolutionary movements (which presuppose volition) are more likely to succeed in "mafiacracies." (These are Wickham-Crowley's variations on what S. N. Eisenstadt [1978, pp. 277–289] has referred to as neopatrimonial regimes: systems in which government is extremely personalized and where the operating principle of the dictator is to encourage rifts and divisions within the political elite and the military in order to safeguard his absolutist rule.)[15] As Robert Dix (1984, p. 443) has pointed out, neopatrimonial regimes can be especially vulnerable to revolution because "a personalistic dictator—isolative, repressive, [often] anti-national, and corrupt" is likely to have an exceedingly small popular base. The neopatrimonial regime's insignificant linkages to the population, as well as the lack of cohesion among its political elite, in turn, can serve to increase the fragility of the state apparatus and to facilitate the formation of cross-cutting alliances between the nation's disparate, oppositional groups. As has frequently been pointed out, such alliances are generally indispensable for dislodging the ongoing system (Dix, 1984; Greene, 1990; Goodwin and Skocpol, 1989).

But it is much easier to generalize about why revolutions succeed or fail than about the circumstances under which they arise in the first place. To supply an answer to the above question, "We have to trespass," as Greene has noted, "boldly in the territory of casual inference. . . . According to the formalities of scientific method, we can never prove causality. At best, we *demonstrate* varying degrees of probability in the relationships of specific phenomena. And the persuasiveness of our causal inference is more a matter of logical self-evidence than empirical certainty" (Greene, 1990, p. 133).

As in the previous section, therefore, we are unable to provide a straightforward answer to the question under consideration. This is so not only because of our methodological limitations, which are admittedly considerable, but also due to the variability of circumstances that have managed to produce revolution.

Even if we merely attempt to show "varying degrees of probability in our relationships," our generalizations cannot frequently apply across time and space. It does not appear likely that we can supply an invariant set of conditions, each commonly associated with the collapse or overthrow of prerevolutionary regimes. In fact, increasing research has made it clear that a multiplicity of differing factors can be associated with both military and administrative breakdowns (which for Skocpol is essentially synonymous with revolution) and the existence of widespread dissatisfaction, which lays the basis for coordinated popular action aimed at toppling the ongoing system (the primary concern of most purposive theorists of revolution).

Writing in 1965, Eckstein observed that "we may have available many interpretative accounts of internal war simply because an enormous variety of objective conditions can create internal-war potential" (Eckstein, 1972, p. 20). This point appears to have been lost on most theorists of revolution, who have, in the words of Tilly, "generally insisted on offering singular models, specifying the invariant conditions under which revolutions [are] likely to occur" (Tilly, 1995, p. 138). Today, however, "our better theorists are conceding in their footnotes the multiplicity and variability of [revolutions] while often continuing to focus their main texts on singularity" (Tilly, 1995, p. 139).

Recognition of variability among revolutions appears to be most keenly appreciated by those who have undertaken the task of comparing actual cases of revolutionary upheavals or the numerous theories that have been proffered in order to account for them. After conducting an in-depth historical analysis of "forcible transfers of state power" from 1492 to 1992 in Europe, Tilly concludes that the "history of revolutionary processes tells us much about the mechanisms of political change, but defeats all neat formulations of standard recurrent conditions . . . Instead, we have learned how conditions for revolution [have] varied and changed" (Tilly, 1993, p. 237). After meticulously analyzing and explaining the various components of revolutionary movements, including the factors that have contributed to their success or failure as well as the conditions frequently associated with their development, Greene turns to assessing the conceptual utility of some of the more prominent theories of revolution. He concludes: "[T]heir respective advantages and disadvantages are a function of self-evidence rather than 'empirical validity' and their conceptual utility is likely to *vary* according to the values of the researcher and the *particular society under study*" (emphasis added) (Greene, 1990, p. 193). With his last statement, Greene implicitly acknowledges the existence of variability among revolutionary situations and outcomes as well as the difficulty of generalizing across time and space.

After thoroughly examining almost all of the hitherto existing theoretical and empirical literature on revolutionary phenomena in his extremely dense and detailed book *Political Violence, Crises, and Revolutions*, Ekkart Zimmerman (1983, p. 405) reaches a similar conclusion. Maintaining that "the sequences leading to and through [revolutions] seem to display considerable variety," Zimmerman states that his analyses have revealed "theorizing on the conditions of revolution" to be highly "heterogeneous . . . [producing] hardly any systemic knowledge." He adds that "this may be disappointing yet perhaps inescapable." Why? Because, as John Dunn has argued, the designation of certain phenomena as revolution on the basis of their common features does not necessarily mean that "they [can] then be explained by common causes specified in general causal statements" (quoted in Taylor, 1984, p. 153).

After conducting a comparative analysis of eight twentieth-century revolutions (Mexican, Russian, Chinese, Yugoslav, Vietnamese, Algerian, Turkish, and Cuban), Dunn concludes that the differences between them "are at least as striking as the uniformities." Moreover, the commonalities "are on the whole more like lexical preconditions for applying the category 'revolution' at all than . . . empirically discovered attributes" (Taylor, 1984, p. 153).[16] In other words, it is exceedingly difficult to generalize, in a nontautological fashion, about the preconditions associated with the development of revolutions (regardless of their variety).

Most recently, *Revolutions of the Late Twentieth Century* (1991), coedited by Jack Goldstone, Farrokh Moshiri, and Ted Robert Gurr, examined ten revolutionary upheavals in the last third of this century and concluded by reiterating the same point. Like Skocpol, Goldstone et al. adopt a top-down view of revolution, asserting that revolutions are tied to state breakdowns and crises of authority. Yet the work's case studies reveal that "a wide variety of state failures—economic, environmental, cultural—can precipitate a crisis of state authority" (Goldstone, 1995b, p. 54). "Thus, at the level of discrete causal factors, generalizations about consequences for political stability may not be possible." If this is so, then "approaches to the origins of revolution that pose the simple question, what are the causes? and seek a list of items that have destabilizing consequences in most states are misguided and not terribly helpful" (Goldstone, Gurr, and Moshiri, 1991, p. 42).

This assertion appears to be borne out by the empirical investigations of Robert Dix. Systematically testing the socioeconomic characteristics associated with cases of successful and failed revolutions in eleven Latin American nations (between 1960 and 1980), Dix (1984, p. 429) discovers no "consistent pattern of differentiation" in average annual growth in GNP per capita, in average annual urban growth rates, or in the distribution of income or land: "In fact, in three of the six failed cases where data are available (Guatemala, Peru, and Venezuela), income distribution was made more inequitable than in Nicaragua. In the case of land distribution, Cuban and Nicaraguan data in fact show greater equality than that to be found in any of the other countries."[17]

The Problem of Revolution Resolved?

In light of the variety and variability of revolutions, is theorizing about this complex concept still possible? Of the scholars mentioned above, only Goldstone has sought to formulate a highly elaborate theoretical framework, which is predicated upon the premise that a multiplicity of divergent preconditions can be associated with the development of revolutions. However, as shall subsequently be seen, Goldstone's scheme is fraught with numerous difficulties and oversights. The task, therefore, is to venture a less defective, albeit more modest, framework, in contradistinction to that of Goldstone.

Goldstone's Framework

Arguing that there cannot be an invariant general explanatory theory of all revolutions, Goldstone (1995a) maintains that "[i]n the study of revolutions and rebellions, a single model might explain much about a particular kind of event, or a small part of many different events; but no single model will explain much about all kinds of events" (Goldstone, 1995a, p. 179)—unless, of course, it is Goldstone's own model, which is sufficiently general and abstract to include within its purview all of the necessary conditions (as deemed by Goldstone) that have to be met before a revolution can take place.

Goldstone's (1995b) point of departure is that unlike the phenomena studied in the natural sciences, the use of theory in the study of revolutions cannot, and indeed should not, be the same for both explanation and prediction. Explanation involves knowing why the necessary conditions for revolution, which will not consistently be correlated with a single cause or a set of preconditions, have come into existence. Prediction, by contrast, entails (merely?) discovering the extent to which such conditions have progressed in tandem.

When it comes to predicting the likelihood of state breakdowns, Goldstone believes that his singular model can more than adequately be used in all types of context, regardless of their variety. According to Goldstone, since "revolution is an unfolding process," analysts who seek to forecast the coming of such events "should aim to monitor how far that process has progressed" (Goldstone, 1995b, p. 44). To accomplish this task, Goldstone advances a "conjunctural process model." The model holds that the conjuncture of three conditions will invariably lead to revolution, although the exact timing of the revolutionary outcome, which may be dependent upon individual actions or accidents, cannot be predicted.

The three components of Goldstone's model are: (1) the state's loss of effectiveness in exacting resources and obedience; (2) the alienation of elite groups from the state as well as the emergence of greater competition among such groups over the distribution of status and power; and (3) the willingness and capability of a vast or strategic proportion of the aggrieved populace to be mobilized for protest against the system. Goldstone asserts that the presence of all these factors in strong form makes the occurrence of revolution highly likely. However, when one or more factors are missing or weak, then the potential for revolution declines substantially (Goldstone, 1995b).

Goldstone acknowledges that it is impossible to determine the nature and intensity of people's feelings toward the system before the onset of revolution. But "to predict it is not critical to measuring with great precision the degree of popular discontent or opposition to the regime. It is enough to ask whether the structure and grievances that create mobilization potential are significantly present" (Goldstone, 1995b, p. 48). According to Goldstone, although the existence of structures that are conducive to mobilization (institutions that are largely immune from the encroachment of the state, such as religious networks and urban working communities) can be readily detected and monitored, people's grievances against the state and elites can, with more difficulty, be logically inferred from the prevailing objective conditions (such as the economic situation and performance, opportunities for social mobility, and the imposition of "exactions beyond common accepted limits" [Goldstone, 1995b, p. 8]). At the same time, the extent of state effectiveness and elite alienation, as with structures that facilitate mobilization, can also be easily established through observable phenomena (losses in war, crippling state debts, unusual taxation, state disagreements with cultural and economic elites, and so on).

Although his framework is primarily aimed at predicting revolutions, Goldstone believes it can also serve to illuminate the causes of state breakdowns. It can accomplish this objective by prompting us to "seek out the specific causal factors—some of which may be unique, or only clear with hindsight—that produced the revolutionary conditions." Explaining revolutions requires one to ascertain "why state effectiveness declined, elites became alienated, and populations became prone to mobilization" (Goldstone, 1995b, p. 46). Assuming an aggrandizing and self-congratulatory tone, Goldstone declares, in regard to his own framework: "Only a theory that starts from the assumption that revolution is a developing process, which can be brought on or hindered by a variety of causes, is capable of being used for *both* explanation and prediction" (Goldstone, 1995b, p. 46).

Goldstone's Model: A Critique

Goldstone's predictive and explanatory "model" is beset with several problems. Its most fundamental flaw is that (like Tilly's resource mobilization model of revolutionary situations) it is essentially a tautology. The three components of the "conjunctural model" (regime ineffectiveness, elite alienation, and popular mobilization), which Goldstone wants us to use in order to forecast and explicate all types of variant revolutions, are in fact the very distinguishing features of revolutionary situations. Contrary to Goldstone's insistence, definitional tautologies are not theories. "Tautological statements, by their very nature, are nonfalsifiable" (Greene, 1990, p. 185)[18] and are therefore bereft of scientific standing. "Explanation of the variations in revolutionary potential . . . must be evaluated by indicators that are independent of the incidence of revolution or political violence"

(Greene, 1990, p. 184). In the case of tautological declarations, however, "although the characteristics of the independent variable . . . are supposed to explain and predict variations in the dependent variable (revolution), the former is in fact measured by the latter" (Greene, 1990, p. 184).

In addition to being circular Goldstone's scheme also tends to slight the at times paramount role of leadership and downplay the influence of culture. Goldstone seems to assume that incumbent political leaders are essentially powerless in the face of material conditions and that they can at best postpone an imminent revolutionary upheaval: "[A]lthough a conjunctural analysis can tell when a state is weak and facing a revolutionary situation, it cannot predict whether accident or an individual's actions will intervene to slow down the impending arrival of a revolutionary crisis, or to rush it forward" (Goldstone, 1995b, p. 60).

However, as Robert C. Tucker (1981) argues, individuals, especially political leaders (particularly those who are absolutist, or in his terms "totalitarian") can exert a determining influence on "historical outcomes by virtue of the way in which they act or fail to act at critical junctures . . . From this standpoint history is open-ended, a fluid field of forces in which results are not rigidly predetermined even though the currents may be running strongly in one direction rather than another" (Tucker, 1981, p. 27).

Capturing the same sentiment, Nikki Keddie asserts: "It is possible that had the Shah moved forcibly against demonstrators in the Spring of 1978 the movement would have been limited to a short series of mass demonstrations rather than becoming a revolution. . . . It is sometimes possible for an individual to determine whether a revolution occurs" (Keddie, 1995c, pp. 73–74).

Going beyond Keddie, Marvin Zonis, a political scientist masquerading as a psychoanalyst, maintains that

> the people of Iran . . . did not so much "win" the revolution as the Shah "lost" it. That is, the Shah's failure to deal effectively with his mounting opposition before and throughout 1978 resulted, not long thereafter, in his overthrow. There was nothing inevitable about the revolution. Neither its timing nor its outcome was ordained. (Zonis, 1991, p. 2)

Zonis employs a nonfalsifiable and (in what appears to be a contradiction of his implied argument that the shah could have acted differently) psychologically deterministic framework to explain the shah's dispositions, including his arrogance, diffidence, narcissism, and indecisiveness in the face of crisis. Nevertheless, Zonis provides an adequate depiction of the shah's character traits and behavior, showing that such traits, regardless of why they had been formed, helped to contribute to the demise of the monarchy.[19]

In response to Keddie and Zonis, Goldstone will probably argue that even had the shah been endowed with greater resolve and political astuteness (what Machiavelli referred to as "princely virtue"), he would have been able only to delay the calendar date of the revolution. However, individuals can occasionally do more than merely slow down the coming of a revolution. Even Alexis de Tocqueville, who originally advanced the brilliant (yet also circular) proposition that "the most perilous moment for a bad government is when it seeks to mend its ways," also stated (in a sentence that is often not quoted) that "only consummate statecraft can enable a king to save his throne when after a long spell of oppressive rule he sets to improve the lot of his subjects" (de Tocqueville, 1955, pt. 3, p. 177).[20]

Goldstone asserts that "past cases do reveal that . . . efforts at reform . . . hastened the development of revolutions" (Goldstone, 1995b, pp. 60–61). Goldstone, of course, is referring primarily to political reform, namely, political liberalization and democratization. But this assertion does not take into account successful cases of reform and transitions to greater pluralism and democracy in such diverse nations as Spain, Portugal, South Korea, Taiwan, Chile, and Jordan. In initiating reform, as Robert Scalapino has noted, "the dilemma is clear: how to allow politics to evolve, yet not lose control" (Scalapino, 1989, p. 78). Scalapino suggests that the answer may be found, in large measure, in competent leadership:

> Effective political leadership in societies moving from authoritarianism to pluralism requires a mix of flexibility and firmness that needs frequent readjustment, a keen sense of timing, an ability to build coalitions from diverse elements, a capacity to garner and retain able advisers, and the skill—and luck—to develop policies that accord with rapidly evolving domestic and international requirements. (Scalapino, 1989, p. 78)

Apart from slighting the role of power holders, Goldstone's framework entirely neglects the occasionally epicentric role of the antiregime opposition leaders. For example, it is important to bear in mind that the shah was able to retain power for some thirty-seven years in part because he succeeded in preventing the forces opposed to him from becoming united. The shah was overthrown when his heterogeneous opponents, many of whom were entirely averse to establishing an Islamic theocracy in Iran, wholeheartedly submitted to the charismatic leadership of Ayatollah Khomeini in order to overthrow the monarchy. As with Lenin, the accidental presence of Khomeini on the historical scene was arguably indispensable to the Iranian revolution. None of the secular opposition leaders or antiregime clerics could even remotely approximate Khomeini in terms of charismatic and popular appeal. In fact, Ervand Abrahamian, a prominent Iran scholar and political historian who espouses a neo-Marxist orientation, declares in the conclusion of his book *Iran Between Two Revolutions* (which is otherwise primarily devoted to examining the structural causes of the Iranian revolution) that "Khomeini is to the Islamic Revolution what Lenin was to the Bolshevik, Mao to the Chinese, and Castro to the Cuban Revolution" (Abrahamian, 1982, p. 531).

Just as Khomeini, Lenin, and Mao played arguably instrumental roles in the Iranian, Russian, and Chinese revolutions, most recently the leadership of Nelson

Mandela has been exceptionally consequential in the tranquil evolution of the formerly white-dominated regime of South Africa. Indeed, "it is actually hard to imagine the [peaceful] transition occurring in South Africa without Mandela. Another black leader or group of leaders may not have had his particular mix of vision, authority, and legitimacy that was necessary both to negotiate with the whites and sell the deal to his own constituency" (Herbst, 1996, pp. 196–197).

Another problem with Goldstone's scheme is its cavalier treatment of culture. Cultural and ideological factors are not at all featured in the aforementioned model because Goldstone believes that they do not contribute to the process of state breakdown. As noted, according to Goldstone, such factors become crucial only after the demise of the established order, when the process of state reconstruction and the struggle for power begin. "It is chiefly *after* the initial breakdown of the state . . . that ideology and culture play a leading role" (quoted in Wasserstorm, 1995, p. 169).

Although acutely cognizant of the variable causes of revolution, Goldstone displays an incomprehensible indifference to the capacity of cultural variables to serve as important contributing preconditions. His dogmatic insistence on treating culture as a residual variable and granting "material roots of state breakdown pride of place in scientific work" (Wasserstorm, 1995, p. 170) might be appropriate to the largely involuntary military and administrative breakdowns studied by Skocpol (1979). But it is surely insufficient to account for other, far more numerous, purposive revolutionary movements. Indeed, most of the prominent analysts of revolutionary movements have singled out the prevailing (explicit and implicit) cultural and subcultural attitudes of the people, along with the resonance of the ideologies propagated by revolutionary organizations and leaders, as important contributing factors to the demise of the old regimes they investigated.[21]

In regard to the Iranian revolution, Khomeini himself has predictably ascribed an overriding value to cultural and spiritual beliefs. In an interview with the Italian journalist Oriana Fallaci shortly after the revolution, he declared: "[The left] did not contribute anything. They did not help the revolution at all . . . They were not decisive for the victory. . . . [The people who were killed by the thousands died] for Islam. The people fought for Islam" (Foran, 1994c, p. 162). In other words, as Max Weber argued in regard to the rise of capitalism, it was "spirit compelling matter, rather than the other way around" (Bloom, 1987, p. 208).

Among scholars of the Iranian revolution, Said Amir Arjomand (1988) has provided the most detailed and persuasive argument for the primacy of cultural and ideological variables for understanding the revolution. A Weberian sociologist, Arjomand attributes the ultimate cause of the Iranian revolution to the corrosion of the legitimacy of the Pahlavi state among all sectors of Iranian society, particularly the Shia hierocracy. According to Arjomand, the policies espoused and pursued by the centralizing Pahlavi state resulted in the increasing alienation and autonomy of the religious institution from the monarchy. Entirely "disembedded" from the system and in possession of an independent organizational and financial base, the radical elements of the clerical establishment took full advantage of their authority and religious symbolism to incite the disaffected masses against the monarchy.[22]

Even Farideh Farhi (1990), a self-proclaimed disciple of Theda Skocpol, borrowing from Antonio Gramsci, maintains that "a broader understanding of ideology" must be combined with Skocpol's earlier emphasis on the structure of the society and the state (along with the position of the state in the transnational political economy) to account for the Iranian and Nicaraguan revolutions. But Farhi focuses only upon Khomeini's interpretation of Islam and treats it as monolithic. Farhi also neglects the "varying cultures that were tapped by diverse groups or the other overarching themes of nationalism and populism" (Foran, 1994c, p. 165). Perhaps the most sophisticated approach to understanding the role of culture and ideology in the Iranian and, by implication, other purposive revolutionary movements is provided by the sociologist John Foran. According to Foran, "[I]t is . . . important to acknowledge and map the variety and complexity of political cultures of opposition throughout a population, as well as to search for the unifying factors that broad sectors can agree upon" (Foran, 1994c, p. 166).

An Alternative Approach to Explicating and Projecting Revolutions

The shortcomings inherent in Goldstone's model have been scrutinized so that they may be overcome, insofar as is possible, in the flexible framework that I will shortly strive to construct. To assess the potential for the revolutionary breakdown of Iran's theocratic regime, the task is to formulate a nontautological framework that is cognizant of both the variety and variability of revolutions. Combining both top-down and bottom-up approaches to analyzing revolutions, the framework should take into account the regime's structural vulnerabilities and defects as well as the potential for coordinated action by the aggrieved social groups opposed to it. Care should also be taken to ensure that the potentially decisive role of cultural and leadership variables are integrated into the framework and not scanted.

The Changing Patterns of Group Support for and Disenchantment with the Regime

After pondering the varying and largely divergent theories of revolution, Keddie concludes: "[T]he only thing that seems sure about revolutions to date is that they express a considerable level of discontent with things as they are and government as it is" (1995b, p. x). Recall that even Skocpol, in her initial involuntary interpretation of classical revolutions, maintained that a revolution does not come about without class-based, notably peasant-based, uprisings from below. Implicit in her argument is the notion that such revolts take place not only because of the existence of structural facilities but also because the peasantry is dissatisfied with its lot. To explain and project revolutionary transfers of power, therefore, one must begin by endeavoring to assess the extent of social support for and discontentment with the prevailing order: "The question of how many people support change is meaningless unless we know also how many people and what sort of people, support the incumbent government" (Calvert, 1990, p. 36). As the society can be divided into various more or less easily identifiable social groups, it is appropriate to focus on each group in turn and attempt to evaluate the level to which they are (dis)satisfied with the system. Here, the utilization of the group approach is advantageous for several reasons. Economic class, cultural identity, and political inclination can all be subsumed under "group." Subsequently, they can each be analyzed in light of the prevailing circumstances in order to attain a rough estimate of a given social group's disposition toward the regime.

Thus, the group approach can quite fruitfully be combined with the premise that a multiplicity of preconditions can be associated with the existence of widespread dissatisfaction of the populace. Indeed, various bottom-up theories of revolution, including Samuel Huntington's (1968) gap theory (revolutionary potential increases if political incorporation and institutionalization do not keep pace with the rate of socioeconomic change and social mobilization), James Davies' (1962) J-curve hypothesis (a slump in the wake of or period of sustained economic expansion heightens the potential for revolution), and Gurr's (1970) relative deprivation theory ("a perceived discrepancy between [people's] value expectations [economic or cultural] and their value capabilities" [p. 13] increases the potential for political violence), can in isolation or in conjunction be drawn upon to explicate a given group's discontentment with the present order.

In fact, this is precisely what several notable scholars of the Iranian revolution have done. Tracing the underlying causes and preconditions of the Iranian revolution, Ervand Abrahamian (1982), Jerrold Green (1982), Mehran Kamrava (1990), Amin Saikal (1980), and Sepher Zabih (1979) have put forward variants of Samuel Huntington's gap theory to account for the 1978–1979 revolution. Among the individuals cited above, Abrahamian has produced the most conceptually and empirically credible study, holding that

> [t]he failure of the Pahlavi regime to make political modifications appropriate to the changes taking place in the economy and society inevitably strained the links between the social structure and the political structure, blocked the channeling of social grievances into the political system, widened the gap between new social forces and the ruling circles, and, most serious of all, cut down the few bridges that had in the past connected traditional social forces, especially the bazaars, with the political establishment. (Abrahamian, 1980, p. 21)

Mohsen Milani (1994), adopting a theoretically diverse and eclectic approach, draws on both the gap theory and Davies' J-curve hypothesis in order to illuminate the preconditions of the revolution. However, he criticizes the practical implications of Huntington's theory, which suggests that the ruling elite must retain control of the institutionalization process. The shah's misguided and abysmally unsuccessful attempts at building institutions designed to absorb the politically awakened masses are cited to illustrate the dubiousness of elite-controlled institutionalization.[23] Others, particularly Robert Looney (1982) and, to a lesser extent, Fred Halliday (1979), have singled out the impact of economic factors, notably rapid, uneven capitalist development, on Iran's social classes as the primary precondition of the revolution.[24]

As Milani has wisely reminded us, however, the presence of revolutionary preconditions is not necessarily sufficient to result in revolutionary outcomes. Although widespread dissatisfaction may create the basis for revolutionary action, by itself it is insufficient to bring about the demise of the old regime. In the words of Leon Trotsky, "The mere existence of privations is not enough to cause an insurrection; if it were, the masses would always be in revolt" (Trotsky, 1961, p. 249). Even Max Weber, who was primarily concerned with the moral underpinnings of political power, acknowledged that "people may submit from individual weakness and helplessness because there is no acceptable alternative" (quoted in Przeworski, 1991). To enhance the conceptual utility of a new framework, one also has to consider the nature as well as the leadership qualities of both the regime and antiregime forces. In addition, it is necessary to scrutinize the net balance of coercive force for the regime.

The Net Balance of Coercive Force for the Regime

Scholars of revolution, regardless of their theoretical inclinations, are unanimous in regarding the military breakdown of the old regime as a necessary prelude to the triumph of revolution. According to Trotsky, "[T]he fate of every revolution at a certain point is decided by a break in the disposition of the army. Against a numerous, disciplined, well-armed and ably led military force, unarmed or almost unarmed masses of the people cannot possibly gain a victory" (quoted in Zimmerman, 1983, p. 316). After analyzing the role of the armed forces in twenty-six major rebellions in the twentieth century, D.E.H. Russell asserts that "in no case of successful rebellion did the regime retain the loyalty of the armed forces" (Russell, 1974, p. 77). After conducting a thorough investigation of regime changes in Europe in the course of the last 500 years, Charles Tilly asks: "When did revolutionary situations lead to revolutionary outcomes? . . . When a state's access to coercion had significantly and visibly diminished" (Tilly, 1993, p. 237).

In 1943, Katherine Chorley argued that "governments of the status quo who are in full control of their armed forces and are in a position to use them to full effect have a decisive superiority which no rebel force can hope to overcome" (quoted in Calvert, 1990, p. 42). Echoing Chorley, Crane Brinton maintained that "no government has ever fallen before attackers until it has lost control over its armed forces or lost the ability to use them effectively" (Brinton, 1965, p. 89). Chalmers Johnson (1966, p. 194) and Ted Robert Gurr (1970, p. 334) have also provided similar arguments. Finally, Skocpol (1994b) has forcefully asserted that "social revolutions . . . could not happen without a breakdown of the administrative and coercive powers of the old regime" (p. 7). "Moreover, the repressive state organization of the pre-revolutionary regime have to be weakened *before* mass revolutionary action can succeed or even emerge" (Skocpol, 1994c, p. 241).

As the Iranian revolution and the 1989 East European revolutions illustrate, however, insubordination, collapse, or neutralization of a nation's armed forces can be a product of, rather than a basis for, the mass mobilization of the populace. In fact, Skocpol's insistence on identifying massive international pressures, often resulting in military defeats, and social structural impediments on effective state actions as the only causes of military breakdown is definitely inaccurate. Such breakdowns can also result, among other factors, from splits within the ruling and the military elite or insubordination in the rank and file.

The Nature and Leadership Qualities of Regime and Antiregime Forces

Unless they come to lose their coercive effectiveness prior to the mass uprising, nations such as Iran, which are at a middle level of economic development and in which urbanization and specialization have become relatively widespread, are unlikely to undergo a regime breakdown without the coalescence of their opposition groups (Dix, 1984; Goodwin and Skocpol, 1989). The opposition groups that represent the society's major classes must form a broadly based revolutionary coalition in order to orchestrate the type of coordinated action necessary to dislodge the ongoing system. To understand whether a given regime's opposition forces are capable of comprising such an effective and wide-ranging revolutionary alliance, it is necessary to examine their leadership, ideology (what Foran has referred to as "political cultures of opposition"), organizational coherence and resources (including access to structures conducive to promoting mobilization), and likely size of their support base.

Ideology can be defined as "a normative theory of action" (Walt, 1992, p. 336). Revolutionary ideology serves to present a devastating critique of the prevailing order and to provide an alternative vision on the basis of which to organize the new society. In essence, the function of revolutionary ideology is to "facilitate the formation of cross-cutting alliances" (Greene, 1990, p. 79). But as the complexity and interdependence of a developing society increases, it becomes more difficult to fashion an elaborate and coherent ideology that can appeal to a vast cross-section of the population. Nations that have undergone rapid modernization might develop a dualistic political culture, with a segment of society holding on tenaciously to the traditional norms, another portion embracing more modern mores, and still others exhibiting dual characteristics. Under such circumstances, the universally acceptable ideology must of necessity be vague and incoherent, thereby making the role and personality of the revolutionary leader in holding the revolution's disparate supporters together all the more important (Greene, 1990, pp. 52–53).

Nearly eighty years ago, Walter Lippmann stated that "to talk about politics without reference to human beings . . . is just the deepest error in our political thinking" (quoted in Greenstein, 1971, p. 7). His point is still valid today. Especially in Iran, where politics has been perennially and predominantly personalized,

> a widespread belief has existed that in the absence of quasi-messianic leaders who [are perceived] to represent good as against evil and their movements nothing much can be done politically . . . But when a charismatic leader appears, then the people will be moved to back him—as with Mossadeq and Khomeini [and Khatami]—and will see him as the great fighter against oppressions. (Keddie, 1995d, p. 63)

Indeed, scholars of the Iranian revolution are unanimous in viewing the formation of cross-cutting alliances as having been essential to the triumph of the revolution. There also appears to be a shared consensus that among the opposition leaders, the towering figure of Khomeini and his dedicated band of disciples, making effective use of the institutional autonomy of the existing elaborate network of the mosques to propagate their vague and all-embracing propaganda and coordinate the actions of the opposition, were indispensable to the success of the populist revolution.

Susceptibility to the formation of cross-cutting alliances, however, does not guarantee that such a coalition will be able to bring about the demise of the established system. Much depends on the nature of the given regime. As noted, neopatrimonial and sultanistic regimes are by nature institutionally weak and therefore vulnerable to being overthrown by revolutionary forces, particularly if their paramount leader is to become weak or incapacitated. In neopatrimonial regimes, state officials and military officers are "deliberately atomized" (Keddie, 1995d, p. 65). Since the paramount leaders serve as the glue that bonds the system together, functionaries are bereft of independent sources of power. To the extent that they have any power, it derives from "the links between [them] and the person of the dictator" (Rouquié, 1987, p. 162). Consequently, "the fabric of authority unravels quickly when the power and status of the man at the top becomes undermined" (Kirkpatrick, 1979, p. 38). By contrast, collective authoritarian regimes are generally organizationally stronger, and their survival is not dependent on the decisiveness of one individual. Consequently, they are not as brittle as personalistic dictatorships.

Although inherently stronger than sultanistic regimes, collective dictatorships are not invincible. Nor is the demise of neopatrimonial political orders preordained. Whereas factions in personalistic regimes generally compete to ingratiate themselves to the dictator (the sole source of power and patronage), in collective dictatorships they are more apt to strive to assert their dominion over the state apparatus. More than 2,500 years ago, Plato asserted that "revolution frequently begins with 'divisions among members of the ruling class'" (quoted in Greene, 1990, p. 143). To maximize the survival of the regime, key decisionmakers in collectivist authoritarian regimes must ensure that their ambition and struggle for power does not overstep the bounds of their commitment to preserving the constitutional integrity of the system: "As long as the elites remain united in support of the regime, and have the financial and military resources to support their rule, they can withstand significant challenges and retain power" (Goldstone, 1994, p. 9). By being internally at odds and not putting up a common front, however, they are liable to forfeit their capacity for what Pareto referred to as effective and timely violence and manipulation (Eckstein, 1972, pp. 17, 26). Thus, elite fragmentation and unrestrained factionalism in collective authoritarian regimes can serve to make the system vulnerable to regime breakdown. As with sultanistic regimes, then, the orientations, skills, and incentives of leaders can be significant for the survival of collective authoritarian political orders.

Moreover, "the armed forces of neopatrimonial dictatorships, their lack of professionalism notwithstanding—may still manage to control dissidence on their territory . . . leaving little space for revolutionaries to mobilize" (Goodwin and Skocpol, 1989, pp. 499–500). Nor is it always the case that "elites and middle classes" in neopatrimonial regimes are "driven into a coalition with revolutionaries . . . especially if the dictator dispenses patronage according to more or less rational and impersonal criteria and does not repress the moderate position in too heavy handed a fashion." In other words, in such systems, the survival (and transformation) of the regime is dependent on the "unrelenting wiliness and vigilance of the individual ruler" (Goodwin and Skocpol, 1989, p. 500). Hence, the qualities and capabilities of key decisionmakers can play a determining role in any type of regime. Ultimately, the relationship between popular dissatisfaction and the regime's downfall may come to rest upon the skills of revolutionary leaders and the incompetence of power holders.

The factors considered salient in the proposed framework, then, include the changing patterns of inter- and intrasocial group support for and discontentment with the regime, the nature of the regime as well as the forces opposing it, the qualities of regime and antiregime leadership, and the net balance of coercive force for the regime. This framework does not purport to be able to provide a precise prediction of revolutions. It is merely a nontautological attempt at assessing and explaining a society's potential for revolution. It examines some of the factors that make revolutions more likely, not inevitable. It recognizes that the revolutionary destruction of an existing regime is generally caused by the confluence of two sets of interrelated variables: the regime's internal defects and vulnerabilities and the coordinated action of the social groups and individuals opposed to it (Arjomand, 1986, p. 383). It is also cognizant of the fact that depending upon the context, the old regime's vulnerabilities can at times result in its breakdown with minimal purposive and coordinated popular exertion. Combining top-down and bottom-up attempts at understanding revolutions, it strives to account for both collapses and overthrows, recognizing that the preconditions associated with each can be variable. Consequently, the relative weight ascribed to each factor in the framework can vary according to the characteristics of the society under consideration.

To sharpen our understanding of the Islamic Republic's potential for revolution, the following chapters will compare Iran's present circumstances with its pre-1979 situation in light of the above framework. Such a comparison is illuminating because, as Alexis de Tocqueville observed, "the mind can gain clarity only through comparison" (quoted in Pope, 1986, p. 33).

Notes

1. This quotation is derived from Skocpol (1979, p. 16).

2. Among the most prominent of purposive theorists are Davies (1962), Gurr (1970), Smelser (1963), Johnson (1966), Huntington (1968), and Tilly (1978).

3. For arguments similar to that advanced by Skocpol, particularly in regard to the collapse of the state, see Goldstone (1980), pp. 425–453, especially p. 449, where he states: "Continued pressure from the international system, conjoined with certain structural characteristics, precipitates revolution." See also Jenkins and Perrow (1977), pp. 249–268, particularly p. 266: "The dramatic turnabout in the political environment originated in economic trends and political realignments that took place quite independent from any 'push' from insurgents." Cited in Kurzman (1992), p. 2.

4. This categorization is used by Goldstone in order to distinguish between theorists of revolution who emphasize "a populace motivated to rebel" as opposed to those who stress "a state too weak to resist." See Goldstone (1995b), pp. 50–55.).

5. For a summary of Skocpol's arguments, see Kimmel (1990), pp. 171–187; Moshiri (1991), pp. 26–29; Taylor (1984), pp. 34–51; and Wickham-Crowley (1991), pp. 151–154.

6. For a summary of the outbreak of the French Revolution, see Greene (1990), pp. 19–24; Palmer and Colton (1995), pp. 367–378; and Wickham-Crowley (1991), p. 152.

7. For a summary of the outbreak of the February Revolution, see Greene (1990), pp. 24–30, and Wickham-Crowley (1991), p. 152.

8. See Keddie (1995b), pp. 11–19, especially p. 11.

9. In spite of the implication of her argument that forecasting collapse is easier than predicting an overthrow (these terms are not Keddie's, but the distinction is inspired by her own comparison), she does not elaborate on the varieties of revolution. Nor does she pursue the topic further. Instead, she devotes the rest of her essay to expounding why it is impossible to predict any revolution and entirely disregards the ramifications of her earlier argument.

10. For similar orientations, see Selbin (1993), Colburn (1994), Rejai (1977), Tilly (1978), and Sewell (1994).

11. See Skocpol's "Rentier State and Shi'a Islam in the Iranian Revolution" (1994d, pp. 240–260).

12. See Skocpol's "Cultural Idioms and Political Ideologies in the Revolutionary Reconstruction of State Power: A Rejoinder to Sewell" (1994a, pp. 199–239).

13. See also Tucker (1970, 1980).

14. See also Rustow (1970), p. 27.

15. According to Eisenstadt, neopatrimonial regimes can be distinguished from patrimonial ones by the fact that they do not derive their legitimacy from tradition. Similarly, Juan Linz (1975), echoing Max Weber, uses the term "Sultanism" in order to refer to systems in which both the military and the bureaucracy serve merely as the personal tools of the autocrat. See also Snyder (1992).

16. Also see Dunn (1972), pp. 241–243.

17. See also Linchbach (1989). Linchbach conducts an extensive analysis of such studies and finds them to be inconclusive. Indeed, he concludes that no prior configuration of socioeconomic preconditions appears to be uniformly associated with revolution.

18. On refutability as the primary criterion of scientific standing, see also Popper (1968), pp. 40–42.

19. Zonis's depiction of (if not his rationale for) the shah's characteristics and qualities is amply confirmed by the recently published confidential diary of Assadollah Alam. As the shah's closest confidant and minister of court from 1966 to 1977 (the year in which he died of cancer), Alam possessed an unusually intimate understanding of the shah's personality traits as well as his modus operandi. See Alam (1991).

20. See also Gurr (1970), p. 117.

21. Even Skocpol, in a recent article, declares that "[f]rom an institutionalist perspective, we should be looking for the cultural and ideological dimensions of all institutions, organizations, social groups, and political conflicts, so that we can integrate those dimensions into all aspects of our explanations and accounts of both the roots and outcomes of social revolutions" (in "Reflections on Recent Scholarship About Social Revolutions and How to Study Them" [1994c], p. 336). See also Arjomand (1988), Foran (1993), Chirot (1992), Wickham-Crowley (1991), Wasserstrom (1995).

22. Arjomand acknowledges that the support of the secular intelligentsia as well as the modern middle class and the oppositional movements representing them was indispensable to the success of the revolution. However, he chides these groupings for having engaged in self-delusion by believing that they would, after the destruction of the monarchy, be able to outmaneuver Khomeini. See Arjomand (1988). See also Dabashi (1993) and Moadel (1993). Both Dabashi and especially Moadel treat ideology as the most significant variable in explaining the Iranian revolution.

23. Among others, Foran (1993, 1994a–c), Farhi (1990), Keddie (1981), and Fischer (1980) also combine diverse theoretical approaches.

24. See also Bashiriyeh (1983) and Katouzian (1981).

3

The Social Underpinnings of Present-Day and Prerevolutionary Regimes: The Intelligentsia, the Clerics, and the Bazaaris

This chapter, along with Chapter 4, will examine the causes and the probable extent of the cleavages between society and the state in prerevolutionary and present-day Iran. Matched comparisons will focus on the distress levels of Iran's politically important social groups, including the intelligentsia, clerics, bazaaris, entrepreneurs, modern sectors of the middle class, and the dispossessed. As noted, although widespread dissatisfaction is insufficient to bring about a revolution, it is a necessary precursor to any revolutionary situation. It is, therefore, illuminating to contrast the present regime's social bases of support with the previous regime's. To the extent that the Islamic Republic is anchored by firmer social roots than prerevolutionary Iran, it is less likely to be overthrown as a result of revolutionary upheaval. Inter- and intraclass divisions are, by definition, inimical to the formation of cross-cutting alliances and therefore diminish the capacity for collective action.

The Intelligentsia

According to Max Weber, the intellectual community is composed of those "who by virtue of their peculiarity have special access to certain achievements considered to be 'culture values' and who therefore usurp the leadership of a culture community" (Gerth and Mills, 1981, p. 176). In this capacity, as Karl Mannheim argues, they take it upon themselves "to provide an interpretation of the world for the social settings in which they find themselves" (Milani, 1994, p. 62). Edward Shils views intellectuals as "those who concern themselves with ultimate values and live in a 'wilder universe'" (Boroujerdi, 1996, p. 20). Edward Said, by contrast, regards intellectuals as those "endowed with a faculty for representing, embodying, articulating a message, a view, an attitude, philosophy or opinion to, as well as for, a public" (Said, 1994, p. 11).

In this study, the term "intellectual" refers to that segment of the formally or informally educated Iranian elite that has a strong proclivity toward dealing primarily in ideas and ideals (Green, 1990, p. 41). Such individuals are most likely to be found among writers, poets, artists, journalists, teachers, and students enrolled in institutions of higher learning. Given to contemplation about the nature and especially the proper order of things, the intelligentsia subscribes to explicit or implicit notions about the characteristics of the good life and the just society. In their utterances, such notions generally serve as alternative visions of the future, acting as mechanisms through which the past and the present are evaluated and interpreted.

As a social group, the intelligentsia is not necessarily a product of modernization. Intellectuals have existed since the rise of civilization. However, the modernization process has undoubtedly served to swell their ranks and to create a pool of newly politically awakened masses, many of whom have shown themselves to be receptive to the pronouncements of intellectuals. In Iran, the literate population has grown from 14.9 percent in 1956 to 47 percent in 1976 to 66.1 percent in 1993 (Milani, 1994, p. 66; Bashiriyeh, 1983, p. 75; "Children of the Islamic Revolution: A Survey of Iran," 1997). Indeed, the declarations of intellectuals, whether articulated by the religious or secular variety (a classification that became meaningful only after the initiation of modernization) have themselves in substantial measure been a response to the modernization process.

Although highly reflective, members of the intelligentsia are not necessarily open-minded. As those who "examine, ponder, wonder, theorize, and imagine" (Hofstadter, 1963, p. 23, quoted in Boroujerdi, 1996), intellectuals are first and foremost dedicated to the propagation of their perception of the existing order of things. "The allegiance of intellectuals, except to their own ideas, is almost always in doubt" (Greene, 1990, p. 47). That is why most Iranian intellectuals, severely constricted by the repressive and watchful eye of the Pahlavi state, initiated and actively took part in the uprising against the shah's rule. Of course, there were those who opted to enhance their economic and political standing by serving as mandarins for and appendages to the monarchy. But the preponderance enthusiastically supported the revolution, assuming that the shah's ouster would result in the construction of a more politically open, egalitarian, and just order in which their complete and unhindered freedom of expression would be assured. They were soon proved to have made a grave error and have, for the most part, suffered immensely under theocratic rule. Nevertheless, as shall subsequently be seen, although variable, the theocracy's tolerance of expressions of criticism concerning governmental policies and performance, as well as debates about alternative ideologies, has generally been greater than what was permitted under the monarchy. Particularly since Khatami's inauguration as president in 1997, the realm of permissible artistic and intellectual expression has expanded considerably. This expansion, however, has not been steady and has been subject to setbacks, even reversals, because of the staunch resistance of the still disproportionately powerful forces of reaction. Nevertheless, bereft of viable alternatives to the present regime, most intellectuals, even those with secular orientations, are rooting for Khatami. They hope that the reformist camp within the Islamic Republic will ultimately prevail in its power struggle with the forces of conservatism and extremism. The fortunes of intellectuals today have thus become beholden to an unpredictable tug of war between the reformist and conservative factions of the theocracy.

Rising Dissatisfaction with the Pahlavi Order

Approximately two years before the 1979 Iranian revolution, the shah initiated a selective, limited, and inconsistent policy of political liberalization. In part designed to curry favor with the newly installed Carter administration, which started off by making its support for human rights and its opposition to over-arming Third World dictatorships abundantly clear, this policy was continued by the shah until the demise of his rule. As a part of his liberalization policy, the shah suddenly decided to loosen the lid on political expression, which he had previously tightened to the point of suffocation. From 1971 (the year in which the shah commemorated the existence of 2,500 years of uninterrupted monarchical rule in Iran by throwing an exceptionally extravagant party) until the final months of 1976, the shah departed from his previous pattern of dealing with dissidence. Starting in 1971, instead of "balancing coercion with co-optation and repression with reform," the shah endeavored "for the first time in his 30-year rule to . . . rest his throne on a brittle policy foundation of repression and coercion" (Bill, 1988, p. 186). His security forces, especially the notorious secret service, SAVAK, were given carte blanche to subdue ruthlessly even the slightest expression of disagreement with and opposition to the Pahlavi regime.

This period proved to be especially deplorable from the vantage point of the intelligentsia, which "witnessed the peak of censorship, horror, and intellectual suffocation. Many *engagé literati* were imprisoned, blacklisted, or denied permission to write or publish" (Boroujerdi, 1996, p. 50). It is not surprising, therefore, that when the shah suddenly decided to partially lift the galling restrictions on political expression, the intellectuals immediately responded by airing their numerous grievances against the regime. They revived the defunct Writers' Association and circulated open letters addressed to the shah and other high-ranking officials in which they expounded the problems afflicting the regime and the nation. They also held various well-publicized poetry nights. It was during such occasions that they made full use of the rich tradition of Persian allegorical poetry to underscore the horrors that tyrannical rule inflicts upon those who suffer under it and to expose the tyrant himself. Such activities are generally regarded by the analysts of the Iranian revolution as the first events in the massive chain of regime and antiregime actions and reactions that eventually culminated in the Iranian revolution.

It is important to recall, however, that most intellectuals, emboldened by President Carter's human rights campaign, initially launched their campaign of civil protest not to dislodge the Pahlavi dynasty but to transform it. Of course, as was soon demonstrated, they had no inherent respect for monarchical rule. At the time, they simply thought that it was impossible to dislodge the shah's seemingly omnipotent regime. Thus, the attempt by the intellectuals to persuade the shah to truly reform his rule by introducing genuine liberalization and democratization policies, once it had spread to other segments of Iranian society and was spearheaded by the intransigent and charismatic leadership of Khomeini, eventually snowballed into a revolutionary movement.

What prompted most intellectuals to close ranks behind Khomeini and push for the ouster of the monarchy was, apart from Khomeini's obfuscation of his ultimate intentions and the intellectuals' indulgence in wishful thinking (that Khomeini and his disciples would retreat to a life of teaching in the Shia holy city of Ghom), was the intelligentsia's extreme alienation from Pahlavi Iran. As noted, the intelligentsia had become particularly disturbed with the prevailing state of affairs between 1971 and 1976. From a self-serving point of view, they despised the arbitrary and severe, at times life-threatening, restrictions on their freedom of expression. During this period, SAVAK, acting under the orders of the shah, effectively exerted its dominion over the Ministries of Culture and Art, Information, Science and Higher Education, and the National Iranian Radio and Television Organization. It became the final arbiter on all matters pertaining to censorship and artistic control. In this capacity, SAVAK was instrumental in banning films and plays and prohibiting the publication of books and journals. It also forbade the functioning of Iran's Writers' Association (founded in 1968) and brought all professional associations and labor unions, including the highly politicized Teachers' Union, under close surveillance (Abrahamian, 1982, pp. 442–443; Graham, 1978, p. 45; Halliday, 1981, pp. 224–225; Milani, 1988, p. 115). According to one estimation, under the impact of these policies, the number of titles published and marketed annually dropped from above 4,000 in 1969 to approximately 700 in 1976 (Boroujerdi, 1996, p. 50, n. 43). Furthermore: "By the end of 1975, twenty-two prominent poets, novelists, professors, theater directors, and filmmakers were in jail for criticizing the regime. And many others had been physically attacked for refusing to cooperate with the authorities" (Abrahamian, 1982, p. 443). A well-known and unrepentant revolutionary poet was executed, while several other renowned writers and social critics died under suspicious circumstances.

The most prominent Iranian intellectual whose death was blamed on SAVAK foul play was Ali Shariati. Along with Khomeini, Shariati is regarded as the most important ideologue of the Iranian revolution. He was one of the most popular intellectuals in contemporary Iranian history; his doctrines and formulations, from which Khomeini drew freely and selectively, were instrumental in inciting Iranian college and high-school students, especially those with provincial and traditional family backgrounds, to rise up against the monarchy. Between 1972 and 1977, Shariati was persistently harassed by SAVAK. To escape persecution, he went into hiding but resurfaced after his father was taken hostage by the authorities. He was then imprisoned for eighteen months and was subsequently put under house arrest. In May 1977, when the shah had instituted his liberalization policy, Shariati was permitted to leave the country for London. He died a month later at the age of forty-four. The British coroner concluded that he had suffered a massive heart attack (Abrahamian, 1982, p. 465; Foran, 1993, pp. 369–370). Most people, however, pointing to SAVAK's extensive record of abusive and homicidal behavior as well as Shariati's radically populist and antiestablishment ideology, chose to believe that he had been murdered.

A Paris-educated sociologist, Shariati was a superb and spellbinding orator with a gift for presenting his central arguments in poetic and allegorical yet relatively accessible language. Heavily influenced by the ideas of Franz Fanon, Shariati devised his ideology through the merging of certain aspects of Shia Islam with aspects of Marxism. Turning Fanon on his head, Shariati maintained that the inhabitants of the Third World would be ineffective in their struggles against imperialism without at first recapturing and realizing their true cultural identity. In the case of Iran, Shariati maintained that the nation's cultural identity was intimately bound up with Shia Islam. As the cultural redeemer and imperialism slayer, however, Shariati took it upon himself to resurrect "true" Islam (what he labeled Alawite Shiaism) and destroy what he understood as being the deviant variety of Islam (Safavid Shiaism). According to Shariati, the deviant form of Shiaism, imposed as the state religion in 1501, had been used continuously to justify royal absolutism, political quietism, and the silent endurance of suffering (Abrahamian, 1982, pp. 465–468; Milani, 1994, p. 82).

True Islam, though, Shariati argued, is on the side of the disinherited, who are enjoined to act in order to bring about the realization of the just society. Shariati equated justice with equality, arguing that it could only be realized in a religiously inclined, classless social order (Arjomand, 1988, p. 93). True Muslims, instead of concentrating on the ceremonial and ritualistic aspects of their religion and preparing themselves for the hereafter, must emulate the example of Iman Hossein (the Third Imam of the Shias), who sacrificed his life in the struggle against tyranny and injustice. Without mentioning the Pahlavi dynasty, Shariati maintained that the forces of injustice in the modern world were embodied in arbitrary despotic rule, imperialism, exploitative capitalism, and Zionism (many derided the shah for his presumed subservience to the United States as well as his tacit alliance with Israel).

Afraid to express themselves directly, Iranian literati increasingly took to the adoption of symbolic and metaphorical allusions in order to achieve a modicum of freedom from the pervasive institution of censorship. According to one leading literary critic: "A life of concealment develop[ed] progressively in the misty atmosphere where all channels of communication [were] held in control. Ingenious forms of protection and secrecy [were] devised" (quoted in Boroujerdi, 1996, p. 49).

The most competent and popular practitioner of the art of symbolic expression in prerevolutionary Iran was Samad Behrangi, a young leftist primary-school teacher and writer from the province of Azerbaijan. Emulating Antoine de Saint-Exupéry and Lewis Carroll, Behrangi made effective use of children's literature and folklore in order to present his devastating assessment of the prevailing political order. *The Little Black Fish* (1968), Behrangi's most famous work, depicts the life of a curious and adventurous young fish who decides to leave the safe confines of his stream in order to investigate the nature of life in the wider sea. The fish's journey of discovery familiarizes him with all sorts of horrendous atrocities perpetrated against fish by varying sorts of large and sinister forces and creatures. His observations prompt him to dedicate his life to fighting such injustice, and after performing several heroic deeds, he is killed while trying to rescue an oppressed companion. Behrangi's simple and straightforward call to action was extremely well received, and his book became the most popular "children's book" of the 1970s. Behrangi's "accidental drowning" at the age of twenty-nine, shortly after the publication of his book, turned him into a martyr and, contrary to his wishes, helped to foster a pervasive sense of pessimism and helplessness in the ranks of the intelligentsia (Boroujerdi, 1996, p. 436–437; Foran, 1993, pp. 372–373).

Reflecting the discontented and despondent mood of the intelligentsia, the most recurrent themes in works of literature during this time concerned such issues as loneliness, nothingness, dread, fear, unfathomable void, and being constrained (Boroujerdi, 1996, p. 49). The prevailing mood of gloom among a large proportion of writers is perhaps best captured in the following poem by Mehdi Axhavan-Sales:

> *They don't want to answer your greetings.*
> *The weather depressing; doors, closed;*
> *heads in collars; hands, hidden;*
> *breaths, clouds; hearts, tired and sad;*
> *trees, crystal-embroiled skeletons;*
> *the earth, lifeless; the roof of the sky, low;*
> *dusty the sun; dusty the moon;*
> *it is winter.*
> —quoted in Boroujerdi, 1996, p. 48

Such dejection by the literary community was largely shared by many of the university professors and students. In line with the shah's objective of promoting civil privatism, the regime prohibited students from taking part in any type of meaningful political activity. Only apolitical student associations were tolerated, and it was widely known that SAVAK had effectively penetrated all segments and institutions of society, including the universities and student organizations (both at home and overseas) (Boroujerdi, 1996, p. 40; Milani, 1994, p. 62; Parsons, 1984, p. 33). Politically active and recalcitrant students were often identified, then dealt with quite harshly. Depending on the nature of their activities, they could be expelled, imprisoned, tortured, or even eliminated.

Under the threat of severe chastisement, professors were also expected to behave in ways pleasing to the authorities. They were prohibited from speaking on subjects considered taboo by the regime and, faced with student informants, were expected to present favorable interpretations of the shah and his policies. A political science professor who was beaten up because he had neglected to refer to the "White Revolution" (a package of reforms, the centerpiece of which was a land-redistribution program, the White Revolution was promulgated by the shah in 1963 in order to neutralize his domestic opponents and placate the Kennedy administration) in his lectures once remarked: "There is nothing special about my case" (Abrahamian, 1982, p. 443). Promotion was more often dependent on having the proper connections and behaving in the politically correct fashion rather than on merit and competence. The reflections of Mehdi Pakdaman, a professor of economics at Tehran University, is indicative of the sentiments of the disillusioned and idealistic educators during this era: "Pakdaman compares the plight of a university Professor in Iran at the time to a man imprisoned inside a steam pipe. . . . The imprisoned man develops a language of symbolism, indulges in self-censorship, and becomes negative minded and isolated" (quoted in Boroujerdi, 1996, p. 41).

The Plight of the Intellectuals Today

Interestingly, Pakdaman's analysis is an apt metaphor for depicting the predicaments facing independent-minded Iranian intellectuals after the establishment of the Islamic Republic, particularly before Khatami's rise to power.[1] Even today, as in the previous system, free thinking in Iran is beholden to the arbitrary whim of the despotic regime's determination of what constitutes sufficient political space in a given moment. Large numbers of writers and poets, both foreign and Iranian, whose work has been deemed inappropriate by the authorities, have joined the ranks of banned authors, and strict official censorship is still imposed on domestic publications, broadcasts, and movies. Effective measures have been introduced to encourage self-censorship. Apart from intimidation and the threat of punishment, the Ministry of Culture and Islamic Guidance has ingeniously employed the prospect of financial ruin as a means of discouraging publishers from investing in politically suspect literature. The ministry has decreed that once a book has been published, it should then be sent to the ministry's Book Review Unit for inspection. Many printed books have been read by inspectors and banned, causing the publishing companies to lose their investments (Mousavi, 1992, p. 18). Since November 1995, however, the regime has dispensed with such arrangements and has, as in the final years of the monarchy, imposed censorship prior to publication ("Deputy Minister Quits over New Censorship," 1996).

Publishing a book in Iran during most of the Post–revolutionary period has been a Herculean task, requiring an inordinate degree of patience. The ministry's meddlesome Review Committee could not only object to a book's general thesis or tone, but it could also quibble about a specific sentence or words that it deems to have improper moral, political, and sexual connotations ("Children of the Islamic Revolution: A Survey of Iran," 1997). In 1996, Iranian writers and publishers maintained that of the approximately 1,500 novels submitted to the censors in the previous year, none had as yet been approved (MacFarquhar, 1996).

Ridiculing the cumbersome restrictions placed on Iranian writers, Hooshang Golshiri, a prominent Iranian intellectual, stated in an interview with the BBC in 1996: "In this country, you could not write a sentence like 'I left my house to buy some cigarettes and on the way I saw a pretty woman.' . . . Here, you could only write that you left your house to buy some cigarettes." Shortly thereafter, he was arrested by the authorities and charged with the crime of spying for foreign entities. Golshiri is a novelist and the founder of the Iranian Writers' Association. A fearless defender of the freedom of expression, he was also jailed under the shah. He is a recent recipient of a Human Rights Watch grant awarded to writers who are in financial need because of political persecution ("Maroufi, Golshiri Awarded Human Rights Watch Grants," 1997; "No Novel Published in Year," 1996).

Golshiri's persecution under both the monarchy and the Islamic Republic indicates that the theocracy can be just as harsh as the monarchy in muffling the voices of outspoken intellectuals. Indeed, the Islamic Republic has also instituted a highly efficient system of surveillance in order to keep its opponents in check. As in the time of the monarchy, all voluntary associations and trade unions, including the Teachers' Union, have been made to operate under the close supervision of the state. As in the past, the Ministry of Information, the present successor to SAVAK, places just as much emphasis on intelligence gathering as on brutality. "Suspect Iranians, which includes academics and writers who stayed on after the revolution, now perform largely on sufferance, constantly watched and listened to. In rather kindly fashion, the bugging system tends to employ paralyzed or disabled veterans of the war with Iraq" ("Children of the Islamic Revolution: A Survey of Iran," 1997).

As in the time of the shah, the disappearance or demise, under mysterious circumstances, of intellectuals propounding dangerous viewpoints from the vantage point of the regime has also continued under the Islamic Republic: "Everyone has tales of people whom the regime considered inconvenient and who have simply vanished." In 1996, Ghaffar Hosseini, a writer critical of the regime, was found dead in his Tehran apartment. The government maintained that Hosseini had died from a heart attack. But the New York–based Poets, Playwrights, Editors, Essayists, and Novelists Association (PEN) maintains that Hosseini, who did not have a history of heart trouble, "was the victim of foul play." According to PEN, Hosseini, whose corpse was covered with bruises, had bled substantially from his mouth before he died ("PEN Says Writer Murdered," 1996).

In a similar incident, the body of another respected writer, Ebraheem Zalzadeh, was discovered in a coroner's morgue in Tehran in 1997. According to Zalzadeh's family members, the morgue was in possession of the body for more than a month before it decided to notify the family. In response to the murder, Human Rights Watch issued a statement expressing concern that "the suspicious death of Mr. Zalzadeh may be part of a pattern of repression directed against independent writers and publishers in Iran" ("Writer's Body Found with Stab Wounds," 1997).

The writer and satirist Ali Akbar Saidi Sirjani, who died in November 1994 under a shroud of secrecy while being held in detention, is the most prominent Iranian intellectual to have fallen victim to the regime's intolerance for iconoclasts. Sirjani was deemed subversive by the regime because in many of his writings, through the use of metaphors and allegories, he questioned the very legitimacy of the system by exposing the pious pretensions of its rulers as a hypocritical scheme designed to exploit the gullible masses for the purpose of attaining and preserving power. In a series of books, he also celebrated the noble qualities of Iran's pre-Islamic civilization. Sirjani's fate finally became sealed when, after his writings had been banned, in a letter of protest addressed to Ayatollah Khamenei, Iran's supreme leader, he insinuated that "hypocrisy, falsehood, discrimination, and injustice . . . had penetrated into the organs of government." Sirjani went on to claim that the charge of undermining the foundations of Islam "had become a pretext for the suppression [and] strangulation" of those who criticized power holders. Shortly thereafter, Sirjani was detained on spurious charges of sodomy, opium addiction, and being in contact with antirevolutionary elements. Eight months later, the regime announced that Sirjani, who did not have a history of heart trouble, had died of a heart attack. They refused to hand over his corpse to his family or to permit an independent autopsy.[2]

In defending his writings against the charge of being anti-Islamic, Sirjani had drawn a sharp distinction between belief in Islam and the attempt to impose a politically motivated, unidimensional interpretation of Islam. Today, aversion against the imposition of such an order is becoming increasingly rampant even among the religious intelligentsia, which had initially wholeheartedly supported the theocratic order. This group wishes to reform the present system in order to reconcile it with pluralism and democracy. The writings and declarations of the Islamist philosopher Abdulkarim Soroush provide the most systematic and coherent delineation of the democratically inclined religious intelligentsia's vision of the appropriate political order.

A professor of philosophy at Tehran University, Soroush is endowed with impeccable revolutionary credentials. During the early years of the revolution, he was a member of the theocracy's Senior Cultural Revolution Panel. In this capacity, he took an active role in directing the university purges and book burnings of the early 1980s (Miller, 1996, p. 455). Today, however, Soroush has abandoned his role as an intolerant prosecutor of suspected antirevolutionaries. No longer a functionary, he now derives his bearings more from the philosophy of his former professor, Sir Karl Popper, than from the utterances of Ayatollah Khomeini. Soroush's popularity is now such that he is increasingly being referred to as the Ali Shariati of his age. Soroush, however, is a far more serious philosopher than Shariati, who was more of an ideologue, committed primarily to inciting rather than presenting coherent and consistent arguments.

Soroush advocates a relativistic understanding of Islam. Arguing that there is not, nor has there ever been, a single absolute interpretation of Islamic precepts and doctrines, Soroush maintains that neither a single cleric nor a clerical group can claim to provide the true interpretation of Islam: "There is no official interpretation of Islam" ("Soroush Talks 'Roots and Fruits,'" 1997). According to Soroush, although the Sharia (Islamic law), which is handed down to us from the past, is divine and sublime, its apprehension, which is always contemporary, is of necessity human and mundane (Boroujerdi, 1996, p. 173). Man's comprehension of the Sharia, therefore, is subject to varying hermeneutical interpretations. Referring to this proposition, Soroush has stated, "I regard this epistemological distinction to be my most important achievement" (quoted in Boroujerdi, 1996, p. 173).[3] Since the understanding of Islam is dependent upon time, space, and circumstance, competing paradigms should not be silenced. Moreover, the clergy should not impose its interpretation of the Sharia on the masses. People should not be forced to practice Islam but should be free willingly to submit to God (Andoni, 1995, p. 6; "An Iranian Martin Luther Preaches Islamic Reforms," 1996; Soroush, 1993).

Such an interpretation can readily lend itself to the reconciliation of Islam with a liberal version of liberal democracy. Yet Soroush goes further. In what appears to be an implicit argument for the separation of church and state, he maintains that religion should never be turned into an ideology. According to Soroush: "[U]sing religion as an ideology makes it intolerant and authoritarian . . . Government and economics are the province of intellect and reason, not religion." If religion assumes ideological connotations, then it is bound to make itself vulnerable to the charge of being responsible for the ills of society. Moreover, the clerics should neither be financially supported by the state or people's contributions nor acquire any gain from political office. To retain their purity and independence, they should earn their livelihood through hard work. "Religion is for the lovers of the faith, not the dealers of the faith" (Wright, 1995). Furthermore, if your interests are secured through religion, then you will defend your interests first and religion will become secondary ("Iran Won't Let Soroush Leave," 1997).

Although Soroush regards himself as a pious believer and a defender of Islam, his ideas are regarded as highly dangerous by conservative defenders of the clerical regime. His implied call for the separation of religion and politics poses a devastating challenge to the underlying principle of the regime, namely, Khomeini's doctrine of *velayat-e faqih*, or rule by the Islamic jurist. Shortly after the revolution, Khomeini himself had declared that "[t]hose intellectuals who say that the clergy should leave politics and go back to the mosque speak on behalf of Satan" ("Speech to University Students," *Itila'at*, September 22, 1979, as quoted in Abrahamian, 1982, p. 530). Soroush, therefore, in the course of the last few years, has been maliciously attacked by the regime's leading conservative figures. Especially prior to Khatami's rise to power, he had been made persona non grata, virtually banned from teaching, publishing, lecturing, or granting interviews. Nevertheless, upset by the manner in which the regime has tarnished Islam, Iranians in increasing numbers, particularly the intelligentsia, continue to be attracted to his ideas. In October 1995, after a group of revolutionary zealots physically attacked Soroush and prevented him from delivering a lecture at Tehran University, 7,000 students took part in a pro-Soroush demonstration. Calling for tolerance and academic freedom, the protest was probably the largest organized implicitly anti-regime activity in Tehran since the revolution ("7,000 TU Students Protest Regime Control," 1995). Even after Khatami's attempts to enlarge the realm of permissible speech, Soroush has continued to be harassed by Hezbollahi thugs. In August 1999, he was attacked and beaten by a Hezbollahi gang after he had delivered a lecture to a group of his supporters at a private house in the city of Mashad ("Soroush Is Beaten After Lecturing," 1999). The ability of Soroush to attract a mass following among students is indicative of the aversion of many students toward the system. Indeed, prorevolutionary student organizations have repeatedly expressed anxiety about the absence of revolutionary devotion by many of their colleagues (Siavoshi, 1995, p. 214).

The Islamic Republic has also treated recalcitrant journalists with disdain. The Paris-based organization Reporters Without Borders has cited Iran as among the countries in which "journalism is a high-risk occupation" because of governmental oppression ("Iranian Press Least Free," 1996). Even if they are aligned with a faction from within the ruling clerical establishment, journals that overstep the bounds of the politically permissible are quickly closed down and their staff is occasionally savagely chastised. In 1995, the newspaper *Jahan-e Islam*, published by the current spiritual leader's estranged brother Hadi Khamenei, who is associated with the radical faction, was shut down. The courts, dominated by the conservative faction, held that the newspaper "created doubts, printed untrue stories, and insulted the religious beliefs of the Muslim nation" (Miller, 1996, p. 459). In 1996 alone, five journals were closed down. Some were charged with such vague accusations as weakening the foundations of the Islamic Republic. Abbas Maroufi, the editor of the literary journal *Gardoon*, was convicted of publishing disrespectful articles about Iran's supreme leader Ayatollah Khamenei. In addition to being sentenced to thirty-five lashes and six months in prison, he was barred from any "journalistic activity for two years." Reacting to the closure of his journal, another editor, who did not want to be quoted by name, asserted that "there is deep fear and absolutely no freedom of expression. Almost everyone has been silenced" ("Backlash of Intolerance Striking Fear in Iran," 1996).

Weary of the constrictions curtailing their ability to express themselves freely, 134 prominent intellectuals living in Iran courageously signed an open letter on October 24, 1995, calling for an end to censorship. Also in 1995, more than 200 filmmakers petitioned the government, urging noninterference in their scripts, production, and distribution. The regime responded by intimidating the writers to withdraw their names and banning the export of any film depicting a negative image of Iran ("Faith in Numbers," 1994, pp. 64–65; Wright, 1995).

But given the largely unfavorable and hostile milieu in which they find themselves, in order to retain their integrity, most Iranian intellectuals, including filmmakers, are precisely interested in projecting a negative image of Iran. The case of Mohsen Makhmalbaf, an internationally renowned movie director, is instructive in this regard. Makhmalbaf is an erstwhile dedicated supporter of the Islamic revolution who comes from a destitute family. Before the revolution, he spent five years in the monarchy's prisons, where he was repeatedly tortured. In the early years of the revolution, his films were largely propagandistic in nature and were highly supportive of the Islamic system. Gradually, however, he stopped celebrating the revolution, concentrating instead on exposing the absence of freedom in the lives of ordinary people. In his *Marriage of the Blessed*, he depicts a disturbingly realistic picture of the devastating impact of the Iran-Iraq war, which, as many critics have observed, did not result in the demise of even one prominent mullah's son. Makhmalbaf's last several movies were banned in Iran ("Makhmalbaf Skips Gabbeh Opening," 1997; Miller, 1996, p. 446).

Other intellectuals who have largely lost faith in the revolution are university students and faculty members. Slightly more than one year after the revolution, the politicized clerics, who were clearly emerging triumphant from the postrevolutionary power struggles, closed all of Iran's thirty-four universities for two years. The closure of the universities was part of an overall campaign designed to overhaul the academic curricula along Islamic lines. Textbooks were rewritten, and all of the nation's teaching staff, including primary- and secondary-school teachers, were purged of those deemed to have anti-Islamic tendencies. The entire university faculty staff of 6,954 was cut in half, and 60,000 teachers were relieved of their positions because of political considerations (Enayat, 1983, p. 177; Miller, 1996, p. 446).

Educators, particularly university professors, many of whom are Western-educated and supportive of the separation of religion and politics, are still viewed suspiciously by the conservatively inclined ruling clerics. In 1996, on condition of anonymity, a professor recently asserted that "the teaching staff is regarded as the most dangerous element [within society, because it] might join the external [opposition] groups in the struggle against the Islamic regime" ("Clergy Calls for Purifying Westernized Professors," 1996). As in the time of the shah, the regime's secret agents have penetrated the universities. Those who even obliquely question the political role of the mullahs may be fined, detained, or "have their teaching disrupted by rent-a-crowd gangs" ("Children of the Iranian Revolution: A Survey of Iran," 1997). Again, as in the previous regime, in both the recruitment of faculty and students, preference is accorded to those committed to the officially sanctioned ideology rather than to those with superior intellectual and professional capabilities (Amuzegar, 1995, p. 10).

In 1996, Ansar-e-Hezbollah (the Partisans of the Party of God), a quasi-official vigilante group composed of revolutionary zealots (associated with the ultraconservative faction of the ruling elite), issued a proclamation justifying its use of force to combat those it regards as counterrevolutionary. Highly anti-intellectual in tone, the proclamation castigates free-thinking intellectuals as enemies of Islam, "who resort to their gift of gab to undermine revolutionary standards" ("Ansar: Violence Good—and You Better Like It," 1996). The spiritual guide of the Ansar is Ayatollah Ahmad Janati, who, apart from serving as the secretary of the Council of Guardians (a twelve-man body that must clear all laws enacted by the Parliament), also heads the Islamic Propaganda Organization. Janati has charged the universities with undermining religious values and has publicly called on conscientious (i.e., pro-Hezbollahi) students to snitch on their professors and classmates. He has also endorsed vigilantism by zealous students:

> I do not think anybody denies the fact that those who enter universities with beliefs and morals . . . have lost much of those Islamic values when they leave. . . . If students see a lecturer questioning our values and attacking these values, they [the students] must have the right to defend these values. No one must reprimand them for this defense and no one should deny them the right to defend our beliefs. ("Call out for New College Purges," 1996)

Relatedly, Ayatollah Khamenei's representative in the nation's universities, Hojatoleslam Gholam Reza Mesbahi, who is charged with overseeing the proper "Islamic" functioning of Iran's 114 colleges and universities (with 150,000 students and 13,700 teaching staff), has asserted that new foreign-educated faculty recruits must be "ideologically quarantined in order to prevent the expansion of their thought" ("Purge Has Eyes on Foreign Educated," 1996).

As in the Pahlavi era, students continue to be prohibited from engaging in any type of political activity that is not officially sanctioned. Whereas the shah sought to promote civil privatism, the present regime even seeks to control the students' private lives. Numerous hurdles have been placed on intermingling between the opposite sexes and the pursuit of frivolous forms of entertainment. Unlike the shah's era, however, since the regime houses various forms of ideological tendencies within its purview, the students are presented with a greater number of officially tolerated political groupings and activities in which to take part. But even such groups are not free to express themselves with impunity and can incur the wrath of Hezbollahi purists. In 1997, Heshmatollah Tabarzadi, leader of the democratically and radically inclined Union of Islamic Associations of Students, was assaulted by a Hezbollahi gang for arguing that the powers of the supreme leader of the country should become limited ("Hezbollahi Gang Goes on Rampage," 1997). According to Ramin Jahanbegloo, a founder of *Goft-O-Gu*, a scholarly quarterly devoted to promoting dialogue between secular and Islamist intellectuals: "[M]any [young] people [are] now 'totally disillusioned' with religious values. The Islamic revolution [has] succeeded in producing among the young an a-religious generation as well as a 'James Dean syndrome'—'rebels without a cause'—and a sharp generation gap between young Iran and the aging clerics who made the rules" (Miller, 1996, p. 456).

The Sociopolitical Milieu, Then and Now

As in prerevolutionary Iran, members of the intelligentsia have become conspicuously alienated from the regime not only because of the dismal fate that has befallen them. They are also deeply disturbed about the glaring problems that plague their surrounding environment, problems that rather than having been mollified by the revolution have been vastly compounded. While incurring the consternation of the nation's ordinary citizens, these problems are particularly distressing to the intelligentsia, which tends to be most concerned about conditions for the good life and the just society.

Apart from suppression of freedom and overt forms of unsanctioned political activity, the intellectuals regarded the widespread practice of corruption and nepotism in prerevolutionary Iran, particularly among members of the royal family, as reprehensible. To acquire favorable treatment from the government, secure lucrative contracts, and maximize profitability, businessmen who were engaged in commercial and industrial ventures had to offer worthy stakes to the relatives of the shah or the Pahlavi Foundation. The largest conglomerate in Iran, the Pahlavi Foundation was nominally a charitable organization. However, according to the *New York Times*: "behind the facade of charitable activities, the foundation [was] used in three ways: as a source of funds for the royal family; as a means of exerting influence on key sectors of the economy; and as a conduit for rewards to supporters of the regime" (Chittendin, 1979, as quoted in Abrahamian, 1982, p. 438).

In addition to receiving their cut from the foundation and private enterprises, princes and princesses, each of whom was associated with a particular area of development, acted as intermediaries and agents for foreign firms interested in selling goods and services to the Iranian government at inflated prices. Often successful in persuading government officials (many of whom also engaged in unrestrained bribery and influence peddling) to reward their clients with lucrative contracts, princes, princesses, and other high-ranking officials were able to augment their exorbitant fortunes through the acquisition of payoffs and commissions (Graham, 1978, p. 162; Naraghi, 1994, pp. 44, 51, 53, 72; Parsons, 1984, p. 28). In 1969, the shah's closest confidant and minister of court, Assadollah Alam, recorded the following candid and revealing observation in his confidential diary: "I belong to a corrupt and money-grubbing elite. Iran stands little chance under the thumb of such a motley crew" (Alam, 1991, p. 81). Again, in 1972 he asserted: "One only need look around this country to realize that we, the ruling class, behave as if we were conquerors in a vanquished land. The people not surprisingly resent this attitude" (Alam, 1991, p. 209). In June 1972, the U.S. embassy issued a report on corruption in Iran. A section of the report, entitled "American Companies and Influence Peddlers," cited seven U.S. companies, including General Electric, Northrop, Boeing Aircraft, McDonnell-Douglas, and Neill-Price, that were "to the Embassy's certain knowledge, buying the influence of the persons listed with them" (Bill, 1988, p. 209).

Outraged by such behavior, the Islamic revolutionaries promised to bring about the moral regeneration of Iran. Instead, the revolution has led to the institutionalization of corruption. Venality on the part of high-ranking officials has persisted and even expanded. The inheritors of the assets of the Pahlavi Foundation and the enterprises belonging to the shah's cronies (the Foundation of the Oppressed, the Martyrs' Foundation, and 15 Khordad Foundation) continue to function nominally as charitable organizations. Behind the masquerade of charity, however, they continue to perform the same functions as the Pahlavi Foundation. But instead of providing funds to the royal family, they bestow unimaginable economic and political power upon a few well-connected members of the ruling elite.

In 1997, Control Risks Group, Ltd., a respected British research organization, ranked the Islamic Republic as the ninth most corrupt regime (out of 185) in the world. The company defined corruption as "the offering or accepting of bribes or kickbacks, the abuse of official positions for personal gain and the frustration or impediment of public tenders" ("Iran Ranked 9th Most Venal Government," 1997).

Iran today is rife with corruption and scandals involving influence peddling and embezzlement by high-ranking government officials. Indeed, the extent of public disquiet concerning high-level venality has been so high that the ruling clerics have felt compelled to acknowledge and condemn its widespread practice. In one of his sermons, Ayatollah Janati asserted: "Many senior government officials and people have been involved in the smuggling of contraband goods. . . . They were using government facilities for smuggling purposes. They should be punished twice, three times and ten times" (*BBC Summary of World Broadcasts*, 1995). Further, the Speaker of Iran's Majles (Parliament), Hojatoleslam Nategh Nouri, has said: "We have come to implement social justice and Islamic justice. This means all this misuse of power, bribery and violation of the laws must be halted" ("Speeches Point Way to the Future," 1997).

Among the general public, the scale of bribery has gone from bad to worse. A former *New York Times* reporter, who recently visited Iran, maintains that "getting anything done . . . —sending a fax, getting garbage collected, paying a traffic ticket, even, I was told securing an interview with President Rafsanjani—required gratuity" (Miller, 1996, p. 480). Wealthy transgressors can generally escape prosecution by bribing members of the morals-enforcing Komitehs. Although this arrangement is mutually beneficial from the vantage point of both parties, enabling the transgressors to find temporary relief from burdensome social restrictions and the commissars to enhance their meager incomes, it is repugnant to the intelligentsia, which is concerned with the degradation it engenders in human relations.

Another reason the intellectuals were alienated from Pahlavi Iran revolved around the fact that the Pahlavis' efforts at rapid modernization had resulted in an alarmingly massive disparity in wealth and income. In 1969–1970, the International Labor Organization found Iran's Gini coefficient (which measures how an economy's income distribution deviates from perfect equality) to be "higher than any country in East and Southeast Asia, considerably higher than in Western countries and probably as high or higher than in Latin American countries for which data are available" (cited in Foran, 1993, p. 331). In 1973, the most economically prosperous 10 percent of the urban households accounted for 38 percent of spending, while the bottom 30 percent were responsible for only 7 percent (Boroujerdi, 1996, p. 27). Today, the most recent figures put out by the Islamic Republic itself show that the disparity in income between rich and poor in Iran is twice the average for underdeveloped countries. The collective income of the wealthiest 10 percent of the population is presently 27.3 times greater than the poorest 10 percent ("Iran's Richest Are Still Richer Than Most Rich," 1996).

The intelligentsia was also particularly distressed with Iran's dismal human rights record during the shah's rule. In 1974, the secretary-general of Amnesty International described Iran's repression of human rights as "worse than any other country in the world" (Graham, 1978, p. 146). In 1976, the respected International Commission of Jurists published a well-documented report stating that "there can be no doubt that torture has been systematically practiced over a number of years against recalcitrant suspects under interrogation by SAVAK" (cited in Bill, 1988, p. 187). Even the shah himself obliquely acknowledged in the mid-1970s that his regime was inflicting torture upon dissidents: "I am not bloodthirsty. I am working for my country and the coming generations. I can't waste my time on a few young idiots. I don't believe the tortures attributed to SAVAK are as common as people say, but I can't run everything" (quoted in Bill, 1988, p. 186). In 1977, Amnesty International also asserted that there were 100,000 political prisoners in Iran. This, however, appears to have been an inflated figure, derived due to propaganda by Iranian dissidents overseas and the policy of Iranian officials to restrict severely any overt monitoring of the nation's human rights record. The actual number was probably closer to 4,000, still a staggering figure (Naraghi, 1994, p. 77).

The revolution was supposed to have put an end to such atrocities. Iran's human rights record, however, continues to be bleak, although the severe brutality of the revolution's early years, when thousands of suspected antirevolutionary elements were summarily executed, has subsided. Since its inception, the Islamic Republic has consistently been ranked as one of the worst violators of human rights. Human Rights Watch has cited Iran as one of only ten nations on the globe where it is prohibited from engaging in any type of overt monitoring of human rights ("Iran Ignores Own Offer to Open Prisons to View," 1995). According to a recent estimate, the number of Iran's political prisoners stands at 19,000 (Teimourian, 1994, p. 70). Although the Iranian Constitution forbids arbitrary arrest and confinement, the authorities, when they deem fit, do not shrink from imposing incommunicado detentions, which can continue indefinitely.

In a 1997 report submitted to the UN, Maurice Copithorne, the UN's special representative on Iranian human rights, asserts that the number of executions in Iran doubled between 1995 and 1996. Referring to amputations and the stoning of women for adultery as examples, Copithorne also notes that "cruel, inhuman or degrading treatment or punishment continues in Iran . . . In general, Iran does not recognize the equality [before the law] of men and women, and tolerates discriminatory conduct towards women" ("UN Says Executions in Iran Now Are Doubling Annually," 1997). In a 1998 interview with Inter Press Service, Copithorne asserted that "there has been little change in [Iran's] human rights situation since president Khatami took office" ("UN Again Raps Iran over Rights," 1998). Meanwhile, summing up the UN human rights official 1998 report on Iran, Copithorne stated: "For many . . . [Khatami's domestic reform process] was slow in bearing fruit and the improvements were too uncertain. For others [the conservative establishment], the process was moving too quickly, and the Islamic nature of society was in jeopardy" ("UN Rights Report: Iran Needs to Learn Tolerance," 1998). Many political dissidents have been executed for taking part in such nebulous and "preposterous but judicially sanctioned crimes as 'apostasy,' 'warning against God,' and 'corruption on earth'" (Miller, 1996, p. 465).

As in the time of the shah, the use of torture continues to be pervasive. According to the U.S. State Department's human rights report: "Credible reports indicate that [Iran's] security forces continue to torture detainees and prisoners. Common methods include suspension for long periods in contorted positions, burning with cigarettes, and, most frequently, severe and repeated beatings with cables . . . on the back and on the soles of the feet" ("U.S. Sees No Human Rights Improvement," 1997). Human rights specialists maintain that Iran has recently adopted a new torture technique, known as "the bell," in order to obviate inflicting physically visible scars on tortured parties. A glass dome placed over its victims, "the bell," when utilized under the sun, can act as a magnifying glass, causing its hapless prisoners to suffocate and bake. Reacting to such accusations,

Assadollah Ladjevardi, the previous head of Iran's prison system, asserted that not only does Iran not have any political prisoners but torture is never used in Iranian prisons. Ladjevardi argued that activists who condemn Iran's treatment of the accused are "sick people, and there is nothing you can do with a sick person" ("Most Prisoners Just Disappear," 1996).

The above comparisons have shown how the generally hostile and constraining environment in which free-thinking intellectuals have found themselves since the revolution is not appreciably different from that which they confronted during the shah's rule: Corruption, maldistribution, censorship, and repression have abounded. Whereas the shah referred to independent thinkers as "idiots," some members of the current regime castigate them as "sick" individuals. But the parallels between present-day and prerevolutionary Iran as they relate to intellectuals should not blind us into disregarding the differences, however subtle, between the two eras. These differences generally revolve around the nature of the regime's appeasing overtures in response to the rising tide of intellectual dissatisfaction. It is to the examination of such responses that we shall now turn.

Appeasing Overtures of the Monarchy Versus the Theocracy

The shah was only willing to resort to political and economic bribery in order to induce the intelligentsia to cooperate with his regime. Those who were willing to compromise their convictions and sing the praises of the Pahlavi dynasty were handsomely rewarded. The co-opted members of the intelligentsia were generally put in charge of producing and disseminating the officially sanctioned ideology. This ideology, however, did not appeal to the intellectual community, which generally found its central tenets repulsive. The secular intelligentsia, seeking political participation and civil liberties, was especially appalled by the ideology's emphasis on strict loyalty to the person of the shah and depoliticization of the citizenry. In addition to being averse to the above, religious intellectuals were also bothered by the state ideology's celebration of Persian chauvinism and glorification of Iran's pre-Islamic past (Arjomand, 1988, p. 68; Boroujerdi, 1996, p. 30). "In the age of republicanism, radicalism, and nationalism, the Pahlavis appeared in the eyes of the intelligentsia to favor monarchism, conservatism, and Western imperialism" (Abrahamian, 1989, p. 17).

Most of those employed at senior levels in institutions of higher learning and outlets of the mass media, whose primary function "was to propagate and propagandize the activities of the monarchy and the monarch's policies as carried out by the government," received substantial financial rewards for their sycophancy. Subservient artists and writers were also awarded with royal patronage. Furthermore, those intellectuals who went out of their way to prove their loyalty to the shah were singled out for political as well as economic rewards. Such individuals were "allowed to walk in the corridors of power" as chancellors of universities, ambassadors, senators, ministers, and even prime ministers (Boroujerdi, 1996, p.

44). Once in positions of authority, many of these individuals turned against their disaffected and uncompromising brethren, persecuting them with a vengeance. Amir Abbas Hoveyda, the shah's longest-serving prime minister (1964–1977), a highly cultivated and eloquent man who undoubtedly deserved the label of intellectual, once referred to alienated members of the intelligentsia as "little crybaby communists trained at the London School of Economics" (quoted in Bill, 1988, p. 166). Only toward the end of his rule did the shah decide to enlarge slightly the almost nonexistent realm of permissible political discourse to appease the Carter administration, with a secondary aim being to cultivate the support of the intelligentsia.

Like the shah, the current regime continues to reward proestablishment and submissive intellectuals with high-level political appointments and economic advantages. In contrast to the monarchy, however, the theocracy quite cleverly allows, within limits whose parameters are always in doubt, a significant expression of political and social dissent. A plethora of mostly professional and apolitical magazines and newspapers now operates in Iran. But there are also a surprising number of journals with explicit and implicit political orientations. Most of these publications are aligned with specific factions from within the fractious political establishment. However, there are also those that attempt to steer a relatively independent line and are not explicitly aligned with any of the factions in the ruling elite. These publications are usually allowed to criticize specific policies of the government as well as the utterances of public officials. In addition, there are a number of scholarly journals that, though dealing mostly with esoteric topics, have also daringly scrutinized such notions as the viability of the present form of Islamic government. Increasingly, they have come to favor the adoption of Soroush's "reformist Islam, which strongly resembles what Western intellectuals call 'secularism'" (Miller, 1996, p. 454) as the best means for overcoming Iran's problems. "Islamic feminists" are also allowed to espouse their views in their journals. Indeed, at times, their "criticisms of the government's treatment of women [can be] as scathing as that of any non-Muslim foreign critic" (Miller, 1996, p. 454). But, as noted, the regime keeps members of the intelligentsia guessing about how far they can go before they are silenced. One thing is certain, however. Those who question the legitimacy of the Islamic revolution or the actions and declarations of Ayatollah Khomeini or his successor, Ayatollah Khamenei, are harshly chastised.

Although this situation is unlikely to be altered in the foreseeable future, Iranian intellectuals, most of whom are clearly alienated from the prevailing order, are hopeful that the realm of permissible political expression and participation may yet be enlarged. Their relative optimism derives from the inauguration of Iran's new reformist president, Hojatoleslam Seyyed Mohammad Khatami, whose landslide election victory is widely viewed as a protest vote against the status quo. Khatami is a former minister of culture and Islamic guidance, who resigned from his position in 1992 after being widely criticized by the conservative faction of the ruling clerics for being excessively tolerant of politically subversive and corrosive forms of expression. Both before and after his election, Khatami made abundantly clear his support for the institutionalization of the rule of law, creation of a vibrant civil society (although he has never defined precisely his understanding of this concept), tolerance for diverse viewpoints, and expansion of civil liberties and personal freedoms.

In his book *Fear of the Storm*, published before his election victory, Khatami asks rhetorically: "[E]ven if we did not allow one bad book to be published in our society, or if we prevented every newspaper or magazine from publishing anything contrary to our wishes and tastes . . . when we banned and prevented all these at an official level, will they not be put at the disposal of the people through any other means?" (quoted in Halliday, 1998). In a very significant speech marking the first anniversary of his victory, Khatami drew attention to the struggle between faith and freedom, bluntly conceding that "the lesson of history was that in any conflict between faith and liberty, liberty would win. Two attempts had been made to impose faith coercively: the Christian Inquisition in the Sixteenth Century, and communism in the twentieth, and both had failed; and so, too, would any Islamic attempt to do so now" (Halliday, 1998). And in a speech that is representative of many of his other utterances and writings, Khatami, only a few months after his inauguration in 1997, declared: "All of us—both the government and the people—must strive to respect the law. All of us must perform our duties within the framework of the law. The law has specified the people's rights. The law has also defined the *limits* of government's authority" ("Gov't Must Obey Law for a Change," 1997). He further stated: "To avoid the arbitrary interpretation of regulations, the law [must be] institutionalized to guide cultural and artistic activities" ("Newsmen Vote for New, Free Unions," 1997). The Iranian Constitution, which comprises a strange blend of theocratic and democratic elements, can indeed be interpreted to provide for far greater civil rights and liberties than have ever existed in the Islamic Republic. Khatami has consistently maintained that he intends to work within the confines of Islam and the law. "What we are aiming for," he has maintained, "is freedom within the framework of the constitution and the Islamic regime" (quoted in "Those Behind Cried Forward," 1998). But he has always emphasized the more democratic components of both the Constitution and Islam.

The intellectuals, of course, do not base their partial optimism on Khatami's utterances alone. During his two and one-half years in office, Khatami has taken some concrete measures to curb censorship. Within the first year of his presidency, the Islamic Republic's Ministry of Culture and Islamic Guidance, under the direction of its liberally inclined minister Ataollah Mohajerani, approved some 200 new charters for newspapers and periodicals.[4] This explosion of new journals, most of which were sympathetic to the reformist camp, raised Iran's daily circulation by one-third. Khatami's government also restored the publishing licenses of three previously banned newspapers, including the radical *Pyam-*

e Daneshjoo, which ran investigative reports on corruption and abuses of power. Meanwhile, the censors allowed the publication of some books that had previously been regarded as anathema, including the sexy novels of Milan Kundera, a Czech writer living in France (although these books were severely censored, excluding all but the general outlines of the stories). The new chief of the state office for cinema, himself a filmmaker who had encountered difficulties with previous censors, diminished the burden of restrictive regulations on filmmakers. And Khatami himself reportedly personally intervened in order to allow Soroush, whose passport had been confiscated, to travel out of the country (Amuzegar, 1999, p.78; "Iran: Time Matures," 1999; "'Saint Diana' Leaves Many Questions After 100 Days," 1997).

Taking advantage of the less restrictive milieu, many journalists, scholars, and even ordinary citizens writing in editorial columns began to delve into and explore the negative aspects of life under the Islamic Republic. Articles began to regularly appear on various topics ranging from corruption, nepotism, injustice, and inequality to the "housing shortage, marriage hurdles, and stifling restrictions on recreation and entertainment" (Amuzegar, 1998, p. 79). Much more significantly, however, topics that up to then had been considered taboo or had only been obliquely addressed in the back pages of obscure scholarly journals began to be directly analyzed in the popular press. For example, writers and editors began to wonder publicly about the wisdom of active political involvement by the clerics, the power and credentials of the supreme leader Khamenei, the benefits of reestablishing relations with the United States, and even the desirability and viability of the concept of *velayat-e faqih* ("Iran's Whiff of Liberalism," 1998; "Why Isn't Khamenei Doing More to Avert an Explosion in Iran?" 1999). Moreover, emboldened by the lifting of the limits on free expression, several nominally "Islamic" student associations proposed that severe restrictions be placed on the powers of the supreme leader. In addition, they maintained that the supreme leader, rather than being appointed for life by the Assembly of Experts, be elected directly by the people for a limited tenure of office. They also called for the nullification of the powers of the Council of Guardians, which is empowered to assess the Islamic credentials of prospective office seekers as well as the compatibility of legislation enacted by Parliament with the tenets of Islam and the constitution (Amuzegar, 1998, pp. 78–79).

The freedom to express such bold pronouncements was indeed unprecedented in the history of the Islamic Republic. Yet as far as the intellectuals were concerned, there was no guarantee that it would be sustained, let alone expanded. Indeed, there had been no meaningful institutional changes, and conservative forces, in spite of their unpopularity, still controlled most of the country's significant levers of power. Khamenei, who up to then had increasingly aligned himself with the xenophobic and anti-intellectual conservative faction, continued to be both constitutionally and practically more powerful than the new president. Furthermore, the conservative faction continued to exercise exclusive control over

Iranian radio and television, the security forces, the Council of Guardians, the Assembly of Experts, and the Friday Prayer Leaders. It also constituted the largest block in the Majles and wielded enormous economic power through its control of the tax-exempt revolutionary foundations.

The hard-liners and many conservatives, moreover, perhaps not without justi- fication, viewed Khatami's reforms with great suspicion, fearing that such liber- alization would ultimately undermine their power base and even bring about the demise of the Islamic Republic. There thus developed a strong backlash against reform, and the fortunes of the intellectuals came to be tied to an increasingly bitter and unpredictable tug-of-war between the conservatives and reformers within the Islamic regime's establishment (curiously, many of Khatami's staunchest proreform allies were now composed of former radicals, who had taken an active role during the early years of the revolution in viciously persecut- ing the intellectual community). In the summer of 1998, the Majles impeached Abdullah Nouri, the moderate interior minister and close Khatami confidant, who had authorized a number of peaceful demonstrations by reformist "Islamic" student associations.

At the same time, Iran's conservative-dominated judiciary closed down several of the most avowedly reformist newspapers, which had begun to test the limits of freedom by featuring stories on previously taboo topics. The most prominent of these newspapers was the daily *Jame-eh* (which changed its name to *Tous* after its publishing license was suspended pending a trial). *Jame-eh*'s bold liberal line had earned it a readership of some 300,000, after only seven months of publication. Following the trial, the newspaper was shut down permanently, and its editor, Mahmoud Shamsolvaezin, and the director of its publishing company, Hamid Reza Jalalipour, were jailed for thirty-five days (MacLeod, 1998). Seeking to in- timidate its opponents, the hard-line fringe of the conservative establishment even went so far as to unleash the Islamist vigilante thugs to beat up intellectuals with whom it disagreed, forcibly close down cinemas showing "un-Islamic" films, and even rough up reformist clerics, whose sermons they found to be morally lax ("Iran Comes Clean," 1999).

Even more ominously, however, seeking to embarrass, discredit, and perhaps set the stage for the ouster of Khatami, hard-liners from within the conservative camp brutally murdered a number of secular dissidents and intellectuals in late November and December 1998. The seventy-one-year-old secular nationalist crusader and liberal democratic political leader, Dariush Foruhar, who headed the banned National Party of Iran, and his wife, Parvaneh Eskandari, were sav- agely decapitated in November. Shortly thereafter, Majid Sharif, a journalist and translator with distinctively liberal leanings, was killed. Then, within a period of two weeks, two prominent intellectuals with impeccable secular credentials, Mo- hammad Mokhtari and Mohammad Jafar Pouyandeh, were strangled with a leather strap or belt. Mokhtari was a poet and a literary critic; Pouyandeh was an essayist and translator, renowned for his translation of the Universal Declaration of Human Rights. They were both among the 134 intellectuals who had signed an open letter in 1994 calling for the lifting of censorship. Prior to the murders of Pouyandeh and Mokhtari, five of the signatories had already been killed or had died under mysterious circumstances. As recently as October 1998, Mokhtari and Pouyandeh had been summoned before a revolutionary court and warned strongly to desist from their attempts to revive and organize the Writers' Association (Dickey, 1999, p. 36; Appiah, 1999, p. A15; Sciolino 1999).

The killing spree petrified the intellectuals, many of whom correctly suspected that the security forces were involved and promptly went into hiding. Khatami, however, acted expeditiously to protect his reforms and reassure his supporters. He declared that the murders had been designed to undermine the efforts of his administration to institutionalize the rule of law and create a civil society. He also ordered an inquiry designed to identify the culprit(s). Shortly thereafter, those who had been charged by the president to investigate the murders released a startling and uncharacteristically candid report, asserting that the murders had been perpetrated by a death squad operating inside the Islamic Republic's Ministry of Intelligence (a longtime bastion of the conservative establishment, which operates under the direct supervision of the supreme leader). Such an admission was indeed unparalleled in the long annals of Iranian history. It served to embarrass the conservatives who, prior to the declarations of the Khatami investigating committee, had blamed the murders on their usual targets, the "Zionist entity" and the United States. In a sharp reversal of rhetoric, they now conceded that "irresponsible, misguided, and unruly personnel" from within the ministry had been responsible for the murders; even Ayatollah Khamenei went so far as to characterize the murders as "crimes against the national security of the country" (Sciolino, 1999).

Emboldened by such declarations, the liberal press asserted that the death squad had devised a list of 180 undesirable individuals, whom it had earmarked for assassination. According to press reports, the "enemies" list comprised not only secular dissidents and intellectuals but also contained the names of Islamist intellectuals (Soroush) and prominent figures from the reformist camp (including the former interior minister Abdullah Nouri and Faezeh Hashemi, an "Islamic feminist member of parliament who is also former President Rafsanjani's daughter ("The Islamic Republic of Iran Turns 20," 1999; Sciolino, 1999).

Although seminal in its departure from precedent and a clear symbolic victory for the reformers, the aforementioned startling admission did not provide sufficient assurance and solace to intellectuals, who, according to the novelist Hooshang Golshiri, continued to "feel the threat of murder" (Sciolino, 1999). Nor did it prove to be more than a temporary setback to the conservatives, who continued their attempts to thwart Khatami's efforts at social and political liberalization. Indeed, in their efforts to undermine reform, the president's conservative adversaries widened their assault against the moderately inclined media, which has expanded substantially since Khatami's rise to power. Aware of their disturbingly fragile levels of support and acceptance, the conservatives fear and detest the reformist press, regarding it as a potent instrument through which the more moderate forces seek to wrest control from them. The reformist press, after all, although not monolithic and composed of those with varying levels of commitment to democracy and secularization of politics, is clearly more in tune with the mood of the populace, publicizes the vision of Khatami and his allies, launches a highly effective criticism of the conservative agenda and personalities, and exhorts the people to vote for the reformist camp. In 1999, the conservatives in the Majles, attempted, but failed, to impeach Khatami's moderate minister of culture and Islamic guidance, Ataollah Mohajerani, who succeeded in retaining his position by a slim margin. The conservatives, however, did succeed in closing down several prominent reformist newspapers, including *Zan* (woman) run by Faezeh Hashemi, *Neshat* (which was edited by Shamsolvaezin), and *Hoviat Khish* (one's identity) administered by Heshmatollah Tabarzadi, director of the Council of Tehran University Students (who was also jailed) ("Iranian Opposition Leaders Arrested over Riots," 1999). Hashemi's newspaper was shut down by the conservative-dominated press court in part because it had published excerpts from the New Year's message of the former empress, Farah Diba, to the Iranian people. Interestingly, though, no actions were taken by the courts against a conservative newspaper, which had also quoted Farah at length. Undeterred, Shamsolvaezin, however, promptly started another publication.

Illustrating the increasingly pronounced extent of intra-elite rivalries within the regime was the closure, in 1999, of the *Salam* newspaper. Published by Hojatoleslam Mohammad Musavi-Khoeiniha, one of the pillars of the revolution (who had served as a feared prosecutor general as well as the spiritual adviser to the students who seized the American embassy and held its personnel hostage for 444 days), *Salam* was one of the most popular and widely circulated dailies in Iran. Like many other Khatami supporters, Khoeiniha has overcome his initial overzealous radicalism, for which he had gained infamy, and become a staunch proponent of moderate reform. *Salam* was closed down by the special court for the clergy after the proreform newspaper (seeking to embarrass conservative Majles deputies) published a memo written by Saeed Emami, a disgraced intelligence officer identified by the regime as the ringleader of the death squad operating inside the intelligence ministry, to his superiors shortly before his arrest. In his memo, Emami, whose subsequent death in prison under suspicious circumstances was officially ruled to be a suicide, had advocated the adoption of a tough press law designed to muzzle the increasingly vocal reformist press. As the readers of *Salam* quickly discovered, Emami's memo, which (among other things) called for holding editors and writers, including newspaper editors, responsible for breaches of the press court, bore an amazing resemblance to a draft legislation that had just been pushed through the Majles by conservative legislators ("Iran's Pro-Reform Press Warns Crackdown Could Spark More Unrest," 1999; "Director of Iranian Paper Which Sparked Riots Says Closure 'Illegal,'" 1999).

Finding Khoeiniha guilty of defamation, misleading public opinion, and publication of a "classified" document, the special clerical court issued a ruling banning the publication of *Salam* for five years and proscribing Khoeiniha from engaging in journalistic activities for three years. In recognition of Khoeiniha's valuable contributions to the revolution, however, the court, comprised of eight clerics, suspended a three-year prison sentence (along with a humiliating and harsh infliction of lashing) that it had also imposed on Khoeiniha (Abdo, 1999a, p. 13). Speaking in his own defense, in a statement that is reminiscent of Khatami's utterances, Khoeiniha declared: "I say from the bottom of my heart and soul that our Islamic republic can remain [survive] only if it guarantees the maximum of legitimate freedoms in the framework of the constitution" (quoted in "The Meaning of Freedom," 1999). Illustrating the conservative apprehension about reform, Hamid Reza Taraghi, a Majles deputy who had played a leading role in bringing suit against *Salam*, maintained: "*Salam* is trying to create turmoil and instability in the basic pillars of the system and the revolution" ("The Meaning of Freedom," 1999).

Ironically, however, it was the initial banning of *Salam* in July 1999, which precipitated the most serious turmoil to beset the Islamic Republic since the socialist Islamist Mojahedin opposition group had attempted to overthrow the theocratic order back in 1981. Protesting the closure of the popular daily, a group of about 500 students staged a peaceful sit-in at Tehran University. This sit-in might have gone unnoticed, however, had Hezbollahi vigilantes not decided to exact revenge upon the students. Later that evening, a group of ultra-right-wing vigilantes attacked students while they were sleeping in their dormitories. The arrival of police and security forces, which operate under the direction of the supreme leader (not the president), did not help matters, as they apparently joined forces with Hezbollahis to severely rough up the students. Several students were reportedly thrown out of second- and third-story windows, and there was at least one casualty (Sciolino, 1999; Jehl, 1999a).

This deliberately provocative act, designed probably to promote unrest and set the stage for the removal of the president and the derailment of his reform campaign, served to incite the students. Although it took place during summer, when most classes were not in session, the provocation prompted the outraged students, impatient and weary at the half-hearted, partial, on-again, off-again, and exceptionally slow pace of reform, to stage six days of massive, spirited, and bitter protests. Had it not been for Khatami, the students, who have become an even more significant force in Iranian politics since the 1979 revolution (65 percent of the populace is below the age of twenty-five, and there are currently more than 1 million students in Iran), would probably have pushed for the demise of the Islamic Republic. For the moment, however, most expressed support for Khatami and the expeditious implementation of his reform agenda. Nevertheless, the more radical students are reported to have chanted: "Either Islam and the law or another revolution" (quoted in Jehl, 1999a). Significantly, many student protesters are reported to have carried pictures of Mohammad Mossadegh, a former prime minister who played an instrumental role in nationalizing the Iranian oil industry in the 1950s ("Fury Mounts as Majles Nips Holiday," 1999). Particularly since his ouster as a result of a CIA-backed coup in 1953, Mossadegh has come to be viewed as a symbol of secular nationalism and democratic nationalism in Iran. A student leader was quoted as saying audaciously, "We are not going to be satisfied until people at the top resign . . . Khatami has to do something or resign" (Jehl, 1999a). Capturing the mood of the majority of disgruntled students, Ali Afshari, a student leader, declared at a news conference in Tehran: "If officials don't respond according to this tremendous call for reforms, the door for peaceful negotiations will shut . . . We may be the last generation that believes in peaceful recourse" (quoted in Faruqi, 1999).

What was truly astonishing, however, was the intense and visceral nature of the demonstrations as well as the rapidity with which they spread to engulf a significant fraction of the nation's major urban centers and even some towns. During the six days of protests, students are reported to have demonstrated in eighteen cities and towns, with at least 15,000 students taking to the streets of Tehran alone (fearful of severe reprisals and not having the stomach for bloodshed, representatives of other social groups appear to have taken a wait-and-see—although broadly supportive—attitude toward the demonstrations) (Jehl, 1999a; Sciolino, 1999). Shouting deliberately provocative, illegal, and insulting statements directed against the supreme leader (the likes of which had not been heard since the revolution), the students called for, among other things, the ouster of Tehran's police chief, the dismantling of Hezbollahi "pressure groups," the unbanning of *Salam*, and the transfer of authority over the police to the Ministry of Interior ("Iran: Conservatives Seen Gaining Upper Hand, But for How Long?" 1999). Some students are reported to have chanted: "Mullahs become God while the people become beggars" and "No more phony parliaments," while others, showering obscenities upon the mullahs, declared, referring to Khamenei, "Commander in Chief—resign!" and "Down with the dictator" (Sciolino, 1999). Some are even reported to have set pictures of Khamenei on fire.

Initially, both Khatami and even Khamenei assumed a favorable attitude toward the students. In a sharp departure from precedent, Khamenei even went so far as to placate the students, asserting that "this bitter incident [the raid on student's dorms] has broken my heart." In a shocking acknowledgment of his own unpopularity, he also admonished his disciples to "remain silent . . . even if they condemn me, and if they set fire to my picture . . . Take no action until the country needs it" (quoted in Sciolino, 1999). But when the protests degenerated into rioting, giving rise to acts of vandalism and arson, both Khamenei and the president changed their tune. Khatami, joining forces with the establishment of which he remains a part, now forcefully declared that he would crush the rioters. Perhaps not coincidentally, Khatami's declaration came after he received a letter from twenty-four senior officers of the Revolutionary Guard Corps, ominously warning him that "our patience [with Khatami's reforms] is at an end . . . We do not feel it is our duty to show any more tolerance" (quoted in Faruqi, 1999). Thus, after six days of massive protests, which represented the most overwhelming crisis of confidence in the regime since the Mojahedin uprising, the security forces of the Islamic Republic (with the full backing of the president) successfully quashed the student uprisings. Subsequently, the president and his supporters asserted that agents provocateurs (associated with extremist figures, connected with those in the Ministry of Information who were blamed for the murder of intellectuals) had infiltrated the ranks of students in order to sow discord, create turmoil, extinguish reform, and set the stage for the ouster of Khatami. The president even went so far as to assert that the riots represented "a declaration of war" against him ("Khatami Says It's Time to Get Rid of Street Toughs," 1999).

Recognizing that he had disappointed, perhaps even lost the backing of some of his radical supporters, the president and his confidants moved quickly after the suppression of the student uprisings to reiterate their firm support for liberal reforms. The harassment of students, especially suspected ringleaders, however, continued unabated. Gholamhossein Rahbarpour, head of Tehran's revolutionary courts, maintained that 1,500 individuals had been arrested in connection with the unrest. But he hastened to add that most had been released on bail pending trial. An organization instituted during the demonstrations, the Student Council of Tehran University Residences, however, asserted that "[p]eople [were] arrested merely for being students, and after hours of interrogation, along with beatings, they were forced to sign confessions with their eyes closed" (quoted in Abdo, 1999a, p. 13). Thus, the struggle for power between the forces of reform, reaction, and conservatism continued.

But even if Khatami is allowed to implement successfully all of his stated objectives, which is not certain, his vision may still fall short of what the disaffected intelligentsia longs for. As Shireen Hunter has pointed out, "[I]t remains unclear whether the reformists are prepared to follow their arguments in favor of greater liberty and freedom of choice to their logical conclusions or will stop once they become the new—if milder—conservatives" (Hunter, 1998). From the perspective of the intelligentsia, however, the realization of Khatami's liberalization measures would be exponentially preferable to what has transpired up to now.

At the same time, it should be recalled that the shah's liberalization policy, far from strengthening his rule by enlarging the social bases of his regime, contributed to the forces that resulted in his ouster. The intellectuals, moreover, took an active role in initiating and sustaining the revolutionary process. One crucial difference between present-day and prerevolutionary Iran is that previously the shah was the state, and his extremely personal approach to governing made it impossible for him to blame others for the shortcomings of the system. It also automatically threw his seriousness about genuinely reforming the system into doubt: "By destroying all balancing elements in Iranian politics and by creating for himself a position of sole leadership . . . there was no one else for the people to blame" (Parsons, 1984, p. 152). Currently, however, there are factions with clearly distinctive differences, platforms, and powers within the ruling establishment. The intelligentsia, more than any other group, is cognizant of this fact.

The intellectuals, then, although disenchanted, are cautiously optimistic about their future prospects. If Khatami fails in his endeavors, they will, in all likelihood, become hopelessly alienated from the prevailing order. Even then, however, by themselves they would be unable to displace the Islamic Republic. To overthrow the theocracy, they would need to make common cause with other social forces. The formation of such an alliance will depend, in part, on the dispositions of other social groups and the capabilities and endowments of the oppositional groupings. Their success, in turn, will, in large measure, hinge on the nature and qualities of the regime. The nature of the regime and the oppositional forces will be analyzed in subsequent chapters. It is to the examination of the orientations of other politically important social groups that we shall now turn.

The Clerics

It is often assumed that the Iranian clergy belong to a unified and homogeneous social stratum, which is universally inimical to the separation of church and state and which recognized Khomeini, even while he was in exile, as its undisputed leader. In fact, nothing can be further from the truth. Among the grand ayatollahs alive at the time of the revolution, Khomeini was one of the least senior figures, and his insistence on merging spiritual and temporal powers (though not entirely unheard of in the history of Shia political thought) went against the predominant current of political quiescence and quietism. Indeed, as shall presently be discussed, the view of Iran's traditional clergy on the appropriate role of religion in politics and society is closer to the propositions advanced by Soroush than to the teachings of Ayatollah Khomeini. It is not surprising, therefore, that Soroush's writings and audiotapes of his lectures are being eagerly sought by the growing numbers of disgruntled clerics and many of the new generation of seminary students.

In prerevolutionary Iran, it was the shah's ill-conceived and repressive policies that served to unify the hierocracy's disparate elements (many of whom joined the revolution as a measure of desperation of last resort and thereafter broke with Khomeini) against the monarchy. At the same time, Khomeini's enormous charismatic and popular appeal, his rigid intransigence, and his ability to appeal to a wide cross-section of the populace, in part through obfuscating and deemphasizing his theological innovations, catapulted him to the position of undisputed leader of the revolution.

The discussion that follows begins by examining how far Khomeini's opinion in regard to the proper role of the ulama (clergy) in politics and society departs from the conservative conventional view, embraced by the vast majority of both rank-and-file and high-level clerics. This discussion will serve as a point of departure for inquiring into why, in spite of Khomeini's radical departures from tradition, the Shia establishment (without whose organizational network and mobilizational efforts the revolution would have been impossible) finally joined him in opposing the shah. After analyzing the dispositions of the clergy toward the monarchy in the later years of the shah's rule, we will examine the outlooks of the various segments of Iran's clergy toward the present regime in order to assess how, and to what extent, their orientations differ from the prerevolutionary period. As we shall see, the Islamic Republic, unlike the monarchy, has deeply divided the clergy. Although the preponderance of Iranian clerics appear to be dissatisfied with the prevailing order, most appear to be reformist in outlook, and none in this order is endowed with Khomeini's charisma. Moreover, the fact that a fraction of the clerical establishment itself now dominates the state apparatus serves to divide the hierocracy. It also enables the ruling clerics to exert far more effective control than the shah over their disgruntled colleagues.

Khomeini's Concept of Velayat-e Faqih

A vast proportion (approximately 90 percent) of the Iranian populace subscribes to the tenets of Twelver Shiaism. The "twelve" in Twelver Shiaism refers to Ali, the Prophet Mohammad's son-in-law and cousin, as well as his eleven male descendants (imams). With the exception of Ali, who served as the fourth caliph for a short period, all of the other eleven imams were prevented from assuming the leadership of the Islamic community. The Shia view this as an usurpation, since they believe the imams to have been divinely inspired and infallible, and therefore the true heirs to the Prophet. According to the eschatological doctrines of the Twelver Shiaism, in 874 A.D., the Twelfth Imam was commanded by God to remain on earth in a state of occultation until such a time as the Almighty deems fit to usher in the Judgment Day. The Twelfth Imam will then reappear as the Mehdi, bringing about messianic deliverance and instituting an absolutely just and legitimate order. The implication, of course, has been that until the return of the Twelfth Imam, all existing governments will, in varying degrees, be unjust and illegitimate.

Meanwhile, in the absence of the Twelfth Imam, Shiaism, as it has evolved in Iran in the course of the last few hundred years, has enjoined all believers to choose a living *marja-e taglid* (source of emulation) and strive to follow his interpretations of the Sharia (religious law) and the hadiths (declarations of the Prophet and the imams).[5] Although there has been widespread consensus among the Shia jurists that during the occultation of the Twelfth Imam their mandates should cover the religious and legal spheres, their direct involvement in political and governmental affairs has been (and continues to be) a subject of enormous controversy.

Those who have historically been elevated to the highest ranks of Shia hierarchy have never approved of Khomeini's *velayat-e faqih* concept. This concept, which constitutes the cornerstone of the current regime's Constitution, justifies the role of the jurisconsult *(faqih)* as the "supreme overseer, judge, and guardian" (Enayat, 1983, p. 161) of the Islamic community. In his formulation of this concept, Khomeini specifically states that the religious jurist has a sacred obligation to become the final arbiter in the state. Enunciated in a series of lectures in 1969, in Najaf, Iraq, when Khomeini was sixty-seven years old, Khomeini's political theory was published in 1970 in a book entitled *Hokumat-e Islami* (Islamic government). Initially, Khomeini had remained ambiguous on whether *velayat-e faqih* should be lodged in one individual or in the entire community of senior religious jurists. Shortly after the publication of his book, however, he "attempted to reduce this juristic pluralism to a unitary theocratic leadership to be installed by an Islamic revolution." In the words of Khomeini, "If one [jurist] succeeds in forging a government, it is incumbent on the others to follow him" (Arjomand, 1988, p. 178).

Khomeini maintained that sovereignty is ultimately derived from God. The Almighty, in his infinite wisdom, had anointed the Prophet Mohammad as his messenger and, through him, set down his rules in the Koran in order to guide the community. The Prophet, in turn, had founded an ideal state dedicated to the propagation of Islamic precepts. After the passing of Mohammad, the imams had inherited his absolute authority to interpret and implement God's laws and the power to serve as spiritual, political, and military leaders of the Islamic community. With the disappearance of the Twelfth Imam, Khomeini argued, all of the imams' powers and prerogatives, with the exception of their capacity to be in communion with God, had devolved to the Islamic jurists and not the kings. In fact, he declared Islam to be inherently opposed to monarchical and secular rule of any type: "In the Prophet's times, was the church separate from the state? Were theologians distinct from politicians?" (quoted in Abrahamian, 1982, p. 477). According to Khomeini, the levers of power should be in the hands of the jurisconsult because only he, as the most learned Islamic scholar in the realm, can ensure that the Sharia is appropriately interpreted and administered (Enayat, 1983, pp. 165–167). As Khomeini put it, "In view of the fact that the government of Islam is the government of law [Islamic law], only the jurisprudent . . . should be in charge of the government" (quoted in Haghayeghi, 1993, p. 37). Indeed, he is the only one "who can govern as God ordered" (quoted in Abrahamian, 1982, p. 477). Disagreeing with the Jurisprudent, then, is tantamount to disobeying God.

To justify his highly controversial position, Khomeini drew on a number of Koranic verses and hadiths. He took the Koranic phrase "the jurists are the representatives of the prophets" to mean: "In the same way the government is embodied in the Prophet, it is also embodied in the Imams and their successors—the Jurist(s)" (Abrahamian, 1982, p. 477). He reminded his audience of Imam Ali's declaration that "all believers [should] obey his successors," by whom, Ali had explained, he meant "those who transmit my statements and my traditions and teach them to the people." He also emphasized the Seventh Imam's lofty praise for religious judges as "the fortress of Islam" and reiterated the Twelfth Imam's admonition to future generations to comply with the commands of those who knew his teachings (as they were his trustees among the populace) (Abrahamian, 1993, p. 25).

In spite of his best efforts to defend his central thesis, Khomeini could not obviate the fact that *velayat-e faqih* constitutes an innovative reformulation of centuries-old predominant Shia thinking and practice. Grand ayatollahs, with the exception of Ayatollah Montazeri, who was designated as Khomeini's successor until being rejected in 1989, have never sanctioned Khomeini's insistence on merging spiritual and temporal powers or entrusting the guardianship of the entire Shia community to a supreme religio-political authority. Although there has occasionally existed a single grand ayatollah whose authority and scholarship have been universally acknowledged to be greater than others, Shia scholars have never argued that this should always be the case. As Roy Mottahedeh notes, traditionally "a few hundred Shiite clergymen have [had] the distinction of being official 'doctors of the law.' None of them [has been] permitted to obey another . . . The masses [have been enjoined to] choose one doctor as their source of authority on correct practice. In short, a fair number of clergymen [have] offered to lead, but no one [has been] obliged to follow" (Mottahedeh, 1998). Yet as we have seen, Khomeini's system seeks to transform Shiaism from a "polycephalic faith to a unicephalic or monolithic one" (Milani, 1992, p. 189). More significantly, senior Shia jurists, drawing on the legacy of the quiescent and scholarly Sixth Imam, Jafar al-Sadeq (700–765) (who by refusing to bestow his blessings upon the reigning caliphs effectively separated theology and politics) (Boroujerdi, 1996, p. 86) have admonished the clergy to engage solely in the interpretation of God's words. The jurists have wisely warned that seeking to participate directly in political affairs is liable to taint both the image of the clergy and Islam. The proper role of the clergy, it has been maintained, is to guard the people against the inherently corrupt state.

Only in times of acute crisis, when law and order have broken down and society stands on the brink of anarchy, have the senior jurists deemed it appropriate for the ulama to enter temporarily the realm of politics in order to restore order (Enayat, 1983, p. 169). Indeed, it has been the desire to avoid chaos that has prompted the preponderance of Shia theologians to accept the institution of monarchy as less vile than the insecurity associated with complete state breakdowns (Abrahamian, 1989, p. 22). Ironically, the concerns and viewpoints of the overwhelming majority of the ulama in regard to the appropriate role of the clergy in society and politics were summarized by Khomeini himself in 1943, long before he had embraced his controversial doctrine of *velayat-e faqih*. In his book *Kashf-i Asrar* (Secrets Revealed), Khomeini declared:

[A] decayed government is better than none at all. . . . the power of the mujtaheds [the most learned ulama] excludes the government and includes only simple matters such as legal rulings, religious judgments, and intervention to protect the property of minors and the weak. Even when the rulers are oppressive and against the people, they (the Mujtaheds) will not try to destroy the rulers. (quoted in Abrahamian, 1982, p. 476)

To underscore the novelty of Khomeini's later formulations, we should also examine the foremost Shia Koran commentaries and works of jurisprudence. From the twelfth to the twentieth century, there has existed a remarkable consistency among major Shia Koran commentaries on the meaning of the "authority verse" of the Koran ("Obey those in authority among you," IV:59). These commentaries have continuously asserted that "'those in authority' are neither the secular rulers (amirs) nor the ulama—neither of whom is immune from error and sin—but rather the infallible *(ma'sum)* Imams, Ali and his eleven descendants" (Arjomand, 1988, p. 177). Similarly, Shaykh Monteza Ansari (d. 1865), one of the primary figures in Shia jurisprudential theory, endeavored, in his analysis of authority, "to demonstrate how absurd it is to reason that because the Imams should be obeyed in all temporal and spiritual matters, the faqihs are also entitled to such obedience; and second . . . that in principle no individual, except the Prophet and the Imam, has the authority to exert *wilaya [velayat]* over others" (Enayat, 1983, p. 162).[6]

It can be seen, then, that Khomeini was not only able to lead a successful revolution against the Pahlavi dynasty but also to bring about a radical transformation in Shia political thought and practice. Khomeini's radical stance raises an intriguing puzzle worthy of explanation. Why, given Khomeini's revolutionary departures from tradition, did the entire Shia hierocracy in prerevolutionary Iran close ranks behind him in opposition to the monarchy?

There are some indications that the leading Shia ulama at the time, though in favor of the general Islamization of the country, did not believe, were unaware, or did not take seriously Khomeini's intention (which he was underplaying at the time) to go ahead with implanting his vision of the just Islamic order.[7] In the immediate term, Khomeini's genius in instructing his clerical followers inside Iran to stage deliberate provocations with the regime and the monarchy's response to these protests were highly effective in aggravating the wrath of all segments of the Shia hierarchy, including the quietists. This will be examined in the subsequent chapter.

The underlying cause, however, as we shall presently see, should be sought in the shah's cavalier and unwise approach to the entire Shia hierarchy as well as his ineptitude in exploiting the divisions among the ulama.

The Shia Hierocracy and the Pahlavi State

The preconditions for the rift between the hierocracy and the monarchical state were laid during the reign of Reza Shah, the founder of the Pahlavi dynasty and the father of Mohammad Reza Shah. Reza Shah, who, in blindly emulating Kemal

Atatürk, sought to implant an entirely secular state in Iran, sharply reduced the power and influence of the hierocracy and helped to make it largely independent from the state. Shortly after coming to power through a British supported coup d'état, Reza Shah set about to create a powerful, centralized, bureaucratic state in order to bring about the rapid modernization of Iran. This centralized state, working through the policies it espoused, launched a frontal attack on the authority and privileges of the clergy as a whole.

For several hundred years prior to the establishment of the Pahlavi dynasty, ever since Shiaism was declared the state religion of Iran in 1501, there had been an alliance between the Shia hierocracy and the state. Although the hierocracy was clearly subordinate to the state, it was nonetheless granted significant autonomy and power, as it was in charge of administering Islamic law, which was the law of the land. Starting in 1926, however, Reza Shah's judicial reforms "gradually reduced the purview of the religious courts until the Civil and Penal Codes of 1939 and 1940 [modeled respectively after the French and Italian laws] finally omitted all reference to the Sacred Law and to religious courts. The entire judiciary system was secularized and incorporated into the centralized state as the Ministry of Justice" (Arjomand, 1988, p. 66). Although some provisions of Shia sacred law, particularly aspects concerning family law, were retained, their adjudication was entrusted to state judges. In an act designed to do away with the last vestiges of the judicial authority of the ulama and deprive them of a lucrative source of income, Reza Shah created the Bureau of Records Registration in 1932. The bureau delegated itself the tasks of registering ownership documents, issuing deeds of property, and notarizing transaction records, all of which were previously the prerogative of the ulama (Amuzegar, 1991, p. 270).

Reza Shah also took measures aimed at severely curbing the other significant component of the ulama's social and political power—their control over educational institutions. Reza Shah created new secular, in some instances coeducational, primary and secondary schools and made it mandatory for all children of school age to attend such institutions. Although the seminaries were not shut down, they were subjected to severe harassment by the state. The most serious of these offenses, which was an intentional affront to the traditional autonomy of the hierocracy, was the forced conscription, under the provisions of the obligatory military service, of seminarians and young clerics. The establishment of a divinity school in the newly created Tehran University was construed as yet another challenge to the authority and the expertise of the ulama (Amuzegar, 1991, p. 270; Arjomand, 1988, p. 82).

Apart from severely restricting the pedagogic, and undermining the judicial, role of the ulama, Reza Shah's other secular reforms also incurred the collective wrath of the Shia establishment. In 1928, the state, seeking to promote the adoption of Western-style clothing and headgear, imposed severe restrictions on the wearing of clerical garb and engaged in the coercive removal of turbans. To drive the message home, "Reza Shah himself [having earlier authorized the licensing of liquor stores in the holy city of Ghom] traveled to the holy city and publicly humiliated Ayatollah Bafqi . . . by beating him and having him dragged by the beard. Internal exile began to be the fate of an increasing number of disgruntled clerics" (Arjomand, 1988, p. 82).

In 1934, Reza Shah issued a decree forbidding the instruction of the Koran and religious studies in schools. In what was regarded as particularly reprehensible by the entire clerical establishment, in 1935 Reza Shah ordered the abolition of women's veils and required the police to be vigilant, even coercive, in its enforcement. Finally, by incorporating the *owqaf* (religious endowments) into the Ministry of Education, Reza Shah deprived the clergy of another lucrative source of income (Arjomand, 1988, p. 82).

Although enraged, the hierocracy was too baffled, stunned, and effectively suppressed to orchestrate a coordinated response against these measures. Moreover, the undisputed religious leader of the time, Grand Ayatollah Abol Karim Haeri, was implacably opposed to political involvement and concentrated instead on establishing a center of religious education in Ghom (Arjomand, 1988, p. 84). At the same time, Reza Shah's reign came to an abrupt halt in 1941, when the Allies invaded Iran and forced him to abdicate in favor of his son.

Young, inexperienced, and insecure, with a shaky power base, Mohammad Reza Shah at first assumed a conciliatory and accommodationist approach toward the hierocracy. After the death of Ayatollah Haeri, the leadership of the Shia hierarchy passed to the Grand Ayatollah Hossein Borujerdi, another politically aloof and quiescent cleric. From the mid-1940s until his death in 1961, Borujerdi came to be universally accepted as Iran's supreme *marja-e taglid* (source of emulation), a position that had remained vacant since the nineteenth Century. In the 1940s, Borujerdi concluded a tacit agreement with the shah, whereby Borujerdi, in exchange for the shah's relaxation of Reza Shah's secular policies and the lifting of restrictions on the wearing of clerical attire and the veil, agreed to subdue his radical subordinates and support the monarchy (Abrahamian, 1993, p. 8; Arjomand, 1988, p. 84; Boroujerdi, 1996, p. 80).

The relationship between the monarchy and the clerical establishment became even more cordial in the 1950s. In the early years of the decade, the nationalization of Iran's oil under the leadership of the nationalist prime minister Mohammad Mossadegh, created a split in the ranks of the clergy. Some, notably Ayatollah Kashani, who served as the Speaker of Iran's Majles from 1952 to 1953, supported Mossadegh and his admonition that the king, in accordance with the provisions of the 1906 Constitution, must reign and not rule. Others favored the shah in his struggle against Mossadegh. But the severe downturn in the Iranian economy, due to the imposition of a British embargo against Iranian oil, the increasing popularity of the Tudeh (Communist) party among the youth, and Mossadegh's unwillingness to restrain the Tudeh, ultimately served to draw the clerics closer to the royalist camp. The subsequent defection of Kashani as well as the support of Ayatollahs Borujerdi and Behbahani was undoubtedly as significant as the CIA-instigated coup d'état in restoring the shah to power (after the latter had lost his nerve and fled to Rome in 1953) (Arjomand, 1988, p. 81; Parsa, 1989, p. 192). Clerical support was also instrumental in helping the shah to consolidate his power throughout the 1950s.

After regaining his throne, the shah rewarded the clergy by launching an anti-Bahai campaign, which he justified by castigating that religion as being heretical and its adherents as being apostates. He permitted the Hojjatieh, an overzealous anti-Bahai group, to flourish, and stamped out the Communist movement on the grounds that it was "atheistic" and "anti-Islamic" (Abrahamian, 1989, p. 19). He also threw the state's support behind religious educational institutions. In return, Borujerdi and other senior clerics endorsed the shah's suppression of both the Tudeh and the National Front (an umbrella organization comprised of Mossadegh's followers). They also provided approval for such unpopular foreign policy measures as Iran's entry into the Baghdad Pact in 1955 (Foran, 1993, p. 336). Underscoring his intimate working relationship with the shah, Borujerdi stated in 1960, "I pray day and night for the person of the Shah-in-Shah [king of kings], for whom I entertain sincere regard" (quoted in Foran, 1993, p. 365). Indeed, the relationship between the monarchy and the clerical establishment became so close in the 1950s that it prompted one critic to assert that the "clergy had become a 'pillar of the Pahlavi state'" (quoted in Abrahamian, 1989, p. 19).

The de facto alliance between the two institutions, however, unraveled in the 1960s and became irrevocably severed in the 1970s when the shah reverted to pursuing his father's anticlerical policies with a vengeance. The shah inaugurated the 1960s by launching a series of reforms (which he later labeled the "White Revolution") designed to enlarge his social base. Among the reforms was a land-redistribution proposal, which even Ayatollah Borujerdi found objectionable, because of the proposal's violation of the Sharia's sanction of private property. The shah, however, did not implement his reforms until after Borujerdi's death in 1961.

With the passing of Borujerdi, the leadership of the hierocracy once again became multipolar, ranging from liberal constitutionalists to radical nonconformists. The remaining senior clerics were divided on the issue of land reform, with the majority, composed of conservatives, opposing the measure. But the other major component of the reform package, the enfranchisement of women, along with the utilization of a national referendum to legitimize the reforms, was universally abhorred. So was the bestowing of concessions on foreigners (particularly immunity from prosecution granted to American military personnel), which, although not a part of the shah's White Revolution, had recently been enacted. Meanwhile, the shah's increasing political activism, which resulted in the enhancement of his dictatorial power as well as his arbitrariness, served to alarm the constitutionalist clerics. "Thus most of the ulama came together to oppose the Shah, though for widely varying reasons" (Foran, 1993, p. 365).[8]

Among the senior clerics at the time, Khomeini, despite his youth and relatively junior status in the hierarchy, emerged as the fiercest critic of the shah's policies, though not as yet of the institution of monarchy.

His denunciations—unlike those of his more conventional colleagues—avoided the issue of land reform and instead focused on such highly explosive topics as court corruption, constitutional violations, dictatorial methods, election rigging, granting of immunity to foreigners, betraying the Muslim cause against Israel, [and] undermining of Shii values. (Abrahamian, 1989, p. 21)

Having earlier attacked the shah for failing to protect the Koran and the Constitution, Khomeini, on June 3, 1963, launched an open attack on the person of the shah by rebuking him for surrounding himself with ill-informed and heretical sycophants. Khomeini also called on the armed forces to come to his aid "for the salvation of Islam and Iran" (Milani, 1994, p. 50). He stopped short, however, of calling for an Islamic government, but his diatribes were sufficiently harsh to cause his arrest.

Khomeini's denunciations and arrest as well as the complaints of other ulama triggered a series of violent antigovernment demonstrations across the country, with the most serious protests occurring in Tehran. The government, under the direction of the prime minister (and not the shah, who had lost his nerve), responded with overwhelming force and demobilized the protesters. According to an American observer, the number of casualties stood at a few thousand (Abrahamian, 1989, p. 21).

In addition to elevating Khomeini to the position of the most ardent and courageous clerical opponent of the regime, the violent response to the concerns of the ulama resurrected the great wall of mistrust between the Pahlavi state and the hierocracy (which, in the course of the preceding twenty years, was in the process of being gradually dismantled). After serving a brief time in jail, Khomeini was exiled to Turkey, whence he emigrated to Najaf, the center of Shia learning in Iraq. There are unconfirmed reports that Khomeini was saved from execution at the time by the intercession of Grand Ayatollah Shariatmadari.

The 1963 insurrection "helped to polarize the clerical class into those who were advocating confrontational political activism and those in favor of quietist, apolitical, and theologically bound pursuits" (Boroujerdi, 1996, p. 83). Even after suffering yet another humiliating defeat at the hands of the Pahlavi state, most of the grand ayatollahs and, by implication, their followers, continued to shun oppositional activism. There were even those with a wide following and respectability who were willing to lend their support to the shah's reforms, provided they were consulted and treated with dignity. For example, Grand Ayatollah Milani of Mashad had, in a private 1962 conversation, remarked:

The charge that we clerics are opposed to . . . reform . . . is unfounded. The government makes us out to be reactionary and backward. On the contrary, we are prepared to find religious justification for any reform which His Majesty may wish to
initiate. But on one condition: he must recognize the limits of his prerogatives. He
must also be mindful of our rights and obligations and of the constraints which we
face in our dealings with the people; he must not impose his reforms on us by force.
(as related by Naraghi, 1994, p. 8.)

The shah, however, rather than playing the clerics off against one another,
lumped them all together and began to boast that with the squelching of the June
1963 uprising he had once and for all defeated the forces of "medieval black reaction." Throughout the 1960s, the shah continued to escalate his confrontation
with the hierocracy by pursuing policies inimical to the interests of the Shia establishment as a whole. As part of his bureaucratic reforms in 1964, the shah
abolished the clerical fund responsible for paying monthly stipends to clerical
students and their instructors in religious educational institutions. Instead, he
charged the newly established state-controlled Endowments Organization with
the task of providing financial assistance to those engaged in religious pedagogy
and learning. However, "the funds available through this organization were far
less than clerical students had formerly received from religious sources. [Thus]
[m]any students [became] hard-pressed to survive" (Parsa, 1989, p. 195). The Endowments Organization was also placed in control of properties donated to religious organizations and was invested with the authority to do with them as it
deemed fit. It closed down and converted numerous existing mosques and prevented the construction of new ones. Such policies resulted in a decline in the
number of students enrolled in theological schools and the number of mosques
throughout the country. Between 1965 and 1975, the number of mosques in Iran
dropped from 20,000 to 9,015 (Parsa, 1989, p. 196).

The shah's establishment of the Literacy Corps was another component of the
White Revolution in the 1960s and was also universally perceived by the ulama as
yet another blow to their influence. Up to this time, the state's efforts at secularizing education had been largely confined to the nation's urban centers and the
larger villages. In the outlying rural areas, the *maktabs* (religious schools) continued to predominate. With the creation of the Literacy Corps, the shah now
sought to fulfill his father's aim of completely undermining the educational role
of the ulama (Akhavi, 1980, p. 98).

Moreover, to portray himself as a progressive and cognizant monarch, sympathetic to the plight of women in society, the shah ordered the Majles to pass a series of statutes in 1967 that directly contradicted the Sharia. Known as the Family Protection Law, the statutes limited men's authority over their wives. They
allowed men to engage in polygamy only if they could secure written permission
from their other wives and prohibited men from divorcing their wives without
valid reasons. The statutes also gave women the right to obtain employment out-

side the home without their husbands' consent and, significantly, stipulated that women were also entitled to petition for divorce. Subsequently, the Family Protection law was expanded, requiring the marriage age for girls to be raised from fifteen to eighteen and for boys from eighteen to twenty (Abrahamian, 1982, pp. 444–445; Amuzegar, 1991, p. 271). Departing considerably from a strict interpretation of the Sharia, these laws enraged the ulama, regardless of their ideological stripes, especially given the fact that (contrary to Ayatollah Milani's advice) the statutes were imposed upon the clerics without any prior consultation.

The shah's treatment of the Shia establishment in the 1960s, however, was rather mild compared to how he decided to approach them in the 1970s. Seeking to strengthen his exclusive hold on power even further, the shah increasingly resorted to repressive tactics in order to bring all elements of society under his control and subdue those who did not share his vision for Iran. In the 1970s, "the Shah . . . systematically began an all-out attack on the Shi'i religious establishment" (Bill, 1988, p. 187). In August 1971, the shah, who had by then become virtually synonymous with the state, ordered the creation of the Religious Corps. Modeled after the Literacy Corps, the Religious Corps, whose members were drawn from university graduates with degrees in Islamic studies, were charged with the task of going into villages in order to teach the regime's version of Islam and supersede the ulama as propagators of Shiaism (Milani, 1994, p. 64). "The Religious Corps taught peasants that 'true Islam' was distinct from the preaching of so-called black reactionary mullahs" (Parsa, 1989, p. 196).

In another measure designed to diminish, and perhaps ultimately undermine, the influence of the ulama, the regime embarked on the closure of prominent seminaries, theological schools, and Islamic associations. In 1975, "under the pretext of the creation of a green space around the shrine of the Eighth Imam" (Arjomand, 1988, p. 83), the regime demolished most of the seminaries of the holy city of Mashad. Also in 1975, the regime closed down Madresehy-e Fazieh-e Ghom, the nation's foremost clerical school. In addition, it closed the Hedayat Mosque and the Hosseinieh Ershad in Tehran, and forbade several well-known ulama from delivering sermons (Parsa, 1989, p. 196). At the same time, SAVAK moved forcefully to dissolve all religious student associations on university campuses throughout the country. It also shut down publishing houses that put out books on religious and theological issues and began to disseminate officially sanctioned religious publications (Abrahamian, 1982, p. 444; Bill, 1988, p. 189).

As if these moves were not sufficient to antagonize the hierocracy, the shah inaugurated the 1970s by reaffirming his avowed commitment to glorifying the pre-Islamic history of Iran. The staging in 1970 of an unusually ostentatious ceremony, designed to commemorate 2,500 years of monarchical rule in Iran, was frowned upon by the entire Shia establishment. But from the vantage point of the clerics, the most devastating manipulation of symbols by the shah was undoubtedly his arbitrary decision in 1976 to change Iran's Islamic calendar, based on the

Prophet's flight from Mecca to Medina, to an imperial one based on the founding of the Achaemenid Empire by Cyrus the Great.

Also reprehensible from the viewpoint of the ulama (conservative, liberal, and radical alike) was what they viewed as the increasing influence of pernicious Western cultural values and practices on Iranian society. The clerics in general were appalled by the mushrooming of bars, liquor stores, discos, and movie theaters exposing the populace to "decadent" Western modes of conduct. They were also distraught by what they perceived as Iran's subservience to the West, particularly America, and the presence of increasing numbers of foreigners in Iran (which expanded dramatically after the shah went on an arms-buying spree following the fivefold increase in oil prices in 1973).

Predictably, the shah's blatantly aggressive approach toward the hierocracy, as well as his utter lack of concern in regard to the attitudes of the clergy in general, incurred the collective ire of the ulama. An exiled newspaper intimately associated with the ulama commented that the state "was trying to nationalize religion by taking over the vaqfs, recruiting mullas into SAVAK . . . monopolizing the publication of theology books, and sending the religious corps into the countryside to turn the peasants against the country's spiritual authorities" (Abrahamian, 1982, p. 445). The politically active ulama, most of them former students and protégés of Khomeini, now began to openly agitate against the monarchy. The regime responded with severe repression. Three prominent clerics—Ayatollah Hossein Ghaffari and Hojatoleslams Saldi and Ansari—were tortured to death (Abrahamian, 1989, p. 24; Bill, 1988, p. 189). Moreover, several clerics who subsequently played significant roles in the revolution, including Ayatollahs Montazeri and Beheshti along with Hojatoleslams Rafsanjani and Khamenei, were imprisoned. Such blatant abuse against fellow ulama, combined with the harsh climate of state antagonism toward the whole institution of Shiaism, prompted even the normally quiescent senior members of the hierocracy to raise their voices against the system. For instance, the exceptionally conservative Ayatollah Tabatabai-Ghomi denounced the prevailing anticlerical policies of the state as "Jewish conspiracies designed to destroy both Iran and Islam" (Abrahamian, 1989, p. 24).

It can be seen, then, that after 1963 the shah's modernizing state gradually deprived the hierocracy of almost all of its privileges and severed its ties to the state. The Shia establishment, however, did have an autonomous institutional basis as well as a source of income in the form of religious taxes, which were immune to the encroachment of the state. "With the economic prosperity of the 1960s and 1970s, this revenue increased considerably" (Arjomand, 1988, p. 83). Unable, or unwilling, to take over all of the mosques and religious centers throughout Iran, the state could not effectively control the nation's approximately 90,000 ulama (Foran, 1993, p. 337).

Severely alienated from the Pahlavi regime, the ulama were instrumental in the making of the Iranian revolution. Although the political activists (a distinct minority) played a crucial role in organizing and coordinating the antiregime movement, the quietists allowed themselves to be dragged into politics by acquiescing to the revolution. As with many other groups, however, the quiescent clerics, though opposed to the rule of the shah, were not in favor of Khomeini's vision of the just Islamic order.

Clerical Discontentment with the Islamic Republic

Most of Iran's grand ayatollahs are now dead. But in their lifetimes none of them referred to Khomeini as imam, a title that in Iran has been reserved for the twelve direct descendants of the Prophet Mohammad. Khomeini's notion of an omnipotent religio-political leader, who can, if the need arises, even order the violation of the Sharia,[9] was rejected by eleven of the twelve grand ayatollahs living in 1981 (Montazeri excepted). Some of the grand ayatollahs, notably Abol Ghassem Khoi and Kazem Shariatmadari, directly opposed Khomeini, while others, such as Mohammad Reza Golpayeghani, Haj Hassan Ghomi, Mohammad Shirazi, and Najafi Mar'ashi, distanced themselves from the regime and refused to accept official posts (Roy, 1994, p. 173).

The schism between Iran's traditionalist clergy and Ayatollah Khomeini came to the fore shortly after the success of the revolution. The grand ayatollahs were unanimous in expressing disenchantment with the Assembly of Experts (packed with Khomeini's protégés), which had been convened to revise Iran's 1906 Constitution, when the assembly produced an entirely new draft modeled after Khomeini's *velayat-e faqih* concept. By far the most devastating denunciations against the new constitution emanated from the liberal Grand Ayatollah Shariatmadari, who favored the creation of "a pluralistic political system . . . where elected officials, not the ulama, would wield . . . power, and where the clergy would interfere in politics only when the state grossly violated the Sharia" (Abrahamian, 1989, p. 45). Shariatmadari attacked the Constitution for being at odds with the Sharia and the notions of democracy and popular sovereignty. He also reiterated the view that members of the clergy should be above politics so that they can fulfill their essential duty of guarding Islam. Meanwhile, the conservative Grand Ayatollah Ghomi argued that Khomeini and his followers had "monopolized the mosques, [made] a mockery of Islam, and encouraged corruption" (Abrahamian, 1989, p. 45).

Khomeini's response to such challenges and accusations was swift and severe. Shariatmadari was charged with having collaborated with the shah, SAVAK, and the American embassy over the course of some thirty years. It was also alleged that he had been "imposed" as a *marja-e taghlid* on the Shia community by a bunch of "knife-wielding hooligans" associated with the shah's court (Parsa, 1989, p. 293). Reacting to such charges, Khomeini, in an unprecedented event in the history of Shia Islam, publicly humiliated and demoted Shariatmadari, who was then placed under house arrest until his death in 1985. After disagreeing with the continuation of the Iran-Iraq war, Ayatollah Ghomi was also placed under house arrest. After more than thirteen years, he continues to remain in this position even up to this day. According to Amnesty International, Ayatollah Ghomi has been "denied access to medical care for heart disease" ("AI: Iran Suppresses Clergy," 1997).

Currently, apart from Ghomi in Mashad, Grand Ayatollahs Zanjani, Shirazi, and Montazeri are all under house arrest in Ghom. Similarly, prior to his death in 1997, Grand Ayatollah Sadegh Rohani was also forced to spend the last five years of his life under house arrest in Ghom. Rohani, Shirazi, and Zanjani were placed under house arrest because of their refusal to sanction the guardianship of the jurisprudent. Reflecting the extent of its animosity toward the clerics who oppose *velayat-e faqih*, the regime, following Rohani's death, prevented his family from burying him in a cemetery or arranging for any type of public mourning ceremonies ("Rohani Dies in Qom at 78," 1997). Even the Iranian government itself has confirmed that at least one grand ayatollah, Ya'sab al-Din Rastegari, has been imprisoned since 1996. The government has accused Rastegari with the following vague charges: "misinforming and [engaging] in activities against the security and public order of the country" ("AI: Iran Suppresses Clergy," 1997). Concurrently, Montazeri has been ostracized not because of his objection to the rule of the jurist (indeed, Khomeini himself designated Montazeri as his successor in the early 1980s) but because he eventually fell out of Khomeini's favor. Only a few months before he died in July 1989, Khomeini bitterly denounced and defrocked Montazeri because of the latter's frequent criticisms of the regime's suppression of opponents and his implied rebuke of Khomeini for refusing to end the senseless war with Iraq earlier.

Khomeini was able to silence his opponents with impunity because, ultimately, he had the full power of the Iranian state behind him. Yet his undeniable charisma, impeccable educational and religious credentials, and stature as the leader who could unite all elements opposed to the shah in what was at the time a popular revolution also served to dampen clerical opposition against his behavior. But Khomeini's successor, "Ayatollah" Seyyed Ali Khamenei, is bereft of all of his predecessor's qualifications. Khamenei's scholarly accomplishments are too minute to qualify him as an ayatollah, let alone a grand ayatollah. Khamenei was promoted to the rank of ayatollah, in blatant disregard of the long-instituted Shia tradition of pedagogic standards, after he was hastily designated as Iran's politico-spiritual leader following Khomeini's death. Having been promoted as a function of his political, rather than religious, qualifications, he is regarded in the eyes of many religious scholars as a phony ayatollah.

Indeed, in 1996 even Ayatollah Azari Ghomi, a former confidant of Khomeini and one of the pillars of the revolution, who has served as an Islamic judge and a member of the Assembly of Experts (which anointed Khamenei to the position of faqih) is reported to have expressed doubts about Khamenei's suitability as the supreme leader. In a letter addressed to the editors of the daily *Salam*, after argu-

ing that "a majority of Iranians no longer identify with the regime and that 'they have no one to whom to turn,'" Azari Ghomi asserted, referring to Khamenei, that "I do not consider him senior enough in theological learning to be a *mujtahid* (a commentator on the Koran)" (Teimourian, 1996, p. 126). Although he went on to propose Grand Ayatollah Behjat as a more appropriate successor to Khomeini, Azari Ghomi "stresse[d] that he [will nevertheless] obey the law and accept Ayatollah Khamenei as the political leader" (Teimourian, 1996, p. 126). Evidently, the doctrine of *velayat-e faqih* has not yet been firmly institutionalized in Iran.

Nor is it likely to be. Because of his junior position in the religious hierarchy, Khamenei has now been forced to acknowledge that he cannot serve as the sole source of emulation for Iranians. Therefore, contrary to Khomeini's initial formulations, he has partially severed religious from political leadership. Khamenei's meager religious credentials have largely undermined the regime's theocratic basis of legitimacy (Ashraf, 1994, p. 149), serving instead to expose it to greater fragility and vulnerability. Consequently, the regime has come to assume a highly stern attitude toward those who question Khamenei's religious credentials. According to Amnesty International, "[H]undreds . . . of [Ayatollah Shirazi's] supporters and relatives [who had expressed doubts about Khamenei's religious abilities] have suffered harassment, and scores, if not hundreds [including his two sons] have been arrested, some on more than one occasion. The arrests have been ongoing since 1994, and many reportedly have been tortured" ("AI Iran Suppresses Clergy," 1997). In response to inquiries from Maurice Copithorne, the UN human rights rapporteur for Iran, the Iranian Foreign Ministry has listed the following charges against the imprisoned followers of Ayatollah Shirazi: "Defaming and insulting the leadership and other officials [and] disseminating lies and rumors" ("Shirazi Entourage Has Police Run-In," 1996). In a related development, a group of exiled Iranian clerics recently reported that sixteen clerics were arrested in Ghom because they were purported not to have recognized the absolute authority of Khamenei ("Mass Arrests of Clerics Reported," 1995).

Probably emboldened by the landslide election victory of Khatami, which was widely perceived as a protest vote against the status quo, Ayatollah Montazeri most recently broke his eight years of silence by questioning the credentials of Khamenei. Shortly thereafter, in a letter addressed to Khatami after the president's landslide victory in May 1997, Montazeri declared: "Your election was no ordinary one." He went on to categorize Khatami's triumph as "a popular revolution against the existing conditions . . . and a clear message to all the authorities and officials of the country" (quoted in Fairbanks, 1997). Speaking to a band of his followers inside his home in Ghom in November 1997, Montazeri, whose remarks were taped and widely disseminated, asserted that "the sweeping controls over political and social matters on which Ayatollah Khamenei and his followers insist [have] made people 'disgusted with the clerics'" (Jehl, 1997). He went on to argue that the powers of Khamenei should be limited to supervising and over-seeing the political system, and that he should be prevented from exercising pol-icymaking authority.

Khamenei and his conservative supporters responded by inciting hundreds of Hezbollahi zealots to take part in street protests, which involved ransacking of the homes and offices of Grand Ayatollahs Montazeri and Ghomi (who had ex-pressed sympathy with Montazeri's pronouncements). Designed to intimidate like-minded clerics into silence, the demonstrations lasted for one week. Khamenei then urged calm and threatened to prosecute Montazeri for treason, the penalty for which is death. Referring to Montazeri as a "politically bankrupt, pathetic and naive cleric [who] has acted against the security of the country and committed treason," Khamenei stated that "those who create discord . . . have committed treason . . . [and] should be dealt with according to the law" ("Khamenehi: Halt Protests," 1997; "Regime Seeks to Cow Reformers," 1997). In 1999, the special court in charge of prosecuting clerical misdeeds forbade the na-tion's media from even mentioning Montazeri's name (*Iran Times*, September 3, 1999).

With the legitimacy of the system increasingly in peril, even some thoughtful politicized clerics have come to contemplate whether a partial retreat from power by the mullahs would be salutary for the long-term survival of the theocracy. The most prominent member of the regime to have entertained such an idea is Aya-tollah Mohammad Reza Mahdavi-Kani, the influential secretary general of Tehran's Combatant Clerical Association (MRM), a conservative fraternal orga-nization whose members compose a large proportion of Iran's present key deci-sionmakers. While in London in 1994 in order to seek medical treatment for his heart condition, Kani is reported to have declared that Iran's next president should not be a cleric (Shirley, 1995, p. 36). Kani's declaration is noteworthy since it indicates that members of the ruling elite are well aware that the revolution is faltering, and is thereby undermining their once irreproachable position.

Since returning to Iran, however, Kani has recanted his earlier pronounce-ment. In a speech delivered in Tehran in December 1995, he declared, "The state-ment that the clergy, in order to save their purity, must retreat from the scene [power] emanates from the mouth of the U.S." Kani went on to say that if the Almighty had deemed it appropriate to entrust the reins of power to mere politi-cians, then the Prophet of Islam and Imam Ali would have never acceded to be-come leaders of the Islamic community (quoted in *Iran Times*, December 22, 1995). Kani's reversal indicates that a general consensus has emerged among the top echelon of the ruling elite on the necessity of acting in concert to ensure the continuation of the *velayat-e faqih* principle. Iran's ruling clerics have apparently come to the conclusion that the greatest danger to the survival of the system and the perpetuation of their rule comes from the doctrines of Soroush and his fol-lowers, including an increasing number of mullahs, because they challenge the regime from a religious vantage point. Indeed, Khamenei has considered the threat sufficiently significant to respond to it personally. In an obvious reference to Soroush, Khamenei recently stated: "If someone confronts the clergy, he gladdens the Zionists and the Americans. . . . They want the clergy to cease to exist . . . This kind of talk is sedition . . . the Islamic system will slap these people hard in the face" (quoted in Wright, 1995). Kani's reversal seems to have been prompted by the desire to dissociate himself completely from Soroush.

Nevertheless, disenchanted with the decline in their stature in the eyes of a large proportion of the populace, the clergy now constitutes one of the most avid readers of Soroush. According to Hojatoleslam Mohsen Kadivar, who ran (prior to his imprisonment in 1999) Ghom's Howzeh Islamic Center, one of the most prominent seminaries in Iran, "[N]inety-eight percent of the more than 100,000 clerics in Iran who [are] not involved in running the state [are] now losing legitimacy among the masses because of the ruling clergy's unpopularity." Kadivar maintains that "the clergy does not want its fate to be that of the Marxist parties in the former Communist States" (quoted in Miller, 1996, p. 456). Capturing the same sentiment and lamenting the decline in mosque attendance, a cleric preaching at a small mosque in Tehran was recently quoted by the *Financial Times* of London as saying: "If you want to be charitable, build schools instead of mosques. Our schools are overflowing but our mosques are empty" (quoted in "Insider's Perspective," 1997).

Having witnessed Iran's numerous failures with Islamic government, even clerics who at one point had unquestionably accepted Khomeini's political philosophy have come to appreciate the traditionalist clergy's warnings, as well as Soroush's philosophical arguments, in regard to the debasing nature of direct political involvement. For example, Hassan Eshkevari, a cleric and a former prominent member of Iran's postrevolutionary Majles, whose efforts at mobilizing the masses had resulted in his imprisonment by the shah's regime, was recently quoted by the Associated Press as saying that "a religious government is not necessary" ("Even Clerics Question Regime," 1996). Similarly, Ayatollah Hariri-Yazdi, a philosophically inclined cleric whose father was Khomeini's teacher, has advanced an argument that is remarkably similar to that of Soroush. According to Yazdi, since the Prophet did not force people to follow him, any government based on force (even if it happens to be a religious tyranny) is illegitimate. Yazdi hastens to add, however: "[B]ecause the Islamic Republic tries to live by Islamic rules and traditions, he would continue obeying it, as his faith commanded. But he would never stop criticizing what he saw as wrong. For these convictions, he [says], 'I am ready to die'" (Miller, 1996, p. 458).

By far the most prominent cleric to have publicly espoused views similar to those of Soroush is Hojatoleslam Mohsen Kadivar. As noted, Kadivar is a leading religious scholar, who was imprisoned before the revolution for opposing the shah's regime. Shunning partisan politics, he has, since the revolution, concentrated on scholarly endeavors, particularly as they relate to theories of Shia jurisprudential governance (which, of course, constitute the core ideological basis of the regime). In a series of revisionist and reformist articles published shortly before his arrest in February 1999, Kadivar maintained that political power should be entrusted to the people, not to a small group of Shia jurists. In one of his essays, Kadivar made the following stunningly candid, yet politically explosive, declaration: "One of the incentives of the revolution was to give power to the people . . . it is not fair to have a revolution in the name of religion and to promise a people-oriented government and then gradually change directions" (quoted in "Islam's Balancing Act," 1999). Condemned by the special clerical court for disseminating propaganda against the Islamic Republic, indirectly insulting Ayatollah Khomeini, and confusing public opinion, Kadivar was sentenced to eighteen months in prison. During Kadivar's trial, Khamenei delivered a speech to senior members of Iran's armed forces, asserting that "the real enemy intends to attack us from within with the aim to weaken our determination, faith, and firm resolution" (quoted in "Kadivar Tried: Critic or Criminal," 1999). What was truly surprising, however, was the fact that Kadivar's arrest and imprisonment incurred the wrath not only of Islamist intellectuals and pro-Khatami reformers but also of several proregime conservative clerics ("Kadivar Is Sentenced to 18 Months," 1999; "Kadivar Says He's Ready to Go Attack in Court," 1999).

It is important to note that Soroush's views do not simply appeal to senior religious figures, who have always been wary of direct political participation, or erstwhile politicized clerics, who have become disillusioned with the Islamic Republic's record of failure. An *Iran Times* journalist who met with a group of *talabeh* (seminarians) in the holy city of Ghom in 1996, was informed by the *talabeh* that approximately 80 percent of the city's 25,000 students agree with most of Soroush's propositions. The religious students appeared to be particularly attracted to Soroush's argument that although the Koran and the Sharia are eternal, their understanding is limited and relative. They had also taken to heart Soroush's admonition that the clerics must confine themselves to serving as spiritual and moral guides to the faithful. One seminarian observed: "Politics by its very nature is dirty, and if the clergy get involved with governing too deeply, then this is bad for Islam." Ironically, however, the *talabeh* who were interviewed did not perceive a contradiction between the ideas of Soroush and the institution of *velayat-e faqih*. Defining the institution as a "spiritual, not a political one," the *talabeh* asserted that "the ideal faqih would function for Islam like the Pope functions for Roman Catholicism. And they insisted this was how Khomeini behaved" ("Even Clerics Question Regime," 1996).

The Bazaaris

Antagonism against the clerical order is also becoming increasingly rampant among Iran's traditional middle class, the bazaaris. "Bazaar" is a Persian word meaning "market," and the "bazaaris" are those individuals who work in the bazaar, a demarcated territory throughout the nation's urban centers. A vast array of individuals, therefore, ranging from lowly street vendors, shop assistants, artisans, and small shopkeepers to very well-to-do domestic and international traders, merchants, and money lenders, are subsumed under the rubric of bazaari. Historically, there has existed an intimate sociological, ideological, filial, and financial link between bazaaris of every sort and the Iranian clerical establishment. This has been so because, "by virtue of their way of life, the bazaar people [have] depended completely on religious personalities, whose support and approbation [have] raised their standing and helped their business affairs" (Naraghi, 1994, p. 11).

Today, however (as with the clerical establishment itself), a large proportion of the bazaari community, which played a pivotal role in the triumph of the revolution, is dissatisfied with the current state of the Iranian economy as well as the harsh manner in which it is being treated by the regime. Members of the bazaar are appalled at the theocracy's policy of blaming them, as in the final years of the shah's rule, for the regime's own inept management of the Iranian economy. Unlike the shah's era, however, a small, well-connected segment of the bazaar has benefited (and continues to benefit) enormously from clerical rule. Whereas the shah's policies, particularly in the final four years of his rule, helped to unify and cohere the bazaar's diverse groups and elements, the present regime has been particularly adept at exploiting the economic and personal rifts between the bazaaris. Moreover, the Islamic republic, unlike the monarchy, has not completely severed its ties with the bazaaris, nor has it sought deliberately to destroy their way of life and livelihood. As a result, bazaari politics have diversified, resulting in a diminished capacity for bazaaris to engage in collective action.

The Shah's Mistreatment of the Entire Bazaari Community: Solidification of Solidarity

The varying utterances of the leading personalities of each regime can be regarded as one indicator of the regime's differing dispositions toward the bazaar. The shah himself had frankly made his disdain and animosity toward the bazaaris abundantly clear:

> The bazaars are basically unhealthy environs. The bazaaris are a fanatic lot, highly resistant to change because their locations afford a lucrative monopoly. I could not stop building supermarkets. I wanted a modern country. Moving against the bazaars was typical of the political and social risks I had to take in my drive for modernization. (quoted in Milani, 1994, p. 63).[10]

By contrast, Khomeini, who never allowed his concerns for the downtrodden to practically interfere with his respect for private property, had on numerous occasions warned against antagonizing the bazaaris. For example, in 1984 Khomeini declared that the "revolution would be undone if the republic lost the support of the bazaaris, who, he stressed, had played such a critical role in overthrowing the Shah" (Abrahamian, 1993, p. 40). Similarly, Khomeini's successor, Khamenei, upon acceding to power, asserted: "Islam respected the bazaar, [that] the Koran had favorable things to say about trade and commerce, and [that] socialists, not Muslims, associated business with theft, corruption and exploitation. 'The bazaaris,' he declared, 'helped the Islamic Revolution and continue to be staunch supporters of the Islamic Republic'" (Abrahamian, 1993, p. 40).

Actions, however, speak louder than words. True to his ideology, the shah pursued policies that were inimical to the interests of the bazaaris as a whole. The shah's intentional decision to promote the modern sector of the economy resulted in the creation of cooperatives, banks, supermarkets, department stores, and chain stores, all of which posed a mortal blow to the livelihood of the bazaaris. As a direct consequence of the rise of such institutions, the bazaaris' share of "domestic trade" in GDP declined from 9.4 percent in 1963–1964 to 5.7 percent in 1977–1978 (Foran, 1993, p. 335). Even back in 1966, an astute observer had argued: "Today, the bazaar, which has survived vicissitudes of invaders, is dying. It is dying even though the volume of retail trade has increased within the bazaar, for retail trade outside the bazaar has increased at an even greater rate" (quoted in Bashiriyeh, 1983, p. 67).

The bazaaris were also highly resentful of the state's increasingly interventionist policies in their affairs. Preferring to bestow their charitable contributions on the ulama of their choice in order to enhance their standing in the eyes of the community of believers and potential customers, as well as the Almighty in the hereafter, the bazaaris despised making required financial donations for state-sponsored secular celebrations (such as the shah's birthday). They also disliked governmental attempts at controlling their books and taxing their profits (Amuzegar, 1991, p. 277). The bazaaris became particularly enraged in 1970, when "the Majles granted the government the prerogative to appoint the director of the *asnaf* [guilds]" (Milani, 1994, p. 63).

In 1975, the shah's treatment of the bazaaris took a distinctive turn for the worse. From the time of his restoration to power in 1953 until 1975, the shah had encouraged the functioning of a two-party system, which had nonetheless degenerated into a farce. In 1975, he suddenly decided to turn the country into a one-party system. His aim was apparently to strengthen the institutional basis of his rule by organizing the society's various strata into a proregime political party. The shah maintained that those who did not wish to join his new Rastakhiz (Resurgence) party were traitors, and he offered either to put them in prison or to grant them a free passport so they could leave the country immediately (Halliday, 1979, p. 47). The shah's attempts at forced institutionalization, however, proved to be especially disastrous from the vantage point of the bazaaris.

Shortly after its establishment, the Rastakhiz initiated an onslaught against the bazaaris. The party dissolved the bazaar's independent guilds. In their place, it created new guilds beholden to the party "under a chamber of commerce in each city often run by a large non-bazaar businessman" (Foran, 1993, p. 335). Under the pretext of an urban renewal program, the bazaar around Imam Reza's shrine in Mashad was largely destroyed, and Tehran's municipal government unveiled plans for constructing an eight-lane freeway, which necessitated the obliteration of the capital's bazaar. At the same time, the government-controlled press launched a campaign underscoring the need for uprooting the bazaars, tearing down "worm-ridden shops," "replacing inefficient butchers, grocers, and bakers with efficient supermarkets, and establishing a state-run market modeled after London's Covent Gardens." Reacting to such developments, a shopkeeper told an American journalist: "[I]f we let him, the Shah will destroy us. The banks are taking over. The big stores are taking away our livelihoods. And the government will flatten our bazaars to make space for state offices" (Abrahamian, 1982, p. 444).

At the same time, the shah singled out the bazaaris to bear the brunt of his "antiprofiteering" campaign, designed to combat runaway inflation. Following the massive rise in oil prices in 1973 (Iran's oil income, which had gone from $90 million in 1955 to $1.1 billion in 1970, rose to $21.4 billion in 1974) (Alam, 1991, p. 273), the shah, acting against the strong objections of his economists in the Plan Organization, decided to double both the government's budget and the ongoing five-year plan (Bashiriyeh, 1983, p. 86; Zonis, 1991, p. 77). The subsequent injection of exorbitant quantities of money into the economy, with scarcely any concomitant rise in production, substantially increased the rate of inflation. Iran's infrastructure was too rudimentary to cope with the dramatic rise in the importation and distribution of goods entering the country. Consequently, even the most common consumer products came to be in short supply. The government itself admitted to an annual inflation rate of 20 percent, but the actual figure was closer to 40 percent (Bashiriyeh, 1983, p. 87; Parsons, 1984, p. 8). Unwilling to acknowledge that his own ill-conceived economic policies were responsible for inflation, the shah blamed profiteering businessmen, particularly the bazaaris.

At the request of the shah, leaders of the Rastakhiz party inaugurated a "merciless crusade against profiteers, hoarders, and unscrupulous capitalists." About 10,000 students were hired as inspectors to check selling prices against government-ordained "appropriate prices." Discrepancies were reported to the newly created Guild Courts, which subsequently imprisoned 8,000 shopkeepers, banned 23,000 traders from their hometowns, fined 250,000 small businessmen, and brought charges against another 180,000. "By 1976, almost every bazaar family had at least one member who had suffered from this . . . campaign" (Abrahamian, 1989, p. 17; Arjomand, 1988, p. 107; Zonis, 1991, p. 77). At the same time, seeking to undercut local wholesale dealers, the government imported massive amounts of meat, wheat, and sugar.

These policies infuriated bazaaris of all stripes, including the shopkeepers, merchants, workshop owners, and peddlers. When the shah first created the Rastakhiz party, Khomeini had issued a statement from exile castigating it as both anti-Islamic and unconstitutional. He had also encouraged the bazaaris to close down their shops in protest of the new party. The bazaaris, however, had uniformly refused to abide. But three years later, in 1978, following the escapades of the Rastakhiz party, the same request received the wholehearted and unanimous support of the entire bazaari community. During the revolutionary process, "the bazaars were frequently closed and the bazaaris were most active in the anti-Shah demonstrations. Furthermore, they also gave financial support to those striking in the private sector, especially to the journalists' strike in November 1978" (Arjomand, 1988, p. 107).

The Islamic Republic and the Unraveling of Bazaari Solidarity

Contrary to the expectations of the bazaaris, however, the triumph of the revolution did not result in the relinquishment of state intervention in bazaari affairs. The bazaaris have not been exempted from state taxes and custom duties, nor have they been given a free hand in determining prices (Ashraf, 1994, p. 116). Indeed, the theocracy has proved itself to be just as harsh, even more severe, than the monarchy in controlling and repressing segments of the bazaari community. The theocracy has even resorted to executing dissident bazaaris, a course of action not entertained by the shah (Parsa, 1989, p. 276).

What is different now, however, is that one of the predominant political factions within the ruling elite is headed by some of the more traditionalist ulama and their followers, who are disposed toward protecting the interests of the bazaaris, especially their own cronies in the bazaar. Some members of this faction, which is highly conservative, at times xenophobic, in outlook, have occasionally found it expedient to move against the rank-and-file bazaaris, depending upon the exigencies of the day. This has severely disturbed the rank-and-file bazaaris, who are resentful of the special privileges accorded to the bazaari cronies of the regime. Speaking to an American journalist in 1995, an unnamed shopkeeper from the province of Mazandaran is reported to have stated: "It's just like under the Shah . . . only now there are more clerics to pay off" (Miller, 1996, p. 440). But the leadership of the conservative faction, unlike the shah, has always been careful not to alienate hopelessly the interests of the bazaaris as a collectivity. In his lifetime, Khomeini always sought to balance the viewpoints of the conservative faction with those of the radical faction sympathetic to the plight of the dispossessed and the more pragmatic faction disposed toward developing the modern sectors of the economy. Since assuming power, Khamenei has largely followed Khomeini's lead.

An illuminating distinction between the plight of the bazaaris under the monarchy versus the theocracy can be gleaned from the two regimes' respective antiprofiteering campaigns against the bazaaris. In the course of the last several years, the Islamic Republic has been suffering from a case of hyperinflation, comparatively much worse than that which prevailed in the years immediately preceding the revolution. As in the previous regime, the primary causes of inflation can be traced back to the system's own policy initiatives. To aggregate the hard-currency resources needed to meet its debt-service obligations (estimated to amount to $6.7 billion in 1996–1997 and $4.7 billion in 1997–1998) ("Country Report: Iran," 1996, p. 7), the Iranian government has engineered a sharp constriction in its imports. As a result, imports have steeply dropped from a peak of $28 billion in 1991–1992 (the Iranian year begins on March 21) to $12.7 billion in 1994–1995 to $11.5 billion in 1995–96 ("Imports Continue Their Downward Spiral," 1996). The consequent dearth of machinery, spare parts, and consumer goods has spurred inflation.

Moreover, in part because of the departure of the nation's most competent and experienced managers, impelled by the regime's restrictive social and political policies, most of Iran's businesses, particularly those in the bloated public sector, are grossly mismanaged and are therefore a financial and economic drain. According to the reformist daily *Hamshahri*, published by Tehran's municipality, "Government Office workers—many of whom hold two or even three jobs to make ends meet—perform only one hour's productive work a day for the government" ("Wake Me at Five," 1996). To finance its deficits, the government has resorted to the inflationary policy of printing money. Because of these policies and despite the maintenance of subsidies and strict currency exchange rules, the inflation rate has remained high (from 40 percent to 200 percent on basic items) (Wright, 1996, p. 163). As with the previous regime, however, the Islamic Republic has been unwilling to shoulder responsibility for inflation. Seeking to mollify public opinion, the regime has blamed inflation on hoarding and price gouging on the part of bazaaris, among other factors. In addition, it has engaged in the imposition of price controls, which are considered anathema from the perspective of bazaaris.

To combat inflation, the government has, on occasion, initiated antiprofiteering measures to eliminate, in the words of former President Rafsanjani, "the leech-like elements standing between production . . . and consumption." In an action bearing an eerie resemblance to the policies of the Rastakhiz party in the prerevolutionary era, more than a thousand mobile courts were created to enforce government-decreed price controls on the bazaaris. In 1995, more than 3,000 merchants were arrested and fined for hoarding and price gouging. Most ominous from the perspective of shopkeepers, however, was the launching by the regime in 1994 of a potentially devastating competition, from a chain of 1,000 discount stores (Refah) with guaranteed low prices ("Country Report: Iran, 1995, p. 13; "Lost in the Bazaar," 1995).

Yet both the scale and intensity of the Islamic Republic's antiprofiteering campaigns have been much smaller than that which transpired under the monarchy. First, the relatives and close associates of the regime's ruling elite, many of whom are from bazaari backgrounds (representatives of shopkeepers and artisans grew from 2 to 4 percent in the last monarchical Majles to 26 percent in the first Islamic Majles) (Ashraf, 1994, p. 123), have been able to escape prosecution. "Furthermore, the conservative ulama who [have] served as judges in ordinary tribunals [have] declined to issue court orders against bazaaris indicted for price gouging" (Ashraf, 1994, p. 117). Indeed, these same traditionalist pro-*velayat-e faqih* ulama, whose support Khomeini had sought to cultivate by granting them the majority of seats in the Council of Guardians (constitutionally empowered to determine whether Majles legislation is in accord with Islam), had earlier rescued the bazaaris by vetoing the nationalization of foreign trade.

Recognizing the importance of maintaining a powerful line of access to the regime, the Islamic Association of the Guilds and Bazaar of Tehran has financed conservative parliamentary candidates and controls two officially sanctioned newspapers, *Abrar* (the Pious) and *Resalat* (Divine Message) (Abrahamian, 1993, p. 137). From 1992 to 2000, conservatives composed the largest voting block in the Majles. Recently, after very strong lobbying efforts by bazaari merchants, the conservatives were finally able to prevail upon the regime to relax the currency restriction laws that were crippling the businesses of bazaari traders.

In May 1995, Iran's currency, the rial, went into free fall following President Clinton's declaration of a unilateral trade embargo against the Islamic Republic. To assure itself of desperately needed foreign-exchange reserves and to arrest the dramatic decline in the value of the rial, President Rafsanjani's government issued a strict decree on currency repatriation. Exporters were now required not only to repatriate all of their foreign-exchange earnings within ninety days but to sell their currency to state banks at substantially lower rates than the free market. From 1995 to 1997, when one American dollar sold for between 4,500 to 5,500 rials on the free market, exporters were required to sell their hard currency to state banks at the rate of 3,000 rials for each dollar. The result of these restrictions on rug exports was immediate and devastating. The export of Persian carpets, which had traditionally accounted for at least 40 percent of all non-oil exports (carpet weaving employs more workers than any other industry in Iran), plummeted from $1.6 billion in 1994–1995 to $400 million in 1995–1996 ("Majlis Hears Rug Merchants," 1997). This policy was viewed as particularly pernicious by the bazaaris, who are the primary exporters of Persian rugs, prompting one rug merchant to declare: "In other countries, the governments provide great benefits to merchants in order to boost exports. But in this country, it is just the opposite" (quoted in "Carpet Bazaar Goes on Strike," 1996).

To extricate themselves from financial ruin, bazaari exporters orchestrated a wide-ranging lobbying of the executive and, particularly, the legislative (where the conservatives predominated) branches. They achieved their first breakthrough in overcoming strict currency rules in the summer of 1996, when the Central Bank allowed the carpet merchants (and no other exporters) to retain 30 percent of their foreign earnings with which to purchase raw material. The merchants undauntingly persevered until finally in January 1997, the Majles enacted special-interest legislation enabling them to keep all of their foreign exchange, provided the merchants used the earnings to import a wide variety of officially sanctioned foreign goods into the country ("Majlis Hears Rug Merchants," 1997; "Regime Eases Currency Rules," 1996). This is an especially appealing requisite from the vantage point of the merchants, who can cut a special deal with their foreign suppliers to overcharge them so that they can retain a good portion of their earnings in hard currency overseas. They can also realize substantial profits from the import of highly appealing foreign consumer goods and spare parts into Iran.

Merchants are not the only members of the bazaari community, however, who have managed to benefit from retaining a relationship with the ruling elite. Although shopkeepers have suffered because of the regime's antiprofiteering campaigns, they have also been able to reap some benefits by organizing and bringing pressure to bear upon the system. Iran's deputy finance minister publicly admitted in 1997 that his ministry, after negotiating with seventy-five different guilds, finally reached a compromise with them on how much they should pay in taxes. The guilds had apparently agreed to pay only 40 percent of what the law obligated them to pay on their incomes. According to the minister, "[T]he tax rolls carried the names of 3.5 million businessmen and their average payment last year ... $83 at the official exchange rate [was] less than the taxes paid by the average civil servant, whose taxes are withheld by the government" ("Businessmen Pay Pittances for Tax," 1997). According to Hossein Namazi, Khatami's finance minister, compared to their incomes, bazaaris pay only miniscule sums in taxes. Namazi maintains that the tax revenues his government collects from merchants, who own and control a disproportionate share of the country's resources, account for less than 0.1 percent of the revenues the Islamic republic receives from all other sources, including oil sales, taxes, and fees. The government derives the lion's share of its tax revenues from its own employees, who constitute the only workers whose precise income levels are known to the government ("Iran Seeks More Taxes from Bazaar Merchants," 1998).

Favored above all other bazaaris, however, are the relatives and friends of the individuals in key positions within the ruling elite. Ali Khamooshi, the head of Iran's Chamber of Commerce, and Morteza Rafighdoost (an ex-bazaari vegetable and fruit seller), the former head of the Foundation of the Oppressed, are the most prominent of these individuals. By relying on the support of their patrons, the bazaari cronies of the regime have been able to receive trade monopolies, government concessions, and unlimited access to coveted hard currency. They have thus been able to "engage in numerous, highly profitable dealings, compiling large fortunes that [have] harmed the public" (Parsa, 1989, p. 277). President Khatami's chief opponent in Iran's most recent presidential election, Nategh Nouri, is known to have been strongly supported by the bazaari cronies of the regime, who contributed substantially to his campaign. Although he lost the election, as of January 2000, Nouri is still the Speaker of the Majles and, more important, retains the backing of Khamenei.

Notes

1. After the death of Ayatollah Khomeini, the conclusion of the Iran-Iraq war, and Rafsanjani's accession to the office of the presidency in 1989, the realm of permissible expression expanded incrementally until 1992. During this period, Khatami was serving as Rafsanjani's minister of culture and Islamic guidance. The conservative backlash, which, among other things, resulted in Khatami's resignation in 1992, brought the cautious experiment with the relaxation of censorship to an abrupt halt. Intellectual suffocation became particularly acute from 1994 to 1998, during Mostafa Mirsalam's tenure as the Islamic Republic's minister of culture and Islamic guidance (Merat, 1999a–b).

2. See Karimi-Hakak (1994), pp. 516–522, esp. p. 521; Adelkah (1995), p. 15; Edward Albee, Allen Ginsberg, and John Irving, "Writer's Death in Iran Calls for an Inquiry," letter to the editor, *New York Times*, December 4, 1994.

3. See also Boroujerdi (1996), pp. 161–175.

4. Indeed, "[G]iven the absence of political parties, the press quickly became politicized, thus filling a significant gap in domestic politics" (Kian-Thiébaut, 1999, p. 14).

5. The Iranian ulama (clergy) have developed an elaborate hierarchical organization, with ranks corresponding to a cleric's understanding of, and ability to interpret, religious law. The top echelons, in ascending order, are Hojatoleslam, Hojataleslam al-Moslemin, Ayatollah, and Grand Ayatollah. Ayatollahs are essentially co-opted by other Ayatollahs. To become one, a cleric must produce a *resaleh* (akin to a doctoral dissertation). Grand Ayatollahs are the most learned and influential religious jurists, with the greatest number of students and disciples. They serve as sources of imitation for the community of believers, who have been traditionally free to choose from among the most qualified religious scholars which one to follow.

6. See also Arjomand (1988), p. 178.

7. For example, Grand Ayatollah Kazem Shariatmadari, one of the most senior religious figures residing in Iran at the time of the revolution, asserted in an interview with the French radio that his position (in regard to the shah's ouster and the role of the ulama in society) was "ultimately the same" as that of Khomeini. Pressed to clarify his objective and program, he replied, "We have said many times that we emphatically demand the application of the true constitution . . . of 1906" (quoted in Katouzian, 1981, p. 353). But the Constitution of 1906 provided only a supervisory role for the ulama, and it did not oppose the institution of monarchy. According to Article 2 of the Supplementary Laws of the 1906 Constitution, "Majles legislation should [have been] reviewed by an 'ecclesiastical committee' consisting of five ulama with veto power over the Majles" (Milani, 1994, p. 87).

8. See also Arjomand (1988), p. 85; Milani (1994), pp. 50, 86; and Parsa (1989), pp. 194–195.

9. Shortly before his death in 1989, Ayatollah Khomeini, seeking to clarify his concept of *velayat-e faqih*, made the following declaration: "[G]overning is one of the derivatives of the omnipotent authority of the Prophet of God. It is a primary principle of Islam, overriding those that are secondary in nature, including even prayer, fasting and pilgrimage . . . The government can forbid any act, religious or non-religious, when it is against the interests of Islam, for as long as necessary" (quoted in Niknam, 1999, p. 19).

10. See also Amuzegar (1991), p. 277.

4

The Social Underpinnings of
the Monarchy and the Theocracy:
The Business Community, the Middle Class,
and the Dispossessed

The Modern Business Community

Composed of those who own and control non-bazaari private-sector enterprises, the modern business class is primarily engaged in manufacturing, non-oil mining, commerce, construction, and agriculture. Largely a product of the shah's modernization strategy, this group was exceptionally well-treated by the state for most of the shah's rule. After the creation of the Rastakhiz party in 1975, however, the shah's increasing arbitrariness as well as his adoption of populist policies struck fear into the hearts of the capitalists, serving to undermine their confidence in the system. As a result, by 1978 the monarchy came to largely lose the support of the group that could have constituted its most ardent constituency.

Today, even more so than the bazaaris, the private capitalists are almost uniformly alienated from the Islamic Republic. From its inception, the theocracy assumed a negative posture toward the business class. Immediately after the revolution, the properties of the upper echelons of this group, composed of fifty-two leading families with links to the court, were confiscated and were then entrusted, along with the shah's own extensive holdings, to the Bonyads (quasi-governmental corporations). Throughout the 1980s, those whose businesses were not expropriated were hurt because of the channeling of state resources to the war effort (which benefited strategic industries out of private control) and the neglect of infrastructural projects. They also suffered because of the regime's early emphasis on etatism and the imposition of rationing, price controls, and strict limitations on currency exchange as well as import and export. With the end of the war and the inauguration of President Rafsanjani's first administration in 1989, the entrepreneurs began to gain hope because of the president's emphasis on privatization, deregulation, economic rationalization, and infrastructural development as the best means of reconstructing Iran's war-ravaged economy. The business community was deluded into thinking that the reconstruction program would partially restore its fortunes to what they had been in 1960–1975 during the shah's rule, when the state's deliberate promotion of the private sector turned the entrepreneurs into the monarchy's main source of support. Rafsanjani's efforts, however, have long since been stymied by entrenched interests. The entrepreneurs today, as the following comparisons will make clear, are even more disenchanted than they were in the prerevolutionary period, when their confidence in the monarchy had become badly eroded due to the antibusiness policies of the Rastakhiz party.

Entrepreneurs Under the Monarchy: Pampered, Then Abused

In the 1960s and 1970s, the monarchy initiated a crash modernization program with far-reaching socioeconomic and political ramifications. To bring about the rapid industrialization of the country, the state itself became heavily involved in infrastructural development and the construction of heavy industries. Moreover, by providing numerous incentives to the private sector, which included the sale of state-owned factories, it fostered a dependent and prosperous industrial bourgeoisie.

During these years, the government's fiscal and monetary policies were deliberately formulated to favor the modern (non-bazaari) private sector. The government created several banks and other lending institutions for the sole purpose of extending low-interest loans and credits to private companies. Corporations were exempted from taxation in their initial period of operation. They also received exemptions from paying duties on imported capital goods that were deemed essential for the construction of their plants. In addition, to promote domestic production, the government initiated a policy of import substitution, levying hefty duties (averaging 80 percent and reaching as high as 200 to 300 percent) on "nonessential" imports. At the same time, a state licensing system limited competition, making it possible for industrialists, particularly those allowed to take part in outright monopolistic practices because of their close links with the court, to realize profit margins of 50 to 200 percent (Foran, 1993, p. 329; Halliday, 1979, p. 150; Katouzian, 1981, pp. 278–280; Milani, 1994, pp. 59–61).

These policies prompted Ali Rezai, an industrial magnate, to acknowledge openly in the early 1970s that "'without the Shahanshah's help and support I could never attain my present position.' This was because 70 percent of the capital of Rezai and his partners came from low-interest government loans. His companies were exempt from taxes for five years in Tehran" (Bashiriyeh, 1983, p. 41).

Largely due to the shah's policy of encouraging private enterprise, then, "between 1963 and 1977 Iran experienced a minor industrial revolution" (Abrahamian, 1982, p. 430). The number of entrepreneurs increased sharply, as did the share of manufacturing in GNP from 11 to 17 percent and annual industrial growth from 5 to 20 percent. Concomitantly, the number of industrial entities expanded from fewer than 1,000 in 1957 to 6,200 in 1974, accounting for 75 percent of the industrial products in the same year (Abrahamian, 1982, p. 430; Bashiriyeh, 1983, p. 40).

Although less so than the bazaaris, the position of the industrialists deteriorated substantially after the inauguration of the fascistic Rastakhiz party by the shah in March 1975. Seeking to strengthen both the institutional and social bases of his rule (which, ironically, subsequently became even less popular and more personalistic), the shah engineered a shift in both the ideology and policies of his regime. Condemning the economic abuses of the "industrial feudalists" and resorting to populist tactics, the shah endeavored to unleash a controlled class antagonism from above in order to facilitate the mobilization of the lower classes into his single party. An overriding aim of the Rastakhiz, the shah declared, was the prevention of "class exploitation": "We are always more steps ahead in satisfying the workers and peasants' demands than what they would expect themselves. For this is a revolution [the White Revolution] that should always be ahead of the events of the future so that no unexpected event and no social or economic change may catch us unawares" (quoted in Bashiriyeh, 1983, p. 91).

In what was widely regarded as a direct threat to the position of the industrialists, the shah sought to placate the peasants and workers by making the implementation of a previously stated goal of stock redistribution mandatory. Three hundred and twenty of the largest private manufacturing companies were now ordered to sell 49 percent of their shares to their own workers and the general public. Concurrently, the decision to combat the symptoms rather than the causes of inflation was extended from the bazaar to include the modern business class. The prices of approximately 16,000 items were forcefully rolled back to January 1974 levels, and two of Iran's most successful and competent businessmen were arrested for conspiring against the people. The owner of Tehran's largest brick factory was imprisoned for selling defective bricks, and the manager of a nightclub was jailed for "overpriced" cocktails (Bashiriyeh, 1983, p. 92; Graham, 1978, pp. 94–96; Zonis, 1991, p. 77).

At the same time, the regime imposed a profit margin of 15 percent, which in many instances was below the cost of transportation, causing many businessmen to refrain from claiming their goods from customs. Moreover, largely due to the decline in the demand for oil after 1975, Iran's exports declined, diminishing the revenue available to the regime. But the shah, unwilling to contemplate meaningful reductions in his favorite ambitious spending programs, many of which (especially the defense projects) were of low priority, decided to compensate for the government's shortfall by raising the level of taxation. Thus, in a sharp departure from hitherto established practices, the regime substantially increased business taxes. In 1977 alone, private corporate taxes were increased by 80 percent. Furthermore, to fulfill the shah's policy of ensuring a more equitable distribution of wealth, the Ministry of Labor, without regard to linking higher pay to higher productivity, required businesses to increase workers' wages (Alam, 1991, p. 17; Bashiriyeh, 1983, pp. 92, 97, 98; Graham, 1978, pp. 89–90; Halliday, 1979, p. 208). These policies caused businessmen to become painfully cognizant of their ultimate dependence upon a regime entirely beholden to the arbitrary whim of a despotic ruler.

Beset by uncertainty and alarm, industrialists and entrepreneurs largely refrained from investing additional capital in the Iranian economy. With their confidence in the system shaken, they also began to shift increasing proportions of their assets overseas. According to a report issued by the British embassy in 1976, approximately $1 billion of private capital per month was leaving the country (Arjomand, 1988, p. 111). Directly as a result of mounting state abuses after 1975, the capitalists, with a few exceptions, notably Hajji Barkhordar (who provided financial assistance to the revolutionaries), took a neutralist, wait-and-see approach during the revolutionary process, many fleeing at the last moment. In the words of an American journalist, "[T]he rich voted with their money long before they voted with their feet" (quoted in Abrahamian, 1989, p. 28).

Entrepreneurship Under Theocratic Rule:
A Norm of Unnerving Unpredictability and Instability

However bad the previous regime might have been, businessmen operating in Iran today, whose powerlessness vis-à-vis the state has arguably increased, look back wistfully even to the post-Rastakhiz Pahlavi period. After all, the degree of stability, predictability, and prosperity afforded them by the admittedly arbitrary Pahlavi regime, even after the escapades of the Rastakhiz party, was greater than what prevails today. At least the Pahlavi state had one, albeit fickle, head. The country at the time was also endowed with a far superior economic status. The present regime, however, which is more bureaucratic and venal, is composed of several equally arbitrary, competing centers of power. These centers increase exponentially the number of unpredictable variables, making rational decision-making nearly impossible.

Currently, all elements of former President Rafsanjani's economic liberalization and rationalization policies, designed to attract both domestic and foreign investors, are largely in tatters. Privatization has been effectively stymied by priviligentsia associated with the Bonyads, fearful of losing some of their enormous power and prerogatives. In addition, powerful elements from within the regime, including the conservative and radical camps, afraid that privatizing may exacerbate inflation and unemployment, have worked to undermine it. Subsidies remain largely intact due to the ruling clerics' alarm about riots by the poor. The dream of a unified exchange rate has receded as the nation's foreign exchange earnings have been accumulated by the government to service the foreign debt. Instead, multiple exchange rates, controlled by the police, have proliferated

(Karshenas and Pesaran, 1995; "World Bank Leader Says Iran Economy Precarious," 1995). In the words of the *Economist Intelligence Unit*, economic reform has been "sacrificed to the interests of political advantage" ("Privatization Plan a Midget," 1998).

It should be noted that the shah's regime never desisted from promoting privatization, even after imposing its profit-sharing programs. Moreover, in prerevolutionary Iran, there was only a single currency exchange rate of 70 rials to one dollar. Currently, however, there are three rates: (1) the official rate of 3,500 rials to the dollar, (2) the free-market rate of 9,000–10,000 rials to the dollar (the value of the rial plummeted precipitously in 1998 and the first few months of 1999 as a result of the drastic decline in the price of oil, the nation's main source of hard-currency earnings; although the price of oil has doubled since reaching historic lows in March 1999, the rial has not recovered and its value continues to remain depressed); and (3) 1,750 rials to the dollar, granted only to government-controlled strategic industries and the Bonyads ("Rial Resumes Deadly Slide," 1999; "Stocks Down 6%, Rial Down 32% During 1998," 1999).

Among other factors, the Islamic regime's economic engineering scheme of halving imports is now serving as a significant impediment to business performance. Very few of Iran's industries are self-sufficient. Most are dependent on spare parts and equipment, and many are even in need of imported raw material. It is estimated that more than 80 percent of Iran's imports consist of intermediate products and capital goods, which are utilized by the industrial manufacturing sector (Behdad, 1995, p. 105). Because of existing import policy, many industrial imports have simply become unavailable. Those that are accessible, regardless of whether they have been smuggled in from Dubai or legally obtained, have become highly expensive. As a result, low industrial productivity, except in the officially sponsored industries, has become pervasive. Average capacity utilization currently is estimated to stand at 65 percent. In some factories up to three-fourths of capacity is inactive. Even with the partial recovery in the price of oil, by far the largest source of Iran's foreign exchange earnings, the policy of import constriction, which has been detrimental to the nation's industrial and mining sectors, is expected to continue ("Children of the Islamic Revolution: A Survey of Iran," 1997; "Iran: Country Profile," 1996–1997). In prerevolutionary Iran, there were no restrictions on the import of essential industrial goods and commodities.

Although the controversial American sanctions have undoubtedly deterred some businessmen from investing in Iran, they have not been, as an International Monetary Fund (IMF) official observed, as effective as the prevailing conditions within the country ("Iran Hurts Economy More Than U.S. Efforts," 1996). In this regard, an important element in discouraging foreign investment is the absence of clear legal guidelines. There is still no clear framework concerning the areas in which the private sector is permitted to operate. Many private businessmen, bereft of capital and technology, are particularly enthusiastic about the idea of entering into joint ventures with foreign companies. For eight years, the Rafsan-jani administration attempted to prompt Iran's Majles to enact legislation re-moving the 49-percent ceiling on foreign share ownership, guaranteeing foreign investors against nationalization and assuring them of the right to repatriate their profits regardless of foreign exchange restrictions. But consensus on this is-sue has consistently been lacking. The revolution, after all, was carried out in part in the name of independence and self-sufficiency.

Even if the regime manages to transcend its factional differences to create an appealing legal framework, however, it would still face numerous hurdles in sat-isfying entrepreneurs. One of the most daunting impediments is an arbitrary, corrupt, and apparently rudderless bureaucracy. In 1996, a newly elected conser-vative deputy from Tehran asserted that 2 million of 4.3 million individuals em-ployed by the government were unnecessary ("Downsizing," 1996). As noted, shortly after the revolution, in search of self-sufficiency, the Iranian government nationalized most of Iran's large-scale industries belonging to the royal family and its cronies, as well as the banking and insurance industries. Some industries were appropriated by the government itself, while others were entrusted to the Bonyads (supposedly charitable foundations run in trust for the downtrodden). These foundations have since come to amass enormous power, operating largely beyond government control. President Rafsanjani's privatization efforts (which have been inherited and embraced by the Khatami administration) notwith-standing, about 86 percent of Iran's GDP is currently derived from government-owned businesses. And of the 14 percent nominally in private control, many are dominated by the Bonyads ("Children of the Islamic Revolution: A Survey of Iran," 1997; Ehsani, 1994, p. 21; Karshenas and Pesaran, 1995, pp. 89–111).[1] The biggest Bonyad, the Foundation of the Oppressed, is the largest conglomerate in the Middle East. It employs hundreds of thousands of workers, and its assets are estimated to stand at $100 billion (Carnegie, 1999). The behavior of the privi-leged and unaccountable Bonyads has been particularly pernicious in terms of undermining confidence. Enjoying extensive access to the cheapest exchange rates, they have discouraged competition by monopolizing many industries, in-cluding the lucrative import-export sectors of the economy.

However, the primary complaint of Iran's business community is that it is be-holden to the arbitrary whim of the central bank and other government agencies, which frequently alter their policies. In addition to the unpredictable behavior of the Bonyads, Iran's two dozen ministers often do not coordinate their policies. In the course of 1996, the Iranian government issued 250 regulations on imports and exports alone. Even when the shah's megalomania had assumed monumen-tal proportions, prompting him to rule entirely at whim and shun the advice of his trusted advisors, his policy shifts were never as unpredictable as those of the Islamic Republic's. To achieve a modicum of predictability in their professional lives, Iranian businessmen have sought to become well connected, usually through bribery, with the officials and bureaucrats most directly responsible for regulating their businesses. According to a disgruntled foreign investor, Iran's colossal and corrupt bureaucracy has made "doing business in Iran . . . like coping with the combined bad habits of the old Soviet Union and the new Nigeria" ("Children of the Islamic Revolution: A Survey of Iran," 1997; see also "Ailing Still," 1999).

As mentioned in Chapter 3 in the section on the bazaaris, the Iranian government, as in the final years of the shah's rule, also regularly engages in the imposition of price controls, which are considered anathema by businessmen. In addition to dictating prices, the regime, also as in the last years of the shah, requires businesses to periodically raise workers' salaries to keep pace with the officially estimated rate of inflation. At the same time, however (quite unlike the shah's era), draconian labor laws make it virtually impossible for employers to reduce redundancies through layoffs. This, despite the fact that an official with the Plan and Budget Organization recently acknowledged that 4 million workers (25 percent of Iran's total labor force of 16 million) were superfluous. He added that "it would make no difference to the economy" if they were relieved of their jobs ("Few Jobs for College Grads," 1996).

It can be seen, then, that the Iranian industrialists, businessmen, and entrepreneurs confront an even more hostile environment today than in the prerevolutionary period. As a result, they are alienated from the Islamic Republic. Highly dissatisfied with the prevailing order, many members of the business community, seeing no other alternative on the horizon, were instrumental in financing Khatami's campaign, hoping that he would succeed where Rafsanjani had failed. Since Khatami's inauguration, however, the performance of the Iranian economy has actually worsened. Furthermore, the type of reforms seen as indispensable by the business community, such as genuine privatization, deregulation, and unification of the currency exchange rate, are unlikely to be initiated by the Khatami administration in the foreseeable future. According to the *Economist Intelligence Unit*, "Khatami may be reluctant to antagonize powerful public sector interest groups when he needs their support for his own non-economic programs [expansion of civil liberties], which he sees as more important" (as cited in "Privatization Plan a Midget," 1998).

The Modern Middle Class

The modern intermediate class in Iran was created as a result of the Pahlavi state's policy of rapid modernization, especially in the 1960s and 1970s, when the number of individuals belonging to the group swelled substantially. Under the present regime, the number of people belonging to this group has continued to expand, due largely to their educational and occupational attainments. Composed of technocrats, educated government functionaries, and professionals such as lawyers, engineers, teachers, and doctors, this group, fearful and engrossed with the ever more complicated task of earning a living, has up to now displayed passive and conformist behavior toward the system. But their public conformity betrays their largely negative private attitude.

Along with the bazaaris and the urban poor, the middle class played an indispensable role in the revolutionary mobilization against the shah's rule. This group's crucial decision to collaborate with Khomeini in pushing for the ouster of the monarchy rather than wresting liberal concessions from the fearful shah was instrumental in the demise of the Pahlavi state. In the prerevolutionary period, those in the middle class experienced relative deprivation in economic, political, and cultural terms. Excessively burdened by the boom and bust in Iran's mismanaged economy, they were resentful of the shah's steadfast refusal to allow them to participate meaningfully in the political process. Nationalistic in outlook, they also regarded Mohammad Mossadegh, who nationalized Iranian oil, as a genuine national hero. Consequently, they never forgave the shah or the United States for overthrowing Mossadegh and bringing Iran's first experiment with semidemocratic government to an abrupt halt. Subsequently, they came to view the shah's obsequiousness and perceived subservience to Western powers, particularly the United States, with passionate disdain.

Severely alienated from the prevailing order, members of the middle class and their political representatives, blinded by enthusiasm, chose to wish away their differences with Khomeini in order to bring down the shah. After the revolution, Khomeini and his followers wasted no time in making their utter contempt for those in the middle class, and all that they stood for, abundantly clear. Shortly after returning to Iran, Khomeini (referring to Mossadegh) declared: "They say he nationalized Iranian oil. So what? We did not want oil, we did not want independence, we wanted Islam" (Foran, 1993, p. 400). Khomeini also made it clear that he was not at all interested in instituting a democratic republic. Within only two years after the triumph of the revolution, "tens of thousands of professionals, white collar workers, students and teachers, of both liberal and radical persuasions, supporters of the revolution, were purged, imprisoned, executed, or fled to exile in Western countries" (Ashraf, 1994, p. 118). There can be no doubt that the modern middle class has been one of the main losers of the popular revolution that it helped to foment.

As the following analysis will show, those in the middle class today are by and large substantially worse off than they were in the prerevolutionary period. Their economic position is more precarious, and they continue to be politically constrained. Although the Islamic Republic offers them a larger variety of officially sanctioned political groupings to choose from, they are still prohibited from establishing autonomous organizations or nominating and electing their favored representatives. Although the theocracy is not vulnerable to the charge of being beholden to foreign powers, it has, in the opinion of most middle-class members, gone overboard in isolating the country. Above all, however, members of the middle class, whose behavioral norms and values have become largely secularized (particularly women and the youth), are especially resentful of the Islamic regime's imposition of irksome social restrictions and intrusive meddlings in their private lives. The monarchy, in spite of its numerous other flaws, allowed people to pursue freely their preferred personal lifestyles and modes of behavior.

The Middle Class Under the Monarchy

Economic Grievances. In spite of, or rather because of, Iran's superficially stellar economic growth during the 1970s, a large proportion of the new middle class, especially those from the middle and lower levels living on fixed incomes, became alienated from the monarchy partly because of economic considerations. "In the decade preceding the [OPEC] price rise of 1973, Iran's record of industrial and economic growth was very respectable, with the gross national product (GNP) increasing 9 to 10 percent annually" (Arjomand, 1988, p. 110). During this time, many in the middle class, although politically dissatisfied, appreciated the substantial gains in their standard of living and were thus better prepared to accept their lack of political enfranchisement. Following the staggering rise in petroleum prices, Iran's GNP rose by 30.3 percent in 1973–1974 and 42 percent in 1974–1975 (Arjomand, 1988, p. 110). Ironically, however, the economic status of the middle class took a distinctive turn for the worse.

As noted, following the price rise, the shah suddenly decided to double the nation's pace of economic development. However, Iran's infant infrastructure as well as its limited number of trained personnel made the realization of the shah's objectives impossible. In 1975, at Khoramshahr, Iran's main port, ships had to wait a minimum of 160 days before being able to enter the harbor (Graham, 1978, p. 87). The massive influx of enormous amounts of money, goods, and services (through which Western countries exported their inflated prices back to the Persian Gulf region) resulted in runaway inflation. The inflation eventually gave way to a tenacious recession, which was in effect during the course of the revolution.

During the years of the oil boom (1973–1977), retail prices, which had on average risen 1.5 percent from 1963 to 1967 and 3.7 percent from 1968 to 1972, dramatically increased to 15.7 percent a year (Foran, 1993, p. 331). Meanwhile, the cost-of-living index shot "up from a base of 100 in 1970 to 160 in 1975, and further to 190 in 1976. The rise was even steeper for such essentials as food and housing" (Abrahamian, 1989, p. 28). Indeed, after 1973, food prices rose by as much as 30 percent a year, while "in 1974–5 rents in Tehran rose by as much as 200 per cent and by another 100 per cent in 1975–6" (Halliday, 1979, p. 165). In 1976, the *Economist* calculated that a middle-class family could have been spending as much as 50 percent of its income on housing (Abrahamian, 1989, p. 28).

Compounding the economic plight of the professional middle class, starting in 1975 and gradually accelerating up to 1977, the world demand for oil began to contract, resulting in diminished revenues to the Iranian government. Unwilling to terminate exorbitant arms purchases, the shah instructed the government to postpone certain industrial projects and to partially compensate for the shortfall by raising income taxes. At the same time, to reduce the rate of inflation and stabilize the overheated economy, the government engineered a recession in 1977 through the imposition of tight monetary and credit policies. In the aggregate, these policies had devastating implications for the already struggling middle class. High interest rates (up to 30 percent) and strict control over the money supply, combined with the termination of industrial projects, brought about a reduction in financial transactions. As a result, the unemployment rate rose from 1 percent in 1974 to 9 percent by the end of 1977. Meanwhile, the government's policy of increased taxation resulted in a 71-percent rise in taxes on salaries in 1976 and another 51 percent in 1977, leading to a sharp rise in feelings of relative deprivation among members of the salaried middle class. This sense of relative deprivation and bitterness, which derived from shattered expectations about their own economic position, acquired extra potency in the face of continued ostentatious displays of opulence and conspicuous consumption by the court cronies.

Cultural Grievances.   For those in the middle class, the presence of increasing numbers of well-to-do expatriates in their midst, combined with the shah's close relations with the United States and Israel, also served to underscore the ultimate dependence of the regime on foreign powers. The perception that the shah was indeed a puppet of the United States received additional widespread public acceptance when the United States, in 1974, chose Richard Helms, former head of the CIA, as its ambassador to Iran (Bill, 1988, p. 213). Moreover, even before 1973, Iran's shortage of trained personnel had prompted the government to rely on an increasing number of foreign experts. After 1973, however, the shah's decision to embark on a spending spree resulted in a geometric increase in the number of European and American military personnel, technicians, educators, and advisers. As in the gold rush in the American West, the accelerated pace of economic activity also attracted a large number of outsiders seeking to acquire a vast fortune rapidly: "By 1976 it was reckoned that the majority of the 24,000 Americans in Iran were defence and defence-related" (Graham, 1978, p. 177).

Political Grievances.   Just at the time the nationalist sensibilities of the middle class were being offended and their economic hardships mounting, making the system's dictatorial, corrupt, and capricious nature even less palatable, the shah chose this worst of moments to launch his Rastakhiz party. Since almost losing his throne to a popular representative of the professional middle class, the shah had come to fear and distrust the middle class more than any other social group. After his restoration to power in 1953, the shah, opting for what Samuel Huntington refers to as the "autocratic model of development" (Milani, 1994, p. 67), banned all independent political organizations and sought to prevent the middle class from engaging in any type of political participation. From 1958 to 1975, the burgeoning and politically conscious bourgeoisie (as well as other social groups, for that matter) was given the option to choose between two equally servile political parties. Indistinguishable in ideology, the parties were headed by two of the shah's most obsequious confidants, prompting the *Economist* to dub them the "yes" and the "of course" parties. Despite the fact that the two-party system was never taken seriously, it did provide a rudimentary mechanism for the recruitment and circulation of the political elite (Arjomand, 1988, p. 108).

Dissatisfied with the failure of his political formula to enlarge his regime's social bases of support, the shah, whose sense of megalomania and omniscience had been fanned by the rise in oil prices and the praise of his sycophantic advisers (he had become increasingly averse to disapproval and had shunned his independently inclined counselors), resorted to forced institution building in 1975. In launching his single party, the shah arrogantly declared that it was the patriotic duty of every Iranian adult citizen to join the Rastakhiz party. He maintained that those who did not support his party were either Communist sympathizers, in which case their place was either in jail or in exile, or were suffering from "mental imbalance" (Bill, 1988, p. 196). Predictably, as with other social groups examined in this study, the shah's attempts to absorb the middle class forcefully into his regime were woefully counterproductive. Yearning as they were for meaningful political participation, those in the middle class became further alienated from an arrogant regime, which treated them like unruly children. The stage was thus set for the recruitment of the modern bourgeoisie into the revolutionary camp.

The Middle Class and the Islamic Republic

It can be seen, then, that the middle class was estranged from the Pahlavi regime because of economic, political, and cultural considerations. As already noted, almost immediately after the triumph of the revolution, members of this group came to realize that they had made a grave error in anointing Khomeini as their leader. Their enthusiastic participation in the revolution, after all, was prompted by the negative aim of overthrowing the shah rather than the positive desire to implant Ayatollah Khomeini's vision of the just Islamic order. As one of the ardent dissidents of the shah's rule (and a middle-class activist) asserted: "The mass movements (against the monarch) were not essentially religious. In fact, a large number of people who followed Khomeini were not necessarily practicing Moslems. Nor did they agree with Khomeini's idea of an Islamic republic" (Amuzegar, 1991, p. 24). Along with the intellectuals, the professional middle class has undoubtedly been one of the biggest losers of the revolution.

The Struggle for Survival

How does the predicament of those in the middle class today compare with their plight in the prerevolutionary period? There can be no doubt that the economic position of the middle class is far worse today than before the revolution. Even after the shah's whimsical approach to economic policy following 1973, the rate of inflation in Iran never exceeded 30 to 40 percent per annum. In 1995, the Iranian Central Bank acknowledged an estimated annual inflation rate of 85 percent, while many private economists believed the actual rate to exceed 100 percent (*Iran Times*, January 26, 1996). From the mid-1990s, spiraling inflation has caused some food prices to rise by as much as 4,000 percent, making it exceedingly difficult for wage earners to make ends meet. If, before the revolution, a typical middle-class family had to devote 50 percent of its earnings to rent, today a typical monthly salary of 300,000 rials ($100 at the official and generally unavailable exchange rate) is scarcely sufficient to pay for rent. It now costs at least 200,000 rials per month to rent a two-room apartment, which is prohibitive for most, considering that a primary-school teacher, for example, earns only 120,000 rials per month ("Children of the Islamic Revolution: A Survey of Iran," 1997; "Inflation Fuels Discontent Against Iran's Government," 1994; Sanger, 1995, p. 46). For those who do not already own their places of residence, it has become nearly impossible to save sufficient money to purchase a house or an apartment. Furthermore, although most bazaaris and other self-employed individuals are able to obviate paying or substantially reducing their income taxes, the government automatically deducts the taxes of wage earners in both the private and public sectors directly from their salaries. The wage earners, therefore, are forced to bear the brunt of taxation ("Taxing News," 1997).

Although the price of goods has increased by as much as ten times since the early 1990s, most salaries have risen by a factor of two (Daniszewski, 1996b). Consequently, many government employees (who constitute approximately half of all city dwellers ["Children of the Islamic Revolution: A Survey of Iran," 1997]) and other functionaries have found it necessary to resort to graft or taking second, even third, jobs to supplement their scant incomes. Teachers, for example, provide tutorials, while government-employed engineers and economists make use of their connections to acquire private contracts. Many have found it expedient to pool their resources in order to purchase and operate taxicabs. In a speech delivered in 1999, even former President Rafsanjani acknowledged the widespread existence of multiple job holdings, when he asserted that the nation must make it a priority to make it possible for workers to provide for their families with the wages of a single shift ("Mending Fences," 1999). Further, it has become common practice for functionaries to accept gratuity in exchange for performing, expediting, or retarding an otherwise impossible or painstakingly slow or injurious task. For instance: "Catching errant teenagers and girls considered to be improperly dressed is now proving to be a big earner for Tehran's numerous and underpaid moral police" (Evans, 1996, p. 12). Thus, venality and overwork "keep the economy rolling and Iranians away from the begging bowl . . . But [they] also help explain the exceptionally low productivity of so many of Iran's government-owned industries. The managers and their staff simply cannot afford to spend much time at their place of work. Besides, having driven a taxi all night they are yawning" ("Children of the Islamic Revolution: A Survey of Iran," 1997). Making ends meet was never this difficult under the reign of the shah.

Living conditions are likely to deteriorate further as Iran's youthful population begins to enter the labor force. Currently, 90 percent of the youth (who compose by far the largest segment of the population, two-thirds of which is under twenty-five) wanting to attend college are unable to do so. As for those who can get into college, the former head of Iran's Plan and Budget Organization recently disclosed that even if the Iranian economy expands by 5 percent per annum (which appears highly optimistic), only 400,000 out of 1 million college graduates will be able to obtain employment by the end of the present five-year plan in the year 2000 ("Leader Says No to Proposal to Set Up Private Colleges," 1996). According to a prominent Iranian economist, now "there is a sense among college students . . . that the doors to success are closed" (Daniszewski, 1996b).

Political Oppression

Discontent among the middle class also derives from the numerous inhibitions the Islamic Republic has placed on political expression and involvement. After all, this group revolted against the shah in part to gain political freedoms and participation. To be sure, in many respects, the present regime is more open and pluralistic than the previous one. Iran's Parliament today is a far cry from the rubber stamp that existed during the reign of the shah. As noted, the range and the diversity of opinions that are allowed expression in the mass media and the Majles, particularly since Khatami's rise to power, are also greater than that allowed in the previous regime. Iran today even has competitive elections, something that was never permitted under the monarchy. However, there are limits (questioning the legitimacy of the system, the principle of *velayat-e faqih*, and the credentials of the present *faqih*). And the elections, although competitive, are certainly not free. Groups and individuals perceived to be even remotely opposed to *velayat-e faqih*, including all middle-class political groupings and associations, are effectively banned.

Among other things, the Council of Guardians, composed of six religious jurists directly appointed by the *faqih* and six lay lawyers selected by the Majles, is empowered to assess the qualifications of aspiring office seekers. The council, whose rulings up to now have been final and not open to appeal, has not been required to submit any formal reasons for its judgments. Drawing on such vague vetting criteria as "practical adherence to Islam," support for the principle of *velayat-e faqih*, and commitment to the political system, the council can and has arbitrarily excluded prospective candidates from taking part in elections. In Iran's most recent parliamentary elections, held in March 1996, the Council of Guardians rejected 44 percent of the candidates. Moreover, it allowed only four out of the more than 230 individuals who had expressed interest in running for the presidency in 1997 to take part in that contest. Ayatollah Janati, a fierce ultra-conservative, the spiritual leader of several Hezbollahi gangs, and the secretary of the Council of Guardians, has maintained that the system of screening candidates is indispensable in "weeding out" enemies of the Islamic revolution. Since the early years of the revolution, the council has persistently prevented individuals associated with secular and liberal political movements, favored by the middle class, to stand for political office. Shortly before his retirement as chairman of the Islamic Republic's judiciary in 1999, Ayatollah Mohammad Yazdi, who became the effective leader of the conservative faction following the defeat of Majles Speaker Nategh Nouri in the presidential election of 1997, addressed the issue of democratic participation in one of his Friday prayer sermons. Yazdi asked rhetorically: "Did the Prophet gain the right to rule and lead because of the support given him by the people? Or was this right granted to him by the divine Qoran?" He then proceeded to provide a prompt response to his question: "[T]he Islamic system is not based on representation . . . The system of government in Islam does not ignore the role of the people. On the other hand, it does not agree with the Western concept that the people are everything and are the source of everything that is good and right . . . The people have a role, which is to facilitate the rule of the leader" (quoted in "God Rules, Not the People: Yazdi," 1999). According to Human Rights Watch, "Iran's election process severely limits citizen participation" ("3,232 Candidates Qualify to Run for Next Week's Parliamentary Elections in Iran," 1996).

In addition to discriminately and arbitrarily banning candidates, the Islamic Republic has placed other hurdles on the political activities of the modern middle class. Although Article 26 of the Iranian Constitution provides for the right to establish political parties and associations, the regime's leadership, fearing the formation of anti-*velayat-e faqih* groups and the widening of ideological cleavages, has banned or placed severe restrictions upon secular associations. Nonsubmissive political organizations "are denied legal registration, access to major media, and the right to meet in public forums or to establish offices. Their public activities, where not banned, are subject to ongoing harassment and violence from groups loyal to various factions in the ruling political and religious leadership" ("3,232 Candidates Qualify to Run for Next Week's Parliamentary Elections in Iran," 1996).

Thus, the modern middle class's overwhelming support for Mohammad Khatami in Iran's most recent presidential election should not be regarded as a sign of its support for the Islamic Republic. The salaried middle class, as well as other dissatisfied groups, voted for Khatami because he came to be viewed, in a manner that neither he nor those who anointed him had anticipated, as the antiestablishment candidate. Iran's most powerful political figures had, after all, lent their support to Khatami's archrival, Nategh Nouri. In the absence of *any* other alternative, Khatami's emphasis on the rule of law and the rights of the individual, as well as his unusual declaration that the government must be responsible to the people, in a regime that flaunts civil liberties, appealed to middle-class voters.

Although the establishment lost the election, it has continued to retain power, controlling the most powerful office in the country *(valy-e faqih)*, the repressive apparatus, the judiciary, and, up to now, the Majles. Khatami (who, even if he was allowed to rule unhindered, would probably not go far enough to satisfy the wishes of most middle-class members), therefore, has very limited room to maneuver. He has to strive to achieve a balance between the desires of Iran's largely disenchanted and youthful population, the conservatives (who are wary of liberal reforms and the expansion of civil liberties), and the Hezbollahi zealots, who constitute the regime's core base of support. Consequently, fundamental transformations in the direction of liberalizing the system, although not impossible, are unlikely in the foreseeable future. And the more they anxiously await such changes, the more disillusioned those in the middle class are likely to become.

Private and Social Restrictions

One of the most significant factors accounting for disillusionment in the ranks of the middle class is the existence of bothersome restrictions and inhibitions (entirely absent during the shah's rule) on their social and private lives. Although the strict enforcement of what the regime deems to be appropriate behavior has slackened since President Khatami's inauguration, morality-enforcing police still roam the streets. They remain powerful and can arbitrarily inflict harsh chastisements on those whom they perceive as being transgressors. Rules governing personal conduct have placed severe limitations on what is permissible in the public, and even the private, realm. These policies are especially bothersome for women and the young.

Members of the middle class in general, but especially the young, are highly resentful of how the Islamic Republic has made it excessively difficult for them to engage in recreation, entertainment, and social contact with the opposite sex. Male and female companionship, except in marriage or within the nuclear family, is strictly forbidden. The ever-present morality police patrol the streets, closely inspecting the areas where young people congregate to mingle with the opposite sex. Unrelated couples who are caught can be subject to humiliating punishments, ranging from caning, imprisonment, and paying a hefty fine to forced marriage. In anonymous interviews with foreign journalists, people increasingly admit to being "fed up" with "brothers and sisters who monitor the streets, checking to make sure that behavior and appearance conform to Islamic standards" ("Young Still Await Khatami Changes," 1998).

Inhibited from freely commingling outside, many have resorted to throwing clandestine parties, seeking to entertain themselves at home. However, not even private gatherings are immune from the encroaching and watchful eye of the theocracy. Those who have not bribed the authorities in advance or are unfortunate enough to fall victim to a random crackdown on "debauched gatherings," can be taken into police custody and, if they have imbibed alcoholic beverages, subjected to lashing. In one galling case, a twenty-three-year-old man, whose apartment was being raided, is reported to have tumbled eighteen stories to his death (MacFarquhar, 1996, p. 41). Although Khatami has repeatedly stated that his administration will seek to protect people's right to privacy, so far raids on social gatherings have continued, albeit with less frequency ("'Saint Diana' Leaves Many Questions After 100 Days," 1997). Reacting to such practices as well as to his general predicament under the Islamic Republic, an old man purportedly told a former *New York Times* correspondent in 1995: "It was better under the Shah. We all miss the Shah . . . If there was a free election tomorrow, the Shah would win" (Miller, 1996, p. 434). Other visitors to Iran have witnessed similar spontaneous expressions of nostalgia for the Pahlavi era.

Perhaps not surprisingly, individuals who are not old enough to have concrete recollections of the prerevolutionary era have also expressed yearnings for the absence of petty social and private restrictions during the shah's rule. In 1998, more than a year after the inauguration of President Khatami, a frustrated twenty-eight-year-old (who was barely seven years old at the time of the revolution) made the following revealing confession to another visiting American reporter: "Young people in Iran are very confused . . . We have no money and no amusement. I haven't seen America but I have heard only good things about it, that you have freedom and an easy life there. Like we hear how it was in the Shah's time— a free-and-easy life . . . This is not true Islam. They don't live the things they demand we do. I wish we could go back to those days." In like manner, a nineteen-year-old middle-class boy declared: "It's summer and it's hot and I don't want to go out with these pants I'm wearing . . . I want to go out in shorts. But it's banned. I came here [a restaurant] last night with my parents, and they talked about how much they loved coming here before the revolution, having beer and wine . . . Why can't it be like that now?" (Sciolino, 1998c).

The boy, of course was engaging in wishful thinking, especially in view of Khamenei's relatively junior religious, as opposed to political, standing. To bolster his meager religious credentials, Khamenei has decided to collaborate more frequently with the faction of the ruling elite that favors a conservative approach to social and cultural issues. He has, therefore, periodically lent his support to the enactment and strict enforcement of additional restrictive policies, which have incurred the wrath of the middle class. Fearful of the political fallout from the exposure of increasing Iranians to dangerous foreign concepts and modes of behavior, in 1995 Iran's Parliament banned the use of satellite dishes. Speaking subsequently in defense of the ban, Ayatollah Janati, the ultraconservative secretary of the Council of Guardians, maintained: "The internet and satellites . . . threaten us . . . They broadcast disgraceful, immoral pictures and threaten all humanity and morality and chastity" (quoted in "Internet, Satellite TV Threaten Chastity," 1999). However, obsession with Western cultural imports has gone underground and continued unabated, particularly among middle-class teenagers, who, having been born after the revolution, were supposed to have become good Islamic revolutionaries (Haeri, 1994, pp. 49–51; Banuazizi, 1994, p. 7; Sacker, 1993, p. 11). In spite of having been exposed to an inordinate amount of Islamic indoctrination and propaganda, the mores of middle-class youth, reflecting those of many of their parents, are remarkably secular and mundane. "Of the 802 men and women the vice squads detained in Tehran in July 1993, 80 percent were under the age of 20. The suppression of culture in the name of defending against the West's 'cultural invasion' and the attempts at coercive 'Islamization' have made [the] youth almost obsessed with the culture they are being deprived of" (Nafisi, 1999, p. 24). Since the banning of satellite dishes, underground video rentals,[2] like networks that specialize in delivering alcoholic beverages, have reportedly become highly popular. Some daring and patient individuals even go through the arduous task of setting up their dishes in the evening and dismantling them before dawn. For most of the middle class, the revolution is now a monumental hurdle to be overcome rather than a set of principles to be believed in.

This is especially true for women, who are openly discriminated against in the courts of law and the workplace. According to a report filed in 1997 by the UN special investigator on Iran, Maurice Copithorne, "Iran does not recognize the equality of . . . men and women and tolerates discriminatory conduct towards women" ("UN Says Executions in Iran Now Are Doubling Annually," 1997). It should be recalled that with the passage of the Family Law in the previous regime, women had acquired some tangible rights in the areas of marriage and work. After the revolution, however, these rights were substantially reversed, as the Islamic Republic once again adopted the Sharia as the law of the land, lowered the legal age of marriage from eighteen to nine, did away with restrictions on polygamy and willful divorce on the part of men, and purged women from many occupations (Abrahamian, 1989, p. 208), most significantly prohibiting them from serving as judges. Today, in spite of having continued their strides in education, women are not allowed to divorce, are almost never granted custody of children, cannot travel abroad without the permission of their husbands, are forbidden from marrying non-Muslim men, and must receive their father's permission prior to being able to marry. In addition, their testimony in court, the compensation due to them as victims of crime, as well as the assets they can acquire through inheritance, are all worth one-half of what is accorded to men. In the eyes of the largely secularized middle-class women, such gross discriminations are only exacerbated by the requirement, at times sternly enforced, that they dress modestly and always cover their heads in public ("Children of the Islamic Revolution: A Survey of Iran," 1997; "Cops Hustle Women Busting Dress Code," 1997).

Since Khatami's rise to power, irksome restrictions on women have somewhat eased, although women continue to be subject to open discrimination. The morality-enforcing police, while still unpredictable, have become distinctively more lenient in their enforcement of the dress code, have diminished their raids into private gatherings, and are less apt to badger male and female companions on the streets. The relatively more relaxed social atmosphere has prompted some women to wear fingernail polish and even to show more hair from underneath their head scarves. Indeed, "young girls in particular have turned the veil into an instrument of protest. They wear it in attractive and provocative ways. They leave part of their hair showing from under their scarves or allow colorful clothing to show . . . They walk in a defiant manner" (Nafisi, 1999, p. 24). The most significant stride from the vantage point of women, however, has been the appointment of four women lawyers as full judges in family courts (which only handle divorce cases) and a woman as an assistant prosecutor judge (authorized to adjudicate civil and criminal cases) ("1st Female Criminal Court Judge Named Since 1979," 1998). Still, although female judges are more likely to be sympathetic to the plight of women, their hands are tied by the laws they administer.

Like the intelligentsia, members of Iran's modern middle class, then, are both hopeful and anxious about their future prospects. They are impatient for far more liberal and meaningful alterations in the nature of the system, which may be beyond the scope of Khatami's power (or even beyond the purview of the reforms he is willing to countenance). Nevertheless, bereft of viable alternatives, most middle-class members are strongly supportive of Khatami and his reformist camp, whom they clearly want to prevail in the ongoing power struggle.

The Dispossessed

Disillusionment and loss of faith in the revolution is also becoming pronounced in the ranks of much of the destitute, whom Khomeini had promised to lift out of grinding poverty. Composed of unskilled and generally uneducated laborers, "[t]he lumpenproletariat refers to the lowest stratum of wage earners in the urban areas" (Milani, 1994, p. 65). The urban poor, if they are able to obtain employment, work in such capacities as construction workers, domestic servants, office tea boys, and load carriers (Kazemi, 1980, p. 44).

In the prerevolutionary era, the essential failure of the shah's land-reform program, as well as the regime's emphasis on industrial and urban development at the expense of the countryside, resulted in the decline of agricultural jobs and massive waves of migration from the rural areas to the cities. Coming to the city in search of the good life, erstwhile peasants were instead confronted with appalling living conditions, mounting inflation, impersonal relations, and disturbingly novel modes of behavior and conduct. Moreover, their marginal existence in the face of opulence and conspicuous consumption served to make them aware of their deprived status vis-à-vis the more privileged segments of society.

Separated from the monarchical order by vast economic and cultural gulfs, therefore, the dispossessed had ample reason for discontentment. However, the urban proletariat was among the last social groups to mobilize against the shah's regime. This can be partially attributed to the fact that these people were preoccupied with the task of making ends meet in order to survive. Indeed, there is evidence to suggest that the squatting community, the poorest of the poor, was less actively involved in the revolutionary process than the settled proletariat (Parsa, 1989, p. 5). In addition, the connection between the state's policies and their own deplorable conditions was not readily apparent to the poor (Kazemi, 1980, p. 89). It was thus left to the oppositional ulama to clarify this nexus and to incite the destitute to rise up against the shah. The ulama, in turn, were considerably aided in their task by the monarchy's curtailment of the secular opposition, the fact that the urban marginals were steeped in the Islamic faith, and Khomeini's charisma as well as his appealing rhetorical utterances.

With such declarations as: "Islam belongs to the *mostazafin*" (the dispossessed and disinherited), "a country that has slums is not Islamic," and "Islam will eliminate class differences" (Abrahamian, 1989, p. 22), Khomeini instilled an insatiable sense of rising expectations in the minds of the poor. The peasants were conspicuous in the Iranian revolution by their absence. But, by serving as foot soldiers of the revolution, the urban proletariat greatly swelled the ranks of the demonstrators and incurred most of the fatalities sustained during the revolutionary process. Persistently worsening economic difficulties, however, have now hopelessly shattered the expectations of the dispossessed as their numbers have expanded, their conditions have deteriorated, and their hardships have mounted. Without heavy subsidies, the poor would be unable to obtain basic subsistence. In the 1990s, seven major spontaneous acts of rebellion involving shantytown dwellers and urban squatters shook Iran.

As we shall subsequently see, however, the present regime, unlike the previous one, has managed to integrate a portion of the proletariat into its political system. The cultural attributes extolled by the Islamic Republic are in greater accord with the dispositions of the destitute (although there are indications that even some of the members of this class are turning to Western modes of recreation and entertainment as well as Western cultural norms and lifestyles)[3] than what was espoused by the monarchy. Consequently, the sense of relative deprivation experienced by the poor today (at least in cultural terms) is not as severe as it was in the prerevolutionary period. More significant, most of the rank-and-file members of Hezbollahi zealots, the last true believers in the sacredness of the Islamic revolution, are primarily drawn from the ranks of the dispossessed. To ensure and reinforce the loyalty of these individuals, the regime showers them with rewards and inducements and puts them through rigorous courses of ideological indoctrination. Thus, the loyalties of slum dwellers have been ripped asunder, making it excessively difficult for opposition groups, even if they could operate without great hindrance, to organize the poor against the regime.

Rural Migration in the Prerevolutionary Era

In prerevolutionary Iran, the massive and continuous influx of peasants to the cities, especially in the 1960s and 1970s, substantially increased the number of urban marginals, facilitating their subsequent mobilization by Khomeini and his disciples. According to one estimation, between 1966 and 1976, more than 2.1 million individuals departed the rural areas for the nation's major urban centers: "The tide of landless peasants pouring into the cities in search of work rose from around 30,000 a year in the 1930s and 130,000 annually from 1941 to 1956, to 250,000 a year for 1957–1966 and 330,000 a year between 1967 and 1976" (Foran, 1993, p. 337). The cause behind these staggering figures can be sought in the gradual destruction of Iran's agriculture, which, combined with the hectic pace of urban economic activity (particularly after 1973), made rural migration almost inevitable. It is, therefore, essential to examine these factors briefly.

Under pressure from the Kennedy administration to enlarge the social foundations of his rule, the shah launched his land-reform program in 1962. Initially, a progressive reform measure was drafted under the premiership of the liberally inclined Ali Amini, a confidant of President Kennedy, whom the shah mistrusted and intensely disliked. Unwilling to be outshone by anyone, the shah, after reaching a compromise with Kennedy, got rid of Amini and proceeded to implement a watered-down and conservative version of the program. Hailing the reform measure as the centerpiece of his "White Revolution," the shah asserted that in addition to improving substantially the lot of the toiling Iranian masses (peasants), his reform would strengthen the unbreakable bond between "his people" and himself. In fact, however, the White Revolution did not bring about an appreciable improvement in the position of the peasantry. Instead, it resulted in the disintegration of Iranian agriculture and contributed to the unraveling of the ties between the court and civil society, including the hitherto politically significant landlords. By substituting sharecropping with wage labor, the land reform undermined the traditional connections between peasants and landlords. "Thus by the 1970s few of the old [landowning] families supported the Pahlavis, and of these few none were in the position to rally large numbers of rural clients behind the embattled monarchy (as they had done . . . in the oil nationalization crisis of 1953)" (Abrahamian, 1989, p. 15).

More important from the vantage point of the peasants, land reform was deficient in several respects. Although by the 1970s a respectable 93 percent of former sharecroppers acquired their own plots of land, those peasants who had not had formal sharecropping agreements with the landlords (approximately half of the peasantry) remained landless. By far the largest proportion of those who were granted titles to their own parcels (three-fourths) either did not acquire sufficient amounts (seven hectares) to enable them to become independent commercial farmers or were given inferior-quality holdings (Abrahamian, 1982, p. 447; Foran, 1993, p. 320). Loopholes allowed large landowners who switched to commercial farming to retain up to one-half of the existing arable land. Moreover, 96 percent of villages remained bereft of electricity, and "land reform did not provide necessary capital for peasants who had acquired lands. [Nor did it] create a sufficient infrastructure in the rural regions to assist the new landowners in managing their lands" (Milani, 1994, p. 258).

Instead, the government allocated substantial amounts of capital to enormous agribusinesses and farm corporations, which the shah, after a trip to California in the late 1960s, had arbitrarily deemed sound business investments for Iran to pursue. But such ventures, which attracted many foreign investors, generally turned out to be failures, and were less productive, in both relative and absolute terms, than medium-sized farms. Being highly mechanized, they also did not function as sources of employment in the "job starved countryside" (Foran, 1993, p. 323; Parsons, 1984, p. 9).

It is no wonder, then, that "actual positive benefits accruing to the peasants as a result of redistributions was virtually non-existent" (Foran, 1993, p. 318). Indeed, in spite, or perhaps because, of the land reform, as well as the spread of mechanization and capitalism, agricultural production in per capita terms remained largely stagnant (Foran, 1993, p. 323). Thus, in the face of the nation's rising population and the expansion in demands generated as a result of the oil boom, Iran, which in the early 1960s had been a net exporter of food, by the mid 1970s was spending as much as $1 billion a year on imported agricultural products (Abrahamian, 1982, p. 447).

The shah had launched his land reform program in order to turn the peasantry into a conservative and contented social force. But the numerous defects of the program examined above, combined with the concentration of virtually all industrial and construction projects in the urban areas (as well as the rise in urban incomes), caused the depressed peasants to pour into the cities. A "survey conducted among male heads of [recently arrived migrant] households (with an average age of 35 years [in the 1970s], indicates that nearly 85 percent left the villages due to unsatisfactory employment and inadequate income" (Kazemi, 1980, p. 44). Between 1966 and 1976, Iran's urban population rose from 38 percent to 47 percent of total population. Meanwhile, after 1973 about 8 percent of the nation's entire rural population departed for the urban centers every year (Bashiriyeh, 1983, p. 88; Boroujerdi, 1996, p. 27).

Living Conditions of the Urban Marginals Before the Revolution

However, as Farhad Kazemi has pointed out, contrary to their expectations, the migrants' sufferings and struggles for survival were not appreciably ameliorated in the cities. "Arriving with great hopes and aspirations, they soon [came] to realize that their new urban life [was] not an escape from marginality but indeed a perpetuation of their struggle for subsistence" (Kazemi, 1980, p. 45). Moreover, as rootless migrants cut off from their closely knit village communities and extended families, they also came to experience additional emotional and psychological distress because of the impersonal and atomized nature of city life.

The squatters' existence and living conditions were especially precarious. Their living quarters often consisted of holes in the ground lined with plastic or dwellings pasted together from discarded scrap metal, cardboard, or oil cans (Katouzian, 1981, p. 271; Kazemi, 1980, p. 55). Not having generally concluded legal arrangements for their residence on the land they were occupying, "the squatters' security of tenure was no better than their living quarters" (Kazemi, 1980, p. 48). Their length of stay in a given area was subject to the whim of the government and the landlords. Shortly before the initiation of the revolutionary mobilization against the shah, attempts by the Tehran municipality to forcibly evict squatters in 1977 and 1978 led to spontaneous eruptions in which the squatters fiercely resisted the authorities. During one of the riots in 1978, which had to be squelched by the army and resulted in 17 casualties, tens of thousands of people were reported to have attacked local police stations (Kazemi, 1980, pp. 86, 87; Zonis, 1991, p. 111).

The settled urban poor, meanwhile, were not much better off than the squatters. A survey conducted in 1977 indicates that only about 18 percent of the urban marginal population of Tehran owned their own, heavily mortgaged, dwellings. Such dwellings, though, consisted of shacks without rudimentary services, such as electricity and piped water (Kazemi, 1980, p. 50). Those without shacks of their own, constituting the majority of the urban poor, had to rent dilapidated rooms, which also lacked basic utilities. With the accelerated pace of inflation following the oil boom, even such meager accommodations became excessively expensive. On average about six members per household lived in one room. Between 1967 and 1977, the percentage of urban families residing solely in one room rose from 36 to 43 (Abrahamian, 1982, p. 447; Kazemi, 1980, p. 50).

While the oil boom had also resulted in an increase in incomes, the annual inflation rate of about 30 percent served essentially to undermine the rise in wages. Among food items, only the price of bread was kept artificially low by the government. As a result, the urban poor increasingly turned to bread as their chief source of sustenance. Overall, those "with little or no skill saw their earnings (despite rising wages) reduced by rising inflation" (Amuzegar, 1991, p. 278). Meanwhile, the income gap, as previously noted, widened. Some have estimated that by 1978 approximately 90 percent of the nation's entire household income was garnered by no more than 30 percent of the income receiving households (Hunter, 1992, p. 58).

In the two years before the revolution, the failure of the oil boom and the credit squeeze generated a downturn in the economy, and thereby served to deprive the urban poor of steady sources of income. The sudden cutback in governmental and construction projects brought about a decline in the demand for labor, diminished real wages and, after 15 years of continuous employment expansion, resulted in large-scale unemployment. Significantly, in 1977/8, one year before the revolution, approximately 10 percent of the working population, comprised mostly of unskilled construction workers, were unemployed (Abrahamian, 1982, p. 33; Foran, 1993, p. 337; Kazemi, 1980, p. 89).

Thus, on the eve of the revolution, with their anguish compounded by the downturn in the economy, the urban proletariat came to be even more disturbed by "living in a society in which the external signs were strange to them" (Hourani, 1991, p. 452). It is no wonder, then, that they sought to assuage their sense of alienation by turning to the only institution that was familiar to them, the mosque. The monarchy, in spite of its imposition of numerous curtailments on the ulama, had allowed them to function in the shantytowns. The slum dwellers, in turn, "who were all recently dispossessed peasants, used religion as a substitute for their lost communities, oriented social life around the mosque, and accepted with zeal the teachings of the local mulla" (Abrahamian, 1982, p. 433).

The genius of Khomeini and his lower ranking religious disciples operating in Iran (all, curiously, released from jail as a result of the shah's liberalization policy) was to make effective use of the existing religious networks in the slums to mobilize the marginal classes. Khomeini's repeated promises that the revolution would inaugurate a new era of social justice was especially effective in helping to incite the masses, whose defiant participation in the anti-shah demonstrations contributed significantly to the triumph of the revolution.

The Dispossessed Today

Nearly 20 years after the triumph of the revolution, however, the oppressed urban masses, in whose name Khomeini declared the revolution to have been made, have clearly not been lifted out of grinding poverty. In fact, their conditions have deteriorated further as the population has nearly doubled, productivity declined, inflation mounted, and unemployment increased. According to some estimates, per capita income today is a third less than before the revolution, while national output in real terms still hovers around the 1979 level. The Iranian currency is now worth 95 percent less than before the revolution, and, according to some economists, the incomes of half of Iran's population places them far below the poverty line (Amuzegar, 1995, p. 30; Miller, 1994, p. 17).

Thus, Iran's spiritual leader, Ayatollah Khamenei, can no longer refute the charge of hypocrisy when he states that "Iranians [have] created a society where 'justice' [has] become the rule ("Khamenehi: Yankees Can't Scare Iranians," 1997). The theocracy has clearly failed to attain its goal of distributive justice. "At present, the wealthiest 10 percent of Iranians earn over 27 times the average income of their poorer compatriots and social inequality, coupled with uncontrolled inflation, is a major source of discontent" (Earle, 1996, p. 7). As for retributive justice, while wealthy law violators are usually allowed to escape prescribed Islamic physical punishments, destitute burglars are "more likely to have their fingers cut off" ("Children of the Islamic Revolution: A Survey of Iran," 1997).

The Impact of the Islamic Revolution on the Countryside

But fearful of the ramifications of rural migration to the cities, the Islamic Republic has travailed to improve life in the countryside (where roughly 40 percent of the population still resides) ("Children of the Islamic Revolution: A Survey of Iran," 1997). Indeed, among Iran's social groups, the villagers have undoubtedly benefited the most from the reign of politicized clerics. Many villagers are now endowed, for the first time ever, with electricity, gas, running water, paved roads, secondary schools, and clinics. A few villagers are even purchasing such gadgets as televisions and refrigerators. Recently, villagers in a remote area in the province of Khorasan were discovered to be using the prohibited satellite dish (Ghazi, 1995; "Now Villagers Are Found Using Forbidden TV Dish," 1995). According to the Iranian Statistical Center, from 1977 to 1987, the average annual income of rural households as a percentage of income of urban households was raised from 37 to 63 percent (Banuazizi, 1994, p. 6). It should be noted that the soaring rate of migration from the rural to urban areas has transferred some degree of rural poverty and unemployment to the cities (Behdad, 1995, p. 115).

But even the regime's triumph in enhancing the quality of life for the villagers has turned out to be a Pyrrhic victory. The regime's policies have failed to stem the tide of migration from the rural areas to the cities, which has continued because of lingering inequities in land distribution (Parsa, 1989, p. 265). In spite of the revolutionaries' criticism of the shah's neglect of agriculture, as well as their avowed goal to make the country agriculturally self-sufficient, Iran today can provide for only 60 percent of its food needs. Land reform has been stymied by the Council of Guardians, and the annual import of foodstuff today amounts to $2 billion (with the availability of resources it can easily top $4 billion). Most recently, Iran's Minister of Agriculture, Issa Kalantari, described the private sector's unwillingness to invest in agriculture as "very serious," revealing that investment in the agricultural sector has declined 2.7 percent in the course of the last eight years. He also asserted that because of the decline in agriculture, capacity utilization in the country's tractor manufacturing plants stands at only 20 percent.[4]

Meanwhile, greater literacy and exposure to modernity have widened the horizons of the villagers. According to one statistic, "In 1996, 93 percent of people between 6 and 24 years of age [in both rural and urban settings] were literate, compared to 50.5 in 1976" (Kian-Thiébaut, 1999, p. 13). Greater knowledge, in turn, has raised their expectations, prompting them to become resentful of their relative deprivation vis-à-vis the more privileged segments of society. It should be recalled that in the 1997 presidential election, even the villagers voted overwhelmingly for Khatami. The political awakening of the villagers, who have traditionally been unconcerned with political affairs, has created yet another potential source of instability for the regime.

Urban Marginals in the Postrevolutionary Era

Since the revolution, Iran's urban population, consisting largely of slum dwellers, has more than doubled. The primary cause behind this expansion has been the migration from the countryside to the cities, impelled by the reduction in agricultural jobs and the mythical attraction of city life. But the reality of life in the cities has been highly degrading and appalling. Housing conditions for both the squatting and settled urban poor remain as sordid today as before the revolution. If anything, shantytowns have expanded in order to accommodate the much larger number of slum dwellers. Many quarters continue to remain bereft of basic utilities, such as piped water and electricity. In the vicinity of Tehran alone, some 3.5 million people live below poverty line in shantytowns that consist of "holes covered with tin sheets and cardboards" (Torabi, 1995). Before the revolution, the entire population of Tehran was not more than 4.5 million.

Meanwhile, inflation and unemployment rates, especially in the last five years, have been consistently higher than what prevailed in the pre-revolutionary era. In his first news conference as Iran's president, held in November 1997, even President Khatami acknowledged the widespread public dissatisfaction with rising prices: "An appreciable part of the nation is having serious difficulties making ends meet. This is a relatively bad year economically" ("Khatami: Chicken Cure for Ill Economy," 1997). But as far as Iran's economic performance is concerned, recent years have been going from bad to worse. The inflation rate on basic items has fluctuated between 50 to 200 percent (vs. a maximum of 40 percent during the economically turbulent years of the oil boom). Some items, such as rice, Iran's preferred but unsubsidized staple, have tripled in price (Jehl, 1996). While the government raises the minimum wage every year based on the *official* estimate of inflation, government statistics always distort and under-report the inflation and unemployment figures. For instance, though unemployment is officially placed at 11 percent, it is privately gauged to stand at least at twice this figure (Amuzegar, 1995, p. 30). It should be recalled that even during the recession immediately preceding the revolution, unemployment never went above 10 percent.

Under such circumstances, the poor have come to rely increasingly on government subsidies in order to survive. As in the pre-revolutionary era, the prices of sugar and bread remain heavily subsidized. During special occasions, such as elections, other items, which the poor can otherwise not afford to purchase (chicken, for example) also become available at centers that distribute subsidized food. The food welfare lines are generally prohibitively long.

Although prostitution is strictly forbidden under the theocratic regime, the profession is experiencing a renaissance in Iran, as increasing numbers of destitute women become prostitutes in order to make ends meet ("Poverty Still Causing Prostitution," 1995). Similarly, while the labor law in Iran makes it illegal for

employers to hire children under 15 years of age, high inflation and low wages
have impelled 266,000 children between the ages of 10 to 14 to stop attending
schools and become cheap wage earners ("Iran Has 266,000 Child Laborers,"
1996).

With no stake in the ongoing system, segments of the urban poor have not refrained from engaging in acts of spontaneous rebellion. In the course of the
1990s, seven major uprisings took place in Iran. As in the previous regime, most
of these events involved urban shanty dwellers and squatters. Generally, price
rises or the demolition of squatters' communities have served as triggering mechanisms, prompting the poor to rise up in an anomic rebellion against immediate
circumstances.

The most significant riot in the history of the Islamic Republic occurred in August 1994 in the industrial city of Ghazvin. The uprising, in which the poor were
joined by other social groups, lasted for four days and produced 400 injuries and
thirty-eight deaths. The riot was sparked when the Majles refused to permit
Farsi-speaking Ghazvin to become a separate province from Turkish-speaking
Zanjan. Some of the young men who took part in the disturbances reportedly
shouted "Death to mullahs." What was most disturbing to the regime, however,
was that the Iranian armed forces, including the dependable Revolutionary
Guards (IRGC), were apparently unwilling to intervene (perhaps because of eth-
nic sympathies). The regime thus had to rely on the Basij (volunteer militia) and
a special antiriot unit from Tehran to crush the revolt (Azneh, 1994; Bayat, 1994,
p. 11; "Don't Count On Us, Ayatollah," 1994; Shirley, 1995, p. 36; "Country Report: Iran," 1995, p. 12).

The Ghazvin riot provided the regime with valuable lessons. Recalcitrant elements from the army and the IRGC were purged. The regime's antiriot forces
were also invigorated and reinforced. These forces subsequently acted with great
efficiency to suppress brutally the riots that erupted in April 1995 in Islamshahr
and Akbarabad, two slums in close proximity to Tehran. This time, the protesters
were apparently reacting against the doubling of bus fares and the lack of appropriate drinking water in their neighborhoods. After killing fifteen to thirty protesters, the authorities fined the families for the cost of the bullets that had killed
their loved ones. They also prevented the families from mourning for the dead.
The bus fares were reduced, however (Sanger, 1995).

In his lifetime, Khomeini, who tended to tailor his rhetoric to fit the circumstances, had said, before the triumph of the revolution, that Islamic government
would do away with class differences. After the revolution, confronted with
groans from the dispossessed about rising prices, he asserted that the revolution
had not been launched to lower the price of watermelons. Indeed, shortly after
returning to Iran, Khomeini ceased using the word *mostazafin* as "an economic
category depicting the deprived masses. Instead, it became . . . a political label for
the regime's supporters and included wealthy bazaar merchants" (Abrahamian,

1993, p. 52). The subsequent history of the Islamic Republic has unequivocally affirmed Khomeini's second statement, but it has made a mockery of the first. Many of the poor do not appear to be amused.

In a random interview with an American reporter who visited Iran on the eve of the twentieth anniversary of the revolution, a thirty-nine-year-old carpet weaver in northwestern Iran declared: "I don't care about the revolution . . . The problem is we can't live . . . We haven't had a good meal in twenty years." Like-wise, an indignant thirty-seven-year-old cleaning person asserted: "Everybody gets angry. These clerics don't know what kind of problems we have. They don't care. So how can they think of solving it? they don't even know what's going on" (quoted in Jehl, 1999b). Providing a glimpse into the extent to which the once popular revolution has faltered (even among its erstwhile devoted adherents), a disabled veteran of the Iran-Iraq war, who called Israel radio's Persian-language program during the student protests of 1999, stated: "I gave my health and my life for this regime and I am crippled today and I don't have anything to eat . . . I ask the students: please go on with your struggle, your demonstrations. You have to change this regime which has betrayed our nation" (quoted in Katzenell, 1999).

Although mounting privations and ascending frustrations are inflicting great suffering on the poor, a segment of this group still remains intensely committed to the revolution and can be mobilized on short notice. This support derives in large measure from the members of fanatical Hezbollahis, represented in such organizations as Ansar-e Hezbollah (a grassroots movement based in Tehran's southern shantytowns) (Barraclough, 1995, p. 5), members of the Basiji (militia) forces, and, to a smaller extent, the Revolutionary Guards, along with many of their immediate families and relatives. "To ensure loyalty . . . 40 percent of uni-versity slots [have been] set aside for families of martyrs, Pasdaran (Revolution-ary Guards) and Basij (war veterans and volunteer militia members). Most of these students [have come] from lower-class backgrounds and lacked the criteria conventionally required by highly competitive university entrance examinations" (Kian-Thiébaut, 1999). Although it is not known how many people belong to Ansar-e Hezbollah, there are 300,000 full-time and up to 1 million part-time Basiji members. These individuals are primarily drawn from the ranks of the dis-possessed. Fully aware of its ultimate reliance on these groups for its survival, the regime is careful to bolster its support in their ranks. Apart from indoctrination, the regime relies on granting of monetary inducements and special privileges in order to keep its constituency loyal.

The government's current five-year plan, scheduled to end in the year 2000, contains funds to subsidize the building of 850,000 low-income housing units. First priority will be given to loyal defenders of the regime ("Home Construction Is Booming in Iran," 1996). Approximately 40 percent of the highly coveted uni-versity admission slots (recall that only 10 percent of those who wish to attend college are able to do so) are reserved for preferred candidates ("Children of the Islamic Revolution: A Survey of Iran," 1997). These include war veterans and their children, the families of those who were martyred in the war, and members of the Basiji and Revolutionary Guards. By contrast, a survey conducted by the Ministry of Education in the prerevolutionary era (1973) indicates that students with urban working-class backgrounds constituted 2 percent, and those from the peasantry 1 percent, of the total students enrolled in the nation's institutions of higher learning (Katouzian, 1981, p. 289). The Islamic Republic even goes so far as to subsidize the haj pilgrimage of its staunch destitute supporters (Fisk, 1995, p. 16). It also extends financial awards to them so that they can provide their children with dowries ("6,600 Poor Are Wed Massively," 1997), an otherwise nearly impossible task, given the fact that they can hardly make ends meet.

It should be noted that the leaders of the Hezbollahis are almost exclusively beholden to the extremist wing of the conservative faction. They do not, therefore, advocate radical socioeconomic transformations. Instead, they reserve their wrath for the Western cultural invasion and improper social and personal conduct. The radical faction, which favored the large-scale nationalization of the economy and redistributive measures, was largely eliminated from decisionmaking posts after the 1992 parliamentary elections. It has now modified its anticapitalist views, has regained most of the seats it lost, and collaborates (along with the pragmatist faction associated with Rafsanjani) with President Khatami. Many in this camp continue to advocate policies supportive of the poor.

It can be seen, then, that unlike the prerevolutionary era, the loyalties of the dispossessed are now quite divided. As with the clerics and bazaaris, a segment of the poor continues to identify closely with the system, whereas others among the poor have become disillusioned and have largely lost faith in the regime. Such inter- and intragroup cleavages have endowed the present regime with a more solid base than that which the monarchy enjoyed, making the formation of cross-cutting alliances against the system much more challenging and difficult. They have also made it easier for the theocracy, provided it does not tear itself apart from above, to inhibit and suppress the formation of such alliances. By closing ranks, the theocracy's various factions were able to rely on their dedicated Basiji and Hezbollahi supporters to effectively quash the 1999 student uprisings before such protests could engulf other sectors of Iran's society. Attempting to illustrate that it is still popular, the regime was even able to bus in a handpicked group of its supporters (numbering approximately 100,000 and drawn primarily from the ranks of the Basiji and their families) in order to stage a pro-Khamenei demonstration following the suppression of the student protests.

The student protests and the ease with which the regime managed to squelch them also underscored the necessity of effective organization and leadership in mounting a challenge against a well-entrenched system. It is to the capacity of Iran's present oppositional forces to mount such a challenge that we shall now turn.

Notes

1. According to a report published by the Heritage Foundation and the *Wall Street Journal* in 1997, the Islamic Republic has one of the least free economies out of 156 countries (Iran ranked 147th) studied by the report. The report maintains that the public sector accounts for an even bigger share of the Iranian economy than some countries in Eastern Europe when they were being ruled by Communist regimes. The report further asserts that "Iran had one of the most advanced economies in the Middle East before the 1979 revolution. The 1980–88 Iran-Iraq war and widespread economic mismanagement crippled it . . . President Rafsanjani had only limited success in pushing for economic liberalization." See "Iran More Statist Than Old Commies" (1997).

2. According to Ahmad Bourghani, who served briefly as Khatami's vice minister of Islamic guidance and culture before being dismissed because of conservative disapproval: "There are an estimated three to five million VCRs in this country [Iran], which means that each week at least nine million people watch a video. Three-quarters of these videos are black market" (Merat, 1999b, p. 37).

3. According to a visiting American journalist, even some of Tehran's shanty residents have "pooled their money to install [satellite] dishes in their homes and sell tickets to neighbors and friends to watch American serials (especially 'Baywatch'). Many of these slum dwellers also [have] powerful protectors among the Hezbollahis and *Komithes*" (Miller, 1996, p. 450). A female rural migrant provided the following revealing comment to a visiting French social scientist of Iranian extraction: "The authorities think that just because we are poor, we do not share the demands of rich people. Well, they are wrong. We, too, want our children to do sports and learn modern art. Our children want to learn English, mathematics and drawing, but the mosques in our neighborhoods only offer religious training, which is too traditional and oudated for our children. They should learn modern sciences and art to become somebody. It is not by reciting the Qu'ran that they will attain this goal" (Kian-Thiébaut, 1999).

4. On Kalantari's remarks and figures on domestic food production, see "Ag Minister Says Farming Is Failing All Over Iran" (1998); on imports, see Hunter (1992), p. 68.

5

The Oppositional Forces:
From Temporary Cohesion to Large-Scale
Demoralization and Disorganization

The Oppositional Forces in the Pahlavi Era

This chapter begins by scrutinizing the conditions of the nation's major oppositional forces on the eve of the revolution, striving to demonstrate how these
groups had by and large been effectively suppressed and cut off from their constituencies, losing their organizational capacities. The discussion then shifts to
analysis of how Khomeini and his small band of dedicated disciples were able to
ingeniously exploit the shah's inconsistent, incomplete, and self-defeating liberalization policy to take over the mosque networks and unify and coordinate the actions of the monarchy's heterogeneous oppositional and social forces. Using the
preceding as an illuminating point of departure, an explanation is offered concerning why Iran's present opposition forces (most of which are even more severely suppressed now than before the revolution) are probably incapable of
forming an effective and wide-ranging, multiclass, revolutionary alliance by examining their leadership, ideology, likely level of support, institutional resources
and networks, and the potential for their consolidation.

The National Front

Founded in 1949 by Mohammad Mossadegh, the National Front of Iran (Jebhe-
ye Meli Iran) comprised a loose alliance of independent organizations, which
spanned the gamut of the political spectrum, ranging from Socialists to liberal
centrists to pan-Iranists and pan-Islamists. Mossadegh, seeking perhaps to augment his cult of personality, never endeavored to turn the National Front into a
full-fledged and tightly knit political party. The groups that made up the National Front, however, were all united by their desire "to establish Iran's unequivocal sovereignty within and without; in other words . . . rule of law within, and

political independence, coupled with full control over natural resources, without" (Chehabi, 1990, p. 12). The attainment of this vision necessitated, first and foremost, the nationalization of Iranian oil, which at the time was exploited and controlled by the British. In the early 1950s, public support for oil nationalization became such that the shah, despite his own misgivings and the fact that the followers of Mossadegh constituted a clear minority in the Majles, reluctantly asked Mossadegh to become the prime minister.

Although the National Front housed a multiplicity of orientations, the dominant strand, espoused by Mossadegh as well as his closest confidants, was a variant of Western-style (secular) parliamentary democracy. Indeed, Mossadegh's famous dictum at the time, which subsequently became the mantra of his followers, was that the king must reign, not rule. Therefore, national sovereignty and democracy have come to be the essential principles associated with the National Front. Not surprisingly, this ideology has consistently appealed to a large fraction of Iran's modern professional middle class, a substantial (though variable) proportion of the intelligentsia and students, and even enlightened segments of the bazaari and religious communities.

During its heyday, coinciding with Mossadegh's brief tenure of power (1951–1953), the National Front became endowed with extensive organizational networks and unhindered access to the mass media, which it used to propagate its message, acquire converts, and mobilize the masses. Following the 1953 CIA-assisted coup and the ouster of Mossadegh, however, the National Front was declared an illegal organization. Most of its prominent members were imprisoned and subsequently exiled. Mossadegh himself was placed under house arrest (until his death in 1967), and Dr. Hossein Fatemi, who had served as Mossadegh's foreign minister, was executed. Due to such repression, the National Front's "capacity for mobilization and political activities was drastically reduced" (Parsa, 1989, p. 170), and its connections to its support base were severed.

In 1961, the shah, under pressure from the Kennedy administration, reluctantly appointed the liberal and independently inclined Ali Amini as Iran's prime minister. Amini's premiership (1961–1962) resulted in the initiation of political liberalization and the curbing of repression. Taking advantage of the more favorable political environment, three of Mossadegh's confidants still residing in Iran, Karim Sanjabi (leader of the Iran Party), Dariush Foruhar (National Party), and Khalil Maleki (Socialist Society), revived their hitherto banned political parties and joined them together to form the Second National Front. Shortly thereafter, a fourth political party, the Liberation Movement of Iran, newly formed by Mehdi Bazargan and Ayatollah Talegani, was welcomed into the National Front. For a while, the National Front was politically active, publishing a popular newspaper, organizing strikes, recruiting members (including influential bazaari guild leaders), and even acquiring two designated locations in which its members met to coordinate their activities. In 1961, underscoring its enhanced organizational capacity, the National Front was able to organize a rally in Tehran in which 80,500 individuals participated (Parsa, 1989, p. 170).[1]

The National Front's effectiveness as an organized opposition force, however, proved to be short-lived. In the absence of its charismatic founder, the National Front became beset with personal and ideological divisions. More important, the ouster of Amini, which the National Front (foolishly thinking that the shah would turn to them to form the next government) applauded and encouraged (Milani, 1994, p. 46), brought the experiment with liberalization to an abrupt halt. Particularly after crushing the June 1963 riots instigated and led by Khomeini, the state cracked down on all forms of dissidence, once again outlawing the National Front, arresting several of its leaders, and forcing the rest underground. In 1965, there was an attempt to establish a third National Front. But SAVAK promptly arrested and jailed the organizers, who were later released when they signed statements agreeing not to engage in political activities. "In the twelve years that followed, the Front did not issue a single statement on the political situation" (Parsa, 1989, p. 170). Although there was a National Front in exile, the organization was plagued by internal divisions, and it had no resources through which to influence developments in Iran.

Largely to placate the newly inaugurated Carter administration, which started off by making certain moralizing and critical foreign policy pronouncements, the shah slightly loosened the lid of political oppression in 1977 by initiating a series of liberalization policies. Sensing that the time was right, the National Front, under the distinctly uninspiring and wavering leadership of Karim Sanjabi, announced its re-formation in December 1977 (Foran, 1993, p. 373). Although the National Front still had many tacit sympathizers in the ranks of the Iranian middle class and in intellectual communities, years of political inactivity had resulted in its having atrophied. Prevented from functioning as a political movement, the National Front's espousal of liberal nationalism was largely unfamiliar to the younger generation of students and intelligentsia, who had turned instead to left-wing radicalism and Islamic extremism (Naraghi, 1994, p. 37). The National Front was endowed with virtually no resources. In addition to having mediocre leadership, it had lost its networks and "had no specific safe location in which members could gather to discuss political issues, communicate decisions, coordinate activities, and mobilize for collective action" (Parsa, 1989, pp. 171, 172). Moreover, it did not as yet (until well into the revolutionary process, when all restrictions on freedom of expression were lifted) have access to the mass media.

Most significant, as late as three months before the triumph of the revolution, the National Front was still not advocating the overthrow of the monarchy, taking the position that it was willing to preserve the monarchy so long as the "monarch reigned, but did not rule" (Parsa, 1989, p. 172). The National Front was interested in reforming the system so as to make it compatible with democracy, civil liberties, and the rule of law. According to a proclamation issued by its Central Council on July 21, 1978, the National Front's basic principle included "independence from all chains of imperialism, personal and social freedoms, and an independent foreign policy" (Parsa, 1989, p. 172).

The Liberation Movement

As briefly alluded to above, Nehzate Azadi-ye-Iran (the Liberation Movement of Iran) was established in 1961 during the brief period of liberalization grudgingly permitted by the shah. Although the Liberation Movement had initially joined forces with the Second National Front, it endeavored to function as an entirely independent political grouping in the aftermath of the 1963 state suppression of all forms of organized political activity. Following the shah's 1977 liberalization policies, the Liberation Movement continued to act as an autonomous entity, and though it collaborated with the National Front, it did not become a part of it.

The Liberation Movement was founded by Mehdi Bazargan (who would become Iran's first postrevolution prime minister), Ayatollah Seyyed Mahmud Talegani, and Yadollah Sahabi. All three came from the higher echelons of the National Front and had been close collaborators of Mossadegh. Bazargan, a professor of engineering at Tehran University and a civil-rights activist, had served as the head of the oil nationalization committee in 1951 (Foran, 1993, p. 371). Talegani had been among the few high-ranking clerics who had remained loyal to Mossadegh until the very end. Sahabi, a geology professor at Tehran University, had also served loyally under Mossadegh. Whereas Talegani had some socialist economic leanings, Bazargan and Sahabi were bourgeois in outlook. What all three had in common, however, was their insistence on establishing a liberal democratic political order within an Islamic framework. Bazargan served not only as the leader of the movement but also as its chief ideologue. His declarations and treatises, therefore, provide a summation of the group's ideology.

Devoted to the accommodation of Islam with modernity, some of Bazargan's writings "allegedly demonstrate the compatibility of many Islamic canons with modern scientific doctrines and findings" (Boroujerdi, 1996, p. 88). Bazargan also strives to show that Shia Islam holds the key to the resolution of many of Iran's contemporary social and political ills. While abhorring certain Western ideas and modes of behavior, he embraces democracy and humanism, seeking to demonstrate the compatibility of Islam with them (Foran, 1993, p. 371). His purely political pronouncements deal with both the struggle for the achievement of the ideal political order (which should not be violent and should, if at all possible, strive to aim at reform) and the form that this order is supposed to take. He envisages a role for the ulama in both the pre- and post-struggle periods. Rejecting political quietism on the part of the clergy, he "regards political activity by the ulama and the faithful as a religious responsibility" (Milani, 1994, p. 81). Tyranny, injustice, and arbitrary rule must be supplanted, and it is incumbent upon the ulama to help inaugurate a more just political order, which should be in accord with Islam (Keddie, 1981, pp. 214–218).

Yet, though the Shia ulama must fulfill their essential duty of remaining politically engaged, they must also be careful not to get directly involved in the day-
to-day running of political affairs. Otherwise, the prestige of the ulama and, more
important, that of Islam itself is likely to be undermined (Akhavi, 1980, p. 115).
For Bazargan, this would constitute a horrendous calamity, which must be
avoided at all costs. Despite his emphasis on establishing an Islamic government,
it is clear that Bazargan was never interested in establishing a theocracy. Government, he feels, should take the form of parliamentary democracy and "be run not
by Shi'i ulama but by experts who are committed Shiites" (Milani, 1994, p. 80).
As envisaged by the 1906 Constitution, the ulama should merely ensure that the
laws enacted by the government are in accord with Islam.

This ideology appealed to segments of Iran's devout traditional and modern
middle class, the intelligentsia, and a small fraction of the clergy, most notably
the progressive Grand Ayatollah Kazem Shariatmadari. The bazaaris, religiously
inclined and largely subscribing to traditional values, found attractive the group's
emphasis on Islam as well as its desire to avoid radical change (particularly in the
economic realm). The religious-leaning members of the professional middle
class and university faculty and students derived inspiration from the Liberation
Movement's attempts at reconciling religious moderation and modernism with
liberal democracy.

From 1963, when the shah harshly cracked down on all forms of political dissidence, to 1977, when he initiated his limited liberalization policy, the Liberation
Movement was officially banned in Iran. The leaders of the party were all imprisoned following the 1963 uprising and, upon release, were kept under close surveillance. Nevertheless, under the undaunting leadership of Bazargan and Talegani, the group continued to function underground and propagate, as far as it
could, its message inside Iran. It also managed to create an extensive organizational network in exile, particularly in Europe and the United States. Although
the Liberation Movement in exile could not exert an impact on the course of developments inside Iran, it actively and successfully recruited many Iranian students studying overseas. Adept in the art of propaganda, it also effectively drew
attention to the shah's dismal human-rights record. During the revolutionary
process, members of the Liberation Movement in exile helped Khomeini to present a moderate and appealing image of himself to the Western media.

In Iran, however, the group's activities were hampered by severe SAVAK repression. Like the National Front, the Liberation Movement had no organizational network of its own. Unlike the National Front, though, it was able to indirectly reach its social base by occasionally making use of the mosques. Although
he was a lay Islamic scholar, Bazargan surpassed even many of the ayatollahs in
terms of his knowledge of and familiarity with Shia theology and jurisprudence.
As a result, he was respected by many in the religious community, who at times
allowed him to hold public meetings and deliver speeches in the mosques (Parsa,
1989, p. 200). In 1978, Bazargan himself attested to his party's ultimate depen-

dence upon the mosques: "In spite of the power of the security forces, the mosques and religious centers were sanctuaries where we met, talked, prepared, organized and grew" (quoted in Gage, 1978, pp. 132, 134).[2] Talegani, of course, was himself an ayatollah and had access to many of the mosque networks. Nevertheless, both individuals were watched closely by the regime and were thus beholden both to the regime and the hierocracy. Neither of them had the charisma of Khomeini, nor did they command a mass following. Although clearly alienated from the Pahlavi state, Bazargan, along with virtually all of the clerics, especially the *marjas*, who controlled much of the mosque networks, were prepared to accept a modified and reformed version of the monarchy. It was under the impact and pressure of Khomeini's leadership that they came to embrace the revolutionary cause.

The Tudeh

The Tudeh (Masses) is Iran's oldest Communist political party. Inspired by and modeled after the Communist Party of the Soviet Union, the Tudeh Party was founded in the 1930s by a group of disgruntled Iranian intelligentsia, among whom were a number of prominent writers, novelists, and journalists. At the time, Reza Shah was ruling the country with a merciless iron fist, and he wasted no time in severely repressing the party. He promptly outlawed the organization and proceeded to murder or jail most of its founders (Milani, 1994, p. 76). In 1941, the invasion of Iran by the British from the south and the Russians from the north forced Reza Shah, who had expressed ambivalence for the allied cause in World War II, to abdicate. From 1941 until Mossadegh's ouster in 1953, an unusual period of semidemocracy and relative pluralism prevailed in Iran. During these years, "with logistical support from the Soviet Union, the Tudeh Party became the most organized and disciplined party of the period" (Milani, 1994, p. 38).

Benefiting from Soviet protection, the Tudeh was able to establish an impressive and efficient organizational network. With no restrictions on its activities and enjoying unhindered access to the media, the Tudeh energetically propagated its variant, "Persianized" Marxist-Leninist ideology. It organized some workers and acquired the support of a sizable proportion of the intellectual, working, and student populations. Rejecting the strategy of violence and armed struggle, the Tudeh embraced the notion of peaceful coexistence with the monarchy. It managed to elect eight of its members to the Majles and even assented to the participation of some of them in Prime Minister Ghavam's cabinet.

However, the Tudeh's brief period of ascendancy came to an abrupt halt following the ouster of Mossadegh. Although the party had given only half-hearted support to Mossadegh, instead pursuing "left sectarian politics" (Abrahamian, 1982, p. 456) (and thereby tarnishing its own reputation), it now received the brunt of the regime's repression. Recall that after Mossadegh's overthrow, only one National Front member had been executed, and the rest had been given relatively short prison terms. But immediately after the coup, forty Tudeh activists were executed, fourteen died in prison while being tortured, and 200 received life-imprisonment sentences (Abrahamian, 1982, p. 451). Moreover, the newly created SAVAK concentrated most of its efforts and resources on discovering and destroying Tudeh's underground cells. In 1954, a secret network of Tudeh members, headed by Khosrow Rouzbeh and composed of some sixty middle- and low-ranking officers, was discovered in the armed forces. Many officers were executed, the armed forces were purged, and the regime expanded its campaign of hunting down Tudeh members (Milani, 1994, p. 43).

Nevertheless, many of the party's high-ranking officials managed to escape, finding refuge in Eastern Europe. The Tudeh in exile, well-funded by the Soviet Union and other Communist parties and states, published two newspapers and operated a radio station. In addition, it was active in the overseas anti-shah Iranian student movement, helping to establish the leftist Confederation of Iranian Students. Also in exile, Tudeh leaders, including Iraj Eskandari, Nurredin Kianouri, and Ehsan Tabari, clearly delineated the group's ideology as well as its strategy. For the first time in its history, the Tudeh classified itself as a Marxist-Leninist entity, called for the collectivization of agriculture, articulated its ultimate aim of setting up a democratic socialist republic in Iran, praised the "progressive clergy" (particularly Khomeini, for opposing the granting of diplomatic immunity to foreigners), and declared its readiness to collaborate with the liberal opposition to establish a bourgeois democracy as a precursor to a socialist order. It also firmly rejected the use of violence, favoring instead infiltration, instigation, and, whenever possible, democratic participation in order to transform the system (Abrahamian, 1982, pp. 454, 456).

Inside Iran, meanwhile, the organization continued to be subjected to persistently high levels of repression, which, combined with internal splits, competition from combative leftist groups, and devastating government propaganda, served to weaken the party dramatically as an organized force. Even the accelerated pace of urbanization and industrialization and the expansion of education worked to the disadvantage of the party, since the 4 million newly arrived peasant migrants and the new generation of intellectuals and students with traditional bazaari backgrounds were resolutely opposed to the Tudeh's atheistic ideology (Abrahamian, 1982, p. 452). At the same time, many of the more secular intellectuals and students became more attracted to the newly instituted leftist guerrilla groups. Moreover, the Tudeh's unquestionable support for Soviet foreign policy, including the sale of weapons to the shah's regime, served to alienate many potential supporters. In addition, "[t]he Tudeh leadership was weakened by deaths, infirmities of old age, and defections" (Abrahamian, 1982, p. 452). Thus, on the eve of the revolution, the Tudeh had lost its organizational networks and much of its social base and capable leadership. By 1975, three years prior to the initiation of the revolutionary process, "lamented Nurredin Kiyanuri, the Tudeh's first secretary (1979–1983), 'we did not have even one connection or unit inside Iran'" (Milani, 1994, p. 76).

The Mojahedin

The Sazeman-e Mojahedin-e Khalgh (Organization of People's Crusaders) was founded in 1965 by six former members of the Liberation Movement, including Mohammad Hanifzadeh, Saeed Mohsen, Mohammad Asgarizadeh, Rasoul Moshkinfam, Ali Asghar Badizadegan, and Ahmad Rezai. Virtually all the founding members were either university students or recent graduates with majors in technical fields who had become disgruntled with the Liberation Movement's moderate stance and interpretation of Islam as well as its strategy of peaceful struggle against the shah's regime. Accordingly, they devised a radical interpretation of Islam and adopted the strategy of armed struggle in order to dislodge the Pahlavi regime (Abrahamian, 1982, p. 489; Foran, 1993, p. 373; Milani, 1994, p. 83; Keddie, 1981, p. 238).

Sharing many common features with the writings and declarations of Ali Shariati, a nonclerical Islamist theoretician, the Mojahedin's ideology was devised through the merging of certain aspects of Shia Islam with those of Marxism. Like Shariati, the Mojahedin argued that true Moslems, instead of concentrating on the ritualistic and ceremonial aspects of their religion, must emulate the example of Imam Hossein, who sacrificed his life in the struggle against tyranny and injustice. The Mojahedin maintained that the forces of injustice in the modern world were embodied in arbitrary, despotic rule as well as imperialism and capitalism. Echoing the arguments of Shariati, the Mojahedin held that "it was the duty of all Muslims to continue [Imam Hussein's] struggle to create a classless society and destroy all forms of oppression . . . [including] imperialism, capitalism, despotism, and conservative clericalism" (Abrahamian, 1982, p. 489; Foran, 1993, p. 373; Keddie, 1981, p. 238; Milani, 1994, p. 83). In a highly innovative and unlikely departure from tradition, the Mojahedin argued that the Nezam-e Tawhid (monotheistic order), which the Prophet and the Imams had endeavored to establish, "was a commonwealth fully united by virtue of being 'classless' and striving for the common good as well as the fact that it worships only one God" (Keddie, 1981, p. 238). Thus, while embracing the Marxist-Leninist political economy (including the appropriateness of the notions of class struggle and the exploitative nature of capitalism as well as the necessity of socializing the means of production and combating imperialism), they continued to regard Islam as the only ideology capable of inciting the masses to rebellion against the monarchical order (Boroujerdi, 1996, pp. 117, 119).

Yet the Mojahedin claimed that true believers do not require any guidance from the ulama, whom they generally held in contempt as agents of tyranny and exploitation, either during the struggle for the achievement of the just order or after its realization. Shariati, whom the Mojahedin revered intensely, had made the following assertion in one of his anticlerical declarations: "If Mossadeq's glory was to define an economy without oil revenue, my pride is to define an Islam without the *rowhaniat* [ulama]" (quoted in Ehsani, 1999b, p. 48). Consequently, they "developed a line of argument whose logical conclusion was to make the whole religious establishment redundant" (Abrahamian, 1989, p. 122). Instead, according to Ahmad Rezai, one of the organization's founders and primary ideologues, "a group of pious and knowledgeable men [should] take over the leadership and power and . . . move the society towards Islam. This group will emerge from the toiling class" (quoted in Bashiriyeh, 1984, p. 73). However, the group's leadership, its devoted rank-and-file members, and its sizable sympathizers (many of whom were inadvertently attracted, thanks to Shariati's sermons) came primarily from the ranks of young Shia intelligentsia and students. Not surprisingly, these individuals had been raised in mostly religiously and traditionally inclined Shia lower- and middle-class (mostly bazaari) families.

In the summer of 1971, the Mojahedin made its existence as an underground guerrilla organization public by declaring open warfare against the regime. The group initiated its operations to coincide with the shah's ostentatious celebration of Iran's 2,500 years of uninterrupted monarchical rule. Designed to demonstrate the vulnerability of the regime and incite the masses to rise up against the system, the acts of terror perpetrated by the Mojahedin at this time included the bombing of Tehran's electrical works and an attempt to hijack an Iran Air plane. Such tactics proved highly ineffective, and the regime responded extremely harshly by arresting and executing a large number of Mojahedin members, including the group's entire original leadership (Abrahamian, 1982, p. 491; Milani, 1994, p. 83).

Demonstrating a high degree of resilience, however, the group managed to survive, replace the older leadership, and recruit new members. It even expanded its violent attacks against the regime, engaging in six bank robberies, assassinating Tehran's police chief as well as an American military adviser, and bombing several foreign-owned business establishments (Abrahamian, 1982, p. 491). In 1975, however, the group became beset with irreconcilable internal divisions when a portion of the new leadership (concluding that Islam was a "middle-class ideology" incapable of bringing "salvation" to the working class) sought to abandon the group's overarching Islamic tendency in favor of a wholesale adoption of Maoism (Abrahamian, 1982, p. 491; Parsa, 1989, p. 201). As a result, the organization split into two groups, with the Islamist wing, active mostly in the provinces, retaining the name Mojahedin, and the Marxist wing (later adopting the name Paykar [Combat]) being mostly active in Tehran (Foran, 1993, p. 374).

The split in the ranks of the Mojahedin served not only to divide its social base; it also diminished the group's organizational capacity by fragmenting its resources. Nevertheless, both factions of the Mojahedin continued to oppose the regime actively, and the regime, in turn, continued to suppress them harshly. After 1975, "the exploits of the Islamic Mojahedin included a bank robbery in Esfehan, a bombing of a Jewish emigration office in Tehran, and a strike in the Aryamehr university . . . Those of the Marxist Mojahedin included the bombing of the offices of ATT [American Telephone and Telegraph] and the assassination of two American military advisers" (Abrahamian, 1982, p. 494). From their formation in 1975 to the triumph of the revolution in 1979, the Marxist Mojahedin lost thirty of their members. In their eight years of armed struggle against the monarchy, the Islamic Mojahedin lost seventy-three members (Foran, 1993, p. 374).

By the eve of the revolution, both groups were endowed with underground organizations across much of the country, had access to firearms and, significantly, had gained experience in fighting the authorities. They were also endowed with a highly committed core of dedicated members and a large band of sympathizers. In addition to being at odds with one another, however, their support base was confined almost entirely to young intellectuals. Their ideology and tactics appealed neither to the traditional or modern members of the middle class nor to the religious establishment. Moreover, despite their best efforts, due to state repression and suspicion from workers, they had not succeeded at all in mobilizing the urban poor.

The Fadaiyan

Sazeman-e Chirikha-ye Fadaiyan-e Khlagh (Organization of the Guerrilla Crusaders of the People), which became Iran's most popular Marxist opposition group in the 1970s, was formed in 1971 through the merger of two small and hitherto distinct Marxist organizations. As with the Mojahedin, which had splintered from the Liberation Movement, these groups were created, respectively, by youthful members of the Tudeh and the National Front, disgruntled (especially in light of the brutal suppression of the 1963 uprising) by the unwillingness of their organizations to take up arms against the Pahlavi regime. The first group was set up in 1963 by five Tehran University students, including Bijan Jazani, Abbas Sourki, and Hamid Ashraf, who had derived inspiration from the success of East Asian and Latin American guerrilla movements. Jazani, the leader of the group, was a political science student who had previously belonged to the youth organization of the Tudeh party. Four years after its formation, however, while the group was still in the process of constructing a secret underground network, it was infiltrated by SAVAK agents. The agents subsequently arrested Jazani and Sourki, as well as twelve other prominent members. However, Ashraf and a few other high-ranking members managed to escape arrest and keep the movement alive. They later named it the Jangal (Jungle) group. The second group was formed in 1967 by two disenchanted university students who had emigrated to Tehran from Mashad. A staunch proponent of Marxism, Masoud Ahmadzadeh, the primary leader and chief ideologue of the group, had at one point been a member of the National Front. He quickly managed to attract a large number of like-minded radical and youthful members to the group (Abrahamian, 1982, pp. 483, 484; Foran, 1993, p. 374; Milani, 1994, p. 76).

In February 1971, some members of the Jangal organization ventured into the forests of Mazandaran, bordering the Caspian Sea, in order to set up a training camp. But when one of their members was accidentally arrested by the police, others, fearful that he might reveal the group's secrets under torture, attacked the police station in the small town of Siahkal. The regime responded with rapid and overwhelming force, nearly decimating the entire membership of the group. Although a dismal failure from a military standpoint, the Siahkal incident was the first act of violent defiance and guerrilla warfare against the shah's rule. Shortly thereafter, the remnants of the Jangal organization and the Ahmadzadeh group amalgamated to form the Fadaiyan-e Khalegh (Milani, 1994, p. 77).

Much like the Tudeh party, the Fadaiyan propagated a strictly Marxist-Leninist ideology, advocating the abolition of private property, socialization of the means of production, and the establishment of the dictatorship of the proletariat. However, they placed their primary emphasis on the strategy that had to be pursued in order to expedite the realization of the just order. As Ashraf, a founding member of the group, put it:

> After much deliberation we reached the conclusion that it was impossible to work among the masses and create large organizations since the police had penetrated all sectors of society. We decided that our immediate task was to form small cells and mount assaults on the enemy to destroy the repressive "atmosphere" and to prove to the masses that armed struggle was the only way to liberation. (quoted in Abrahamian, 1982, p. 485)

Thus, rather than mobilizing the populace through the establishment of organizations, the Fadaiyan emphasized the importance of heroic deeds and the perpetration of random acts of terror against state institutions. They believed that such actions would exert a snowballing effect and serve to prepare the ground for a violent, massive uprising.

The group's avowed ideology and strategy appealed primarily to young, unconnected, and idealistic intellectuals and students who despised the repressive and watchful eye of the Pahlavi state. The Fadaiyan were quite active and popular in exile: "The Iranian Student Association in the U.S. was pro-Fadaiyan and had at least 5,000 members and many more sympathizers in the 1970s" (Foran, 1993, p. 374). Unlike the Mojahedin, Fadaiyan members and sympathizers generally had modern, middle-class family backgrounds and were quite secular, even antireligious, in outlook. Like the Mojahedin, however, the Fadaiyan social base, though not inconsequential, was restricted.

Following the Siahkhal incident, the Fadaiyan, in spite of heavy state repression, created new cells, recruited new members, printed and disseminated two underground newspapers, and, seeking to hasten the demise of the monarchy, carried out a number of armed operations against the regime. Among these operations were five bank robberies and the assassinations of an industrialist, two police informants, and the chief military prosecutor, as well as the bombing of several embassies (including the British and the American), foreign business concerns, and the police headquarters in several major cities (Abrahamian, 1982, p. 488).

The regime responded to the challenge of the Fadaiyan with a massive campaign of propaganda and countersubversion. In the mass media, the guerrillas were denounced as agents of foreign entities and the Tudeh party. Simultaneously, SAVAK infiltrated the organization, discovered many of its safe houses, and launched several brutal raids upon them (Abrahamian, 1982, p. 488; Milani, 1994, p. 77). In the 1970s, 172 Fadaiyan members were killed in Iran, including Jazani and Sourki, who were murdered in prison while "trying to escape" (Abrahamian, 1982, p. 484; Foran, 1993, p. 374).

The enormity and effectiveness of the government's campaign of repression prompted a portion of the group's leadership to question the Fadaiyan strategy of terror, which, rather than demonstrating the vulnerability of the regime, had manifested its strength. As a result, in 1975 the Fadaiyan split into two factions, with one (making common cause with the Tudeh) underlining the importance of creating an organized secret party machinery to mobilize the masses and the other continuing to stress the necessity of guerrilla warfare as a prelude to sparking a mass uprising (Abrahamian, 1982, pp. 488–489; Milani, 1994, p. 77).

Thus, on the eve of the revolution, the Fadaiyan organization was bereft of the essential networks, resources, and the social base needed to serve as an effective rallying point. Most of its leadership had been annihilated or imprisoned. Those who were operating underground were divided among themselves. The party had lost most of its safe houses and, except for a proportion of young intellectuals, did not appeal to or have any connection with other social groups. It did, admittedly, have well-trained, armed, and highly committed members, as well as a large group of sympathizers. Left to their own devices, however (if they had not self-destructed through further internal divisions and feuds), they would have continued to perform a marginal role as mere agitators.

Khomeini: An Indispensable Unifier and Simplifier

The analysis thus far has shown that, collectively, Iran's prerevolutionary opposition groups did represent a significant cross-section of the nation's diverse social strata (each with different reasons for being alienated from the regime), particularly the intellectuals, professional middle class, and segments of the bazaari and religious communities. However, espousing heterogeneous and divergent ideologies, they each had a different vision for organizing society, both politically and economically. Even those with overlapping ideologies disagreed vehemently on the best means for overthrowing the shah and implementing their grand design of the just society. The primary political representatives of the modern, and portions of the traditional, middle class were essentially reformist. Through repression, all of the opposition groups had been organizationally emasculated, and some were even internally at odds. Many of the leaders of the formal opposition groups were in prison, and none were endowed with the charisma, political acumen, and organizational networks necessary for coordinating and leading the actions of the disparate opposition groups and their constituencies. Without Khomeini, who at the time did not even head an organized political party, it is extremely doubtful whether Iran's social and opposition groups would have been able to forge the requisite cross-cutting alliances that made the revolution possible.

Although the shah did have a number of implacable and brave opponents who, like Khomeini, were willing to die for their cause, none could even remotely approximate Khomeini's political shrewdness and charisma. Without the cohering presence of Khomeini and the indispensable coordination mechanism provided by the mosques, Iran's hodgepodge and contradictory opposition could have been divided through co-optation, succumbed to repression, or disintegrated due to personal and ideological cleavages and rivalries.

Khomeini's capacity to convert the mosque networks into centers of revolutionary agitation and organization is all the more remarkable in light of the fact that most of these institutions were initially beholden to grand ayatollahs who, although disgruntled, were highly conservative, nonrevolutionary, or reformist in outlook. This section examines how Khomeini and his small band of followers inside Iran were able to take over the mosque networks, unify and mobilize the heterogeneous opposition forces and their supporters behind the overarching aim of overthrowing the shah, and politicize the urban proletariat and lower-class bazaaris (whom the other opposition groups had conspicuously failed to reach).

In the prerevolutionary era, the mosques had come to constitute the only institutions in civil society largely immune from the encroachment of the shah's absolutist state. Although overtly hostile dissident clerics were frequently hunted down, harassed, imprisoned, tortured, and even murdered by SAVAK, the regime could never (short of taking over the entire mosque networks) exercise complete control over the religious establishment. Thus, "the state within a state which the Shia Muslim clergy had created over the centuries" (Parsons, 1984, p. 154) continued to function as the only relatively safe organizational setting in which like-minded individuals who were generally known to one another could express their grievances. In 1975, there were 983 mosques in Tehran alone, and the number of mosques throughout the country exceeded 8,000 (Akhavi, 1980, p. 208; Milani, 1994, p. 18).[3] In addition to the mosques, there were numerous shrines, religious schools, endowments, and associations spread throughout the country. Moreover, much of the extensive bazaari guilds were intimately connected to the mosques and the ulama, upon whom the bazaaris (concerned to project a favorable image in the community) bestowed their mandatory religious taxes. Highly revered by the masses, the mullahs "could virtually command the people" (Foran, 1993, p. 389) to take part in protests. The clergy were also endowed with channels of communication that permitted them to coordinate their actions throughout the country. Clearly, the religious establishment, with its unmatched human and organizational resources, could, if it became united, serve as the most formidable mobilization force in the country.

Many, extrapolating from the prevailing situation immediately after the success of the revolutionary process, have incorrectly concluded that the hierocracy, which had by then closed ranks behind Khomeini, had all along been bent on overthrowing the monarchy. Nothing can be further from the truth. As we have seen, the hierocracy was multipolar and rudderless, and Khomeini, although a grand ayatollah, was certainly not the most senior religious figure. Although the antireligious climate engendered by the shah (analyzed in Chapter 3) had produced an environment conducive to the politicization of quiescent and fence-sitting clerics,[4] the disaffected grand ayatollahs in Mashad and Ghom urged caution and the implementation of the 1906 Constitution. Khomeini himself was in exile, and the politically active and revolutionary clerics, composed mostly of Khomeini's former students and associates, were clearly in the minority. They were also primarily drawn from the ranks of the middle- and lower-ranking clerics and theology students. Ayatollahs Montazeri and Talegani were in prison, and Ayatollahs Beheshti and Motahari were under close surveillance (Kurzman, 1992, p. 143).

Early on, Khomeini and his associates recognized that taking over the state required, at a minimum, the acquiescence of the reformist and quietist clerics, who controlled most of the mosque networks. Emboldened and inspired by the relative immunity accorded to intellectuals and leaders of the National Front, who had (following the initiation of limited liberalization policies in 1977) called on the shah to truly reform the system, pro-Khomeini clerics resorted to protests and deliberate provocations in order to achieve their aim. The antiregime clerical mobilization was initiated by a group of midranking pro-Khomeini mullahs who had escaped prison sentences and was at first confined to radical theology students and other militant Khomeini sympathizers. The first demonstration was held in Ghom in January 1978, after a leading daily published an insulting article about Khomeini. When skirmishes with the regime resulted in casualties, the subsequent customary Islamic seventh- and fortieth-day mourning ceremonies were deliberately politicized and led to further acts of sporadic regime suppression. Such acts forced the already disaffected grand ayatollahs to align themselves increasingly with the provocateurs, even though the leading clerics approved of neither the militants' tactics nor necessarily their aim of displacing the monarchy. The mobilization of the dissident ulama "pressured the three leading clerics in Qom to use the mosque networks to broadcast the government's violence and repression" (Parsa, 1989, p. 311).

As the demonstrations began to gain momentum, Khomeini's disciples, acting at the behest of their leader, embarked on a campaign of cajoling the remaining quietist clergy in order to insure themselves greater access to the mosques. For instance, in a letter addressed to Ayatollah Khademi, a leading quietist in Isfehan, Ayatollah Mohammad Sadugi, a close confidant of Khomeini inside Iran, declared: "People, especially the young, expect the clergy to lead, and the silence of the clergy in response to the people is contrary to their expectation. The recent silence of the clergy has been extremely costly to the clerical community" (Kurzman, 1992, p. 149). The absence of any meaningful linkages to the shah's regime, apprehension of losing prestige and influence to dissident clerics, and the growing dimensions of the anti-shah movement eventually served to politicize many quiescent ulama. Especially after the shah's monumental blunder of releasing all pro-Khomeini mullahs from prison in September 1978 as part of his expanded liberalization policy, the high-ranking clergy ("fear[ful] of being outflanked by the uncompromising Khomeini" [Parsons, 1984, p. 68]) were prompted to allow the mosque networks under their control to be used by the revolutionaries.

> By early 1979, when the Pahlavi dynasty fell, non-revolutionary Shi'i leaders had been silenced and the entire mosque network was being used for revolution: for organizing demonstrations, coordinating general strikes, for distributing . . . food . . . and for handing out arms in the two final days of the upheaval. (Kurzman, 1992, p. 150)

During the revolutionary process, the mosque networks proved especially conducive to inciting and organizing the religiously committed massive pool of disgruntled urban proletariat and lower-class bazaaris, who had been left behind by the formal opposition groups. In his audiotaped messages to the Iranian people, which were widely disseminated in the mosques and the bazaars, Khomeini extolled the virtues of the *mostazafin* (the dispossessed), promising to extricate them from drudgery. Khomeini's magnetism and his ability to articulate his messages in simple language accessible to the masses was particularly appealing to the lower classes. As Khomeini himself declared during the revolutionary process: "The symbol of the struggle is the one who talks with the people. . . . That's why the Iranian people consider me a symbol. I talk their language. I listen to their needs. I cry for them" (quoted in Foran, 1993, p. 389).

In his pronouncements, "Khomeini gave the masses a sense of personal integrity, of collective identity, of historical rootedness, and feelings of pride and superiority. Second, Khomeini acquired an 'office charisma,' a religious office of the Shi'ite source of emulation" (Ashraf, 1994, p. 102). On top of all this, Khomeini was also a Seyyed, a descendant from the line of the Prophet. Moreover, he was the courageous leader of the popular uprising of 1963, when he had been the only religious leader brave enough to attack the regime openly. Mesmerized by Khomeini's charisma, many believers allegedly saw Khomeini's face on the moon.

Lining the streets in the millions to perform their solemn duty as demanded by the Imam, many thought that Khomeini was the precursor to the Mehdi, if not the Mehdi himself, and expected him to deliver them from poverty, injustice, alienation, and oppression (Arjomand, 1988, p. 101).

Yet as an astute politician endowed with exceptional political insights, Khomeini well understood that in order to succeed, the revolution needed the support of the largest possible proportion of Iran's social and oppositional groupings, not just the urban marginals and the bazaaris. Therefore, in his pronouncements during the course of the revolution, he never even mentioned his doctrine of *velayat-e faqih*. Indeed, even some of his close advisers at the time appear to have been entirely ignorant of the concept (Abrahamian, 1993, p. 30). Instead, he focused on vehemently denouncing the shah and calling for his ouster. He placed his emphasis on "unity of purpose," appearing to embrace and champion, in the abstract, the primary and overlapping causes of all opposition groups, without committing himself to any specific program.

> He spoke of such misty, but universally popular goals as political and religious freedom, independence from pernicious foreign influences [as well as the need to combat imperialism], social justice . . . the obligation to help the poor . . . the villainy of corruption, a need to conserve precious natural resources . . . self-sufficiency in food, and other essentially [populist] goals. (Amuzegar, 1991, p. 259)

He also emphasized the need to improve conditions in the countryside, provide land to landless peasants, protect the bazaaris from foreign competition as well as domestic crony capitalists, and reverse the mounting moral decay (Abrahamian, 1993, p. 30). But he carefully refrained from enumerating specific proposals for addressing these issues. It can be seen, then, that the ideology that justified the Iranian revolution was extremely vague and incoherent.

Yet Khomeini's enormous charismatic and popular appeal as well as his simple utterances worked remarkably well and achieved their intended results. Among opposition leaders, Karim Sanjabi of the National Front, representing a sizable proportion of Iran's secular middle class and intelligentsia, distinguished himself as being the first to capitulate to Khomeini's position that the shah's regime lacked any legitimacy. Before meeting with Khomeini in early November 1978, Sanjabi had merely called for democratic reforms and the implementation of the 1906 Constitution. After his pilgrimage to Khomeini's residence in the outskirts of Paris, he became convinced that the monarchy had to be obliterated and be replaced by a democratic order "based on Islamic rules" (Katouzian, 1981, p. 353; Parsa, 1989, p. 175). Sanjabi was followed by Bazargan, who subsequently acted as one of Khomeini's primary agents in Iran.

In January 1979, the newly appointed secretary general of the Tudeh Party, Nurredin Kianouri, "announced his party's support for Khomeini's Islamic Revolutionary Council, stating that the party program is quite compatible with the

Ayatollah's action program" (Zabih, 1979, p. 44). Although most of the remaining leaders of the Mojahedin and Fadaiyan were not released from the shah's prisons until the final days of the revolution, both groups fought ferociously for the revolution and marched under Khomeini's banner. In fact, the supporters of Ali Shariati, who constituted one of Mojahedin's most ardent defenders and sympathizers, were at the time so enamored of Khomeini that they "took the somewhat blasphemous step of endowing him with the title of Imam, a title that in the past Shi'i Iranians had reserved for the Twelve Holy Imams" (Abrahamian, 1982, p. 534). They seem to have believed that the arrival of Khomeini would pave the way for the realization of a classless society.

None of the opposition groups, and their large number of supporters, appear to have believed that Khomeini had any intention of actually ruling the country. After all, had the Imam himself not asserted that "as in the past he would be guide to the people" (Parsa, 1989, p. 217)? They all, however, appear to have been operating under the delusion that after the demise of the monarchy, they would be able to implant their own vision of the just political order.

The opposition leaders could be faulted for not having had the foresight to recognize that Khomeini was using them as pawns. But with his virtuoso performance, Khomeini managed even to beguile some highly prominent academic experts on Iran, including James Bill. During the revolutionary process, Bill is quoted as having referred to Khomeini as an individual of "impeccable integrity and honesty, who has denied again and again that he will hold office" (Amuzegar, 1991, p. 260).

Perhaps not surprisingly, the opposition groups today are largely composed of the same forces that opposed the shah. Many reproach themselves for having joined Khomeini's chorus of "altogether," while others lament the fact that the revolution was "hijacked" by Khomeini and his clerical followers.

The Opposition Today

Having examined the status of Iran's opposition groups in the prerevolutionary era and Khomeini's paramount cohering impact upon them, we are now in a better position to assess the potential challenge that these groups can mount against the theocracy. There are a number of opposition groups, ranging from absolute monarchists to Communist revolutionaries, seeking the demise of the present political system in Iran. Most of these operate in exile, while within the country there remain several quasi-antiestablishment organizations. None of these groups poses a serious threat to the survival of the Islamic Republic.

The Mojahedin Today

The best-organized and probably the most dedicated of the opposition groups operating primarily outside Iran is the Mojahedin-e Khalq organization. This group, made up of the remnants of the Islamic Mojahedin, is currently led jointly by Masoud Rajavi and his wife, Maryam. As the only living original member of the group's central committee at the time of the revolution, Rajavi emerged, after his release from prison in early 1979, as the organization's primary leader (Abrahamian, 1989, p. 252). The fact that the Mojahedin constitute the most competent of all the oppositional forces today is a devastating commentary on the mobilizational capabilities of Iran's present opposition groups. As will shortly be made clear, the Mojahedin's leadership, ideology, organizational capacity and networks, as well as its support base, are grossly insufficient for posing a serious challenge to the theocracy. Nor is the organization endowed with the capability for creating a wide-ranging, multiclass, revolutionary alliance against the clerical order.

Although the Mojahedin had very closely aligned themselves with Khomeini before the shah's ouster, shortly after the revolution they came into increasing and irreconcilable conflict with the radical clergy. The passage of time eventually made it abundantly clear to the Mojahedin that Khomeini and his entourage were adamant on exerting their exclusive dominion over all levers of power. Despite his diatribes against tyrannical rulers, Khomeini was not at all interested in establishing a democracy or in power sharing with any group, least of all the Mojahedin. Ironically, by expressing full support and solidarity for the anti-imperialist objectives of the radical Islamic students, who (at the behest of Khomeini) occupied the American embassy and took its personnel hostage in November 1979, the Mojahedin helped Khomeini and his followers to displace the liberals and further consolidate their hold on power.

Realizing their mistake, the Mojahedin began in late 1980 to openly denounce Khomeini's entourage for seeking to monopolize power and derail the revolution. The authorities responded by closing the group's newspapers (which, thanks to the organization's young and intellectual social base, were outselling the ruling mullahs' newspapers by sixteen to one [Abrahamian, 1989, p. 1]), banning its activities, and arresting several of its leaders. By 1981, the party had once again been forced underground.

The conflict between the regime and the Mojahedin came to the fore on June 20, 1981. Mojahedin leaders now argued that the "dictatorship of the Mullas" (whom they accused of being beholden to the "petty bourgeois" classes and therefore unwilling to improve the lot of the poor) "was a hundred times worse than the detestable Pahlavi regime" (Abrahamian, 1989, p. 207). Deliberately defying the regime's ban on demonstrations and endeavoring to instigate another revolution, the Mojahedin called on the people of Iran to pour into the streets. According to one estimate, 500,000 Mojahedin supporters and sympathizers demonstrated in Tehran alone against the Islamic Republic (Abrahamian, 1989, p. 218).

Clearly alarmed by the group's schemes to overthrow the theocracy, the regime, unlike the shah, responded with great alacrity and overwhelming force.

"Anyone who speaks against the ulama, Khomeini declared, must of necessity be against the whole of Islam" (quoted in Abrahamian, 1989, p. 210). Referring to the group as *monafeqin* (hypocrites) and castigating them as being inferior to infidels, Khomeini gave carte blanche to the Revolutionary Guards to shoot any demonstrator (regardless of age) on the spot. After suppressing the uprising, which, unlike the revolution, was confined almost entirely to members of the young intelligentsia and students, the regime initiated a campaign of terror against the Mojahedin and proceeded to systematically destroy the organization and most of its members within Iran.

The Mojahedin responded by perpetrating a series of assassinations and daring suicide bombing campaigns. Shortly after the crushing of the June uprising, two massive explosions killed roughly 100 members of the infant theocracy's ruling elite, including Ayatollah Beheshti, the head of the Islamic Republican Party (IRP), the newly elected president Rajai, and the prime minister, Hojatoleslam Bahonar. The present supreme leader of the country, Seyyed Ali Khamenei, who at the time had just replaced Rajai as the president, "was nearly killed in 1981 by a Mojahedin mail bomb. He still walks with a cane and can barely move his withered arm" (Miller, 1996, p. 436).

The Mojahedin's campaign of terror, however, proved to be short-lived and was soon quelled by the theocracy's devoted security apparatus. The new regime was led by resolute and charismatic leadership, had already become well entrenched, and had established resilient institutions. The Mojahedin's primary reliance on terror, in the meantime, only served to "reflect the impossibility of achieving [their] revolutionary goals under prevailing circumstances" (Greene, 1991, p. 74). By December 1982, the regime had succeeded in virtually decimating the Mojahedin's entire organized network inside Iran: "By this date over 10,000 Mojahedin had been killed or were awaiting execution and other organized armed opposition groups had been largely destroyed" (Arjomand, 1988, p. 155). According to one estimate, the individuals who were summarily executed at this time represented approximately two-thirds of the Mojahedin's hard-core activists (Abrahamian, 1989, p. 225). It should be recalled that in eight years of armed struggle against the Pahlavi dynasty, the Mojahedin (the Islamists and the Marxists) had, by comparison, lost 103 of their members.

Implicitly acknowledging defeat, Masoud Rajai, the leader of the Mojahedin, and a band of his remaining loyal followers, fled Iran in 1982. They first took refuge in Paris and then, in 1986, (when a temporary thaw in Franco-Iranian relations resulted in their expulsion from France) in Iraq, where they are currently based and from whose territory their small army wishes to liberate Iran. To cultivate the support of influential foreign governments, particularly that of the United States, and to make themselves more palatable to the Iranian populace, the Mojahedin have recently announced their conversion to the principles of liberal democracy. Seeking to demonstrate their open-mindedness and commitment to gender equality, the Mojahedin declared Maryam Rajavi their co-leader in 1985 and also recently "elected" her as the president of the future liberated Iran. However, serious lingering suspicions remain about to the extent to which the Mojahedin have actually renounced (or are willing to renounce, if they obtain power) their previous ideology. Furthermore, the fact that they do not practice even a modicum of democracy in the administration of their own organization, combined with their widespread practice of nearly worshipping their leaders as demigods, has cast serious doubt on the extent of their commitment to democratic ideals.

The Mojahedin's previous Islamist-socialist ideology, with its denigration of the clergy, is anathema to the Iranian clerical establishment, even those who do not support the concept of *velayat-e faqih* (rule by the Islamic jurist), as well as to merchants, bazaaris, most of the professional classes, and the business community. It might appeal to some segments of the intelligentsia, students, and the poor. By themselves, however, these groups are incapable of overthrowing the present regime.

Moreover, whatever levels of support the Mojahedin might have had within the Iranian population were severely undermined when they decided to collaborate with Iraq during the Iran-Iraq war. The extent of ordinary Iranians' level of animosity toward the Mojahedin was amply demonstrated in the final months of the war, when the inhabitants of a small border town slaughtered, before the arrival of Iranian armed forces, the Mojahedin fighters who had come from Iraq in order to "liberate" them.

The Mojahedin seem to be operating under the delusion that by acting alone, without establishing cross-cutting alliances with other opposition forces, they will be able to overthrow the well-entrenched clerical regime, just as Chairman Mao was able to destroy the nationalist forces of Chiang Kai-shek. Yet the Mojahedin do not disclose the number of soldiers in their liberation army. Instead, they assure inquiring journalists that they have sufficient forces "to topple the present regime." But a former member who recently fled Iraq maintains that the group currently includes fewer than 700 fighters (Waldman, 1994, p. A2). According to Ervand Abrahamian, who published an impeccably researched book on the Mojahedin in 1989, the National Liberation Army of Iran (Artesh-e Azadibaksh-e Melli-ye Iran) had some 7,000 armed militants (both men and women) in 1987 (Abrahamian, 1989, p. 260).

But whether 700 or 7,000, the Mojahedin are clearly no match for the Iranian armed forces. Not counting the Basij (volunteer militia), the police, and the Komitehs (Islamic security guards), the Islamic Republic is endowed with a 320,000-man army. It also has a 120,000-member Revolutionary Guard Corps (IRGC) and spends at least $2 billion a year on its military. There are no indications that the Mojahedin have managed to infiltrate these forces. In fact, both the top echelons and rank-and-file members of Iran's security apparatus appear to hold the Mojahedin in contempt, detesting them for becoming subordinate allies to Saddam Hussein. As a result, the Mojahedin's military campaigns and "operations" against Iranian state targets (Masoud Rajavi has consistently asserted that the Mojahedin would never target civilians),[5] which have been confined to occasional attacks against IRGC border town outposts, have been exceptionally ineffective in threatening the Islamic Republic. Nevertheless, ever since the relocation of the Mojahedin to Iraq, the Iranian regime has been consistent in launching occasional aerial and rocket attacks on Mojahedin bases inside Iraq.[6]

The Mojahedin, however, constitute the only organized Iranian opposition with a small band of highly devoted adherents inside Iran, willing to put their lives on the line by occasionally assassinating prominent members of the Islamic Republic. After a ten-year period of inactivity within Iran, the Mojahedin in 1998 assassinated the theocracy's detested longtime chief warden, Assadollah Ladjevardi. In 1985, Ladjevardi became the warden of Iran's most notorious prison, Evin, and in 1989, he was promoted to head of the nation's entire prison system. From 1981 to 1985, Ladjevardi had served as a prosecutor general, taking a leading role in the prosecution and execution of numerous "counterrevolutionaries," most of whom were members of the Mojahedin. In August 1988, after the Mojahedin launched an attack inside Iranian territory from Iraq, the Islamic Republic embarked upon killing most of the Mojahedin political prisoners it was still holding. As head of the Evin prison, Ladjevardi oversaw the execution of most of the more than 1,000 Mojahedin prisoners, who, according to the UN, were killed over several days. The assassination of Ladjevardi, who had just retired from his position as chief warden and had returned to managing his shop in the Tehran bazaar, was timed to coincide with the tenth anniversary of the execution of the remaining Mojahedin prisoners in Iran ("Mojahedin Slay Ex-Warden," 1998).

In 1998, the Mojahedin also detonated a bomb at the headquarters of the Revolutionary Courts, which resulted in the death of three individuals. In addition, they fired mortars at a Revolutionary Guards garrison in Tehran, which, according to the regime, resulted in no casualties. In another daring move, the Mojahedin assassinated Lieutenant General Ali Seyyed Shirazi, the deputy chief of the General Command Headquarters of the armed forces of the Islamic Republic, as he was driving his son to school in 1999. As with Ladjevardi, Shirazi was apparently deliberately selected by the Mojahedin in order to exact revenge for the prominent role that the general had played in brutally crushing Mojahedin's penetration into Iranian territory in August 1988 at the end of the Iran-Iraq war ("Mojahedin Murder General," 1999).

The Mojahedin, however, have not learned the lessons of Khomeini's masterful art of revolutionary coalition building and continue to fanatically insist that by relying only on the resources of their own organization and its small band of sympathizers, they will be able to dislodge the present system. The group's response to those who criticize such wishful thinking is to dismiss them as pro-Khomeini traitors, which provides a significant insight into the group's narrow-mindedness and dogmatism. According to a former Mojahedin member who is currently a human rights lawyer, "[The Mojahedin] attack all groups and exiles who don't agree with them" (Waldman, 1994).

Usually disagreement with the Mojahedin is most ardently directed against their decision to collaborate with Iraq. Residing in Iraq has not only largely destroyed the last vestiges of the Mojahedin's credibility but has also turned them into potential pawns. The Mojahedin have to operate under the close supervision and scrutiny of Iraqi president Saddam Hussein, who might eventually decide to use them as a bargaining chip. If the relationship between Iran and Iraq improves, it is likely that the Mojahedin could be exchanged for the anti-Saddam forces currently based inside Iran.

Despite their numerous shortcomings, however, the Mojahedin seem to have mastered the art of self-promotion and lobbying in Western democracies. Their decision to operate under several different names, including the National Council of Resistance (which serves as their political wing) as well as their adoption of a neoliberal ideology, seems in part to have been propelled by the desire to acquire greater external support. Indeed, their strategy has borne some fruit. "One petition against the 'bloodthirsty medieval regime,' circulated in Europe and the U.S. in mid 1983, got the endorsement of some 1700 politicians, labor organizers and university professors, including Maxime Rodinson, Eric Hobsbawm, and Charles Tilly" (Abrahamian, 1989, p. 245). More recently, they have been successful in persuading a number of prominent American senators and congressmen of the righteousness of their cause and their capacity to overthrow Iran's theocratic regime. In a letter addressed to Masoud Rajavi in 1993, Senator Howell Heflin (D–AL) commended the Mojahedin's political arm for representing "all those who truly believe in freedom and human rights," while in 1994, majorities of both houses of Congress endorsed the Mojahedin's attempt to bring "freedom and democracy" to Iran (Waldman, 1994). Apparently, the congressmen were unaware of the Mojahedin's involvement in the murder of American citizens in Iran, its previous staunch anti-Western ideology, and its wholehearted support for the taking of American hostages.

To ensure that their agenda would receive favorable backing on Capitol Hill, the Mojahedin have generously donated funds to the campaigns of their favorite congressmen. According to a study conducted by Kenneth R. Timmerman of the Middle East Data Project in Washington, D.C., members of the Mojahedin, including some who are not American citizens, contributed more than $200,000 to congressional campaigns between 1993 and 1996. Evidently, the bulk of its money went to Senator Robert G. Torricelli (D–NJ), Representative James A. Traficant (D–OH), and Representative Gary L. Ackerman (D–NY). Not surprisingly, all three individuals have been strongly supportive of the Mojahedin. Since the early 1990s, they have actively circulated and signed letters promoting the Mojahedin, arguing that the U.S. government should recognize the group as Iran's government in exile.[7]

There are indications, however, that support for the Mojahedin in the United States is on the wane. In a report issued on October 31, 1994, the State Department referred to the Mojahedin as a terrorist group.[8] Seeking to disassociate itself entirely from the group, the State Department added the Mojahedin to a list of twenty-nine other organizations and countries (including Iran) it deems to be terrorist as of October 1997. As a result, entities operating under the name of Mojahedin-e Khlaq organization have been barred from raising funds in the United States, and their bank accounts have been frozen. However, the other aliases under which the group operates, such as the National Council of Resistance and the Muslim Iranian Students Society, are not cited in the State Department report and, therefore, continue to function legally.[9] Nevertheless, the American government has apparently come to the conclusion that the Mojahedin do not constitute a desirable alternative to the present Iranian regime.

Nor are they a viable alternative. Increasingly isolated and declining in numbers, in both the Iranian and international communities, the Mojahedin have metamorphosed into a cult, extolling the virtues of their "infallible" leaders. Various publications put out by the Mojahedin refer to Masoud Rajavi in exceptionally glowing terms, describing him, for instance, as "the heart, the courage, and the soul of the whole organization." They also praise him for having "illuminated history . . . bridging the gulf between . . . mortals and the prophets . . . [and] saving Iran and the world from the false Islam cooked by the corrupt, hypocritical, and power hungry ulama" (Abrahamian, 1989, p. 243). Masoud, they assert, "speak[s] on behalf of all Mojaheds, both living and dead. He [is] both a great leader-thinker and Masoud of his age for every age should have its Masoud" (Abrahamian, 1989, p. 253).

The Monarchists

The monarchists constitute another opposition movement bent on destroying Iran's Islamic theocracy. Operating solely outside Iran, this group attracts a rather large following among Iranian expatriates, particularly those residing in California (mostly Los Angeles) and Germany. The challenge that the monarchists pose to the Iranian regime is even more insignificant than the threat of the Mojahedin, since the monarchists are divided among themselves and are unorganized. Furthermore, although they surely desire to go back to their country and to revive the monarchy, they have not demonstrated the levels of resolve and commitment expected of revolutionaries or counterrevolutionaries in pursuit of their paramount objective.

The monarchists disagree vehemently on the type of monarchy that should be reinstituted in Iran. One faction favors the establishment of a constitutional monarchy, arguing that the king should serve merely as a figurehead and reign but not rule. This faction holds that the monarchy, which has a 2,500-year history in Iran, can serve as the only centripetal force capable of keeping the country's highly diverse and heterogeneous population together. Another faction, sometimes referred to as the Shahollahi sect, maintains that the only form of government suitable to the Iranian national character is absolute monarchy. Still another faction contends that an absolute monarchy should initially be installed immediately after the demise of the theocracy in order to resolve the multitude of problems afflicting the nation. But once these problems have been ameliorated, they argue that the monarch must then loosen the lid of oppression and gradually transform the system into a constitutional monarchy. There are still other factions that subscribe, with greater or lesser intensity, to different variations on these themes.

The pretender to the throne, Prince Reza Pahlavi, has maintained, to the consternation of many monarchists, that although he personally favors a constitutional monarchy, he would abide by the will of the people. If, after the destruction of the present system, the people of Iran decide in a referendum that he should serve as a royal ceremonial head of state, then he will become the shah of Iran (see "Where Are They Now?" 1996). Although this is an admirable statement, it is not the type of inflammatory rhetoric one would expect to hear from a revolutionary leader: "Revolutions are not for those who are filled with self-doubt and moral skepticism. Revolutionaries see the world in shades of black and white" (Greene, 1991, p. 84) and are endowed with what Dostoevsky referred to as a "fire in the mind." Reza Pahlavi, although an intelligent and articulate man, appears to be bereft of the type of uncompromising and charismatic qualities associated with Khomeini and other revolutionary leaders.

Although there are signs that the people of Iran are increasingly nostalgic for the Pahlavi era, it is unclear whether they are willing to undergo the sacrifices necessary to reinstitute the monarchy. At any rate, the monarchists do not possess an institutional or an organizational base inside Iran, and they have failed to infiltrate the armed forces. Prince Reza undoubtedly has a potential base of support within Iran. However, given their disunity, disorganization, and lukewarm commitments, the monarchists, even were they to join forces with the liberal opposition, would be unlikely to be able to bring down the present regime.

The Current Status of the National Front

The secular liberal opposition, composed of the followers of the deposed Iranian prime minister Mohammad Mossadegh and the remnants of the National Front, also operates primarily from overseas. As noted, in 1979 the leadership of this group, by subordinating itself to Khomeini, helped to deliver the majority in the Iranian intellectual and professional class to the side of the revolutionaries and thus played a significant role in the demise of the monarchy. The liberals, apparently engaging in wishful thinking, thought that Khomeini would acquiesce in the establishment of a Western-style democracy in Iran.

Among the opposition groups that united under the canopy of Khomeini's leadership, National Front members were the first to be rudely scanted and cast aside by the ayatollah. Only a few months after the revolution, Khomeini shattered the illusion of the liberals by firmly asserting that "Islam was not to be denigrated by the adjective 'democracy.'" "Anyone wishing Iran to be just a republic, or a democratic republic, or a democratic Islamic republic," Khomeini declared, "was the enemy of Islam and God" (Arjomand, 1988, p. 137). Most of the few secular liberals who had been granted portfolios in the postrevolutionary provisional government resigned in protest. The rest were eased out of power shortly thereafter. Unarmed, moderate in outlook as well as in behavior, and lacking the will to fight, one by one they went into self-imposed exile. Some chose once again to join the ranks of the opposition. Others simply retired from political life.

In spite of their monumental miscalculation during the revolutionary process, the secular liberals have not lost their penchant for parliamentary democracy. Expressing their support for political participation and contestation, they maintain that a system guaranteeing free, fair, and competitive elections as well as civil liberties should be instituted in Iran. This vision is still quite popular among the Iranian intelligentsia, new sectors of the middle class, certain segments of the bazaaris, and even a few clerics.

But its achievement is likely to remain elusive, since the liberal opposition is also disorganized and without institutional networks inside Iran. The leadership of this group has splintered into two different factions. One group is led by Admiral Madani, a congenial yet uncharismatic man. The other faction is led jointly by Abbas Shakeri and Manucher Razmara. Shakeri and Razmara have succeeded Shapour Bakhtiar, the shah's last prime minister, who was brutally murdered in Paris in 1991, as leaders of Nehizat-e Moghavemat-e Meli (National Struggle Movement). At the time of the revolution, Bakhtiar was the only leading member of the National Front who refused to submit to the leadership of Khomeini, attempting to transform the monarchy rather than subvert it. But he was immediately abandoned by other leaders of the group. After the revolution, Bakhtiar fled to Paris and founded the National Struggle Movement in order to overthrow the Iranian theocracy. The Iranian regime, which must have considered Bakhtiar a potential threat, was undoubtedly involved in his 1991 murder. Yet Bakhtiar's successors, who are purported to dislike one another, are unlikely to forgo their personal differences and unify the liberal opposition, let alone create common cause with the other opposition groups, including remnants of the left-wing opposition.

The Tudeh and the Fadaiyan Today

The leftists pose the most insignificant threat to the survival of the Islamic Republic. With the demise of the Soviet Union, their ideologies have become largely discredited, and they have been further weakened by internal feuds. Moreover, they lack any recognized leaders and are largely unorganized. The national Iranian Communist party (Tudeh) was essentially destroyed in 1983, when a few thousand of its key members, including the influential secretary general of the party, Nurredin Kianouri, and roughly 200 army officers were arrested by the authorities of the Islamic Republic. Seeking to strengthen and consolidate their exclusive hold on power, Khomeini and his entourage (after obliterating the Mojahedin) decided to move against the Tudeh, even though Kianouri and other

Tudeh officials had "sycophantically applauded their revolution" (Arjomand, 1988, p. 159). "On April 30, 1983, Kianouri reported on Iranian television that he had maintained contacts with Soviet agents since 1945 and that Iranian members of the Tudeh party had been delivering top-secret military and political documents to the Soviet embassy in Tehran" (Bill, 1988, p. 273).

Ehsan Tabari, the Tudeh's primary theoretician since the 1940s, stated that under the tutelage of the country's Islamic authorities, he had come to the inescapable conclusion that his entire life's work had been "spurious." He admonished the youth to be wary of the "alien ideology" of Marxism, which would separate them from their history, culture, and people. On a subsequent appearance, Kianouri also admitted to having been "dependent" on the Soviets, committing "sins" and "high treason" against Iranian society and religious culture (Abrahamian, 1993, p. 90). Such admissions demolished the credibility of the Tudeh party beyond repair. Nevertheless, to ensure that Kianouri would remain harmless, the Islamic Republic kept him under house arrest until his death in 1999.

The majority faction of the Fadaiyan, which had aligned with and subordinated itself to the Tudeh, was also obliterated in 1983, along with the Tudeh. Its organizational networks were uprooted and the majority of its members killed. During the unprecedented harsh reign of terror (1981–1982), which was directed primarily against the Mojahedin, the authorities also targeted the minority faction of the Fadaiyan, which had opposed the Mojahedin uprising (Abrahamian, 1989, pp. 215, 219). For all practical purposes, the Fadaiyan have been wiped out as an organized opposition force inside Iran.

There are a few other organizations and political parties operating from overseas and seeking the demise of the current regime. Because for the most part they lack organization and popular appeal, they will not be examined in this study. Apart from the groups outside Iran, there are a few quasi-opposition movements operating under the scrutiny of Iranian authorities. As they are closely monitored by the regime, they are unlikely to threaten the stability of the system. In fact, the regime considers these groups so harmless that it allows them to be regularly interviewed by foreign correspondents so as to demonstrate the theocracy's commitment to pluralism and freedom of expression. If these groups become too emboldened in their criticisms of the system, however, they will immediately be silenced by the regime's effective repressive apparatus.

The Liberation Movement Today

One such group is the Nehzat-e Azadi, which, having unquestionably acknowledged and subordinated itself to the leadership of Khomeini, came to play a role in the political affairs of the country immediately after the revolution. Mehdi Bazargan, the group's founder and leader, was asked by Khomeini to head the first postrevolution government. Bazargan enthusiastically obliged and, as prime minister, filled his cabinet with Liberation Movement and some National Front members. From the start, however, there was no question as to where the true source of power lay. With the passage of time, the cabinet's room for maneuver, insignificant from the beginning, came to be increasingly diminished and undermined by Khomeini and his clerical followers, who were bent on monopolizing power.

Slighted and eclipsed, the Liberation Movement was finally squeezed out of power after the seizure of the American embassy by radical students, who described themselves as the followers of the line of the Imam. Indeed, as one of Khomeini's close disciples later revealed, "the whole upheaval [the taking of American embassy personnel as hostages] had been instigated to sweep aside the 'liberals'" (Abrahamian, 1989, p. 57). Seeing the handwriting on the wall, Bazargan made the following comment to the Italian journalist Oriana Fallaci shortly before his ouster:

> Something unforeseen and unforeseeable happened after the revolution. What happened was that the clergy supplanted us and succeeded in taking over the country . . . If, instead of being distracted, we had behaved like a party then this mess wouldn't have occurred . . . yes, it was the lack of initiative by the laity that permitted the takeover by the clergy. (quoted in Arjomand, 1989, p. 137)

After his fall from power until his death in 1995, Bazargan continued to serve as the head of the Liberation Movement. As the group was unarmed and uninterested in overthrowing the Islamic Republic (Milani, 1994, p. 230) (combined with the fact that Khomeini had a modicum of personal respect for Bazargan), the group was tolerated but never licensed as a full-fledged political party or allowed to take part in the political process.

The movement is currently headed by Ebraheem Yazdi, an American-educated physician who served as foreign minister in Bazargan's cabinet. Ideologically, the Liberation Movement is still dedicated to the principles of liberal democracy, so long as they operate within an Islamic framework. Yazdi, who (although articulate and intelligent) is distinctly uncharismatic and incapable of exciting the masses, has made it clear that his organization is not interested in the revolutionary overthrow of the existing system. He has asserted repeatedly that he is merely interested in reforming the ongoing system through liberalization and democratization policies. But the regime has persistently restricted and refused to allow candidates associated with the Liberation Movement to stand for elections. The Council of Guardians allowed only four candidates associated with the Liberation Movement to stand for the parliamentary elections held in spring 1996. However, the government prohibited the organization from disseminating election materials and holding rallies, prompting the approved candidates to withdraw.[10] The Council of Guardians permitted none of the group's aspiring candidates to participate in the May 1997 presidential election. Four candidates from

the Liberation Movement were also permitted to stand for the 1999
ipal council elections, but none were elected ("Endorsements Matt
   The movement's social base is still composed of the religiously ii
bers of the professional middle class and disgruntled bazaaris. If g
even the primarily secular members of the intellectual and professional classes,
repelled by clerical misrule, are inclined to lend their support to the Liberation
Movement. But the group has no autonomous institutional basis inside Iran. Instead, it has to function under the close and watchful scrutiny of the authorities.
Even "its name is banned from mention by national newspapers" (Peterson, 1996,
p. 1). Some had expected the new Khatami administration to demonstrate its
commitment to liberalizing reforms by licensing the group to function as a political party. But the Interior Ministry (apprehensive about the negative and
provocative response of the conservative and extremist factions within the
regime) has refused to issue the group a license, and the movement remains an illegal party.[11] Indeed, Yazdi himself was recently jailed for eleven days for "insults
to sacred religious values." In 1997, Yazdi was detained after he had expressed
doubts about the powers granted to the supreme leader and had signed a letter
addressed to President Khatami, urging that the dissident cleric Ayatollah Montazeri be protected from further attacks by Hezbollahi mobs.[12] He has subsequently been released, but the party is not allowed to publish or disseminate information and its meetings have occasionally been disrupted by Hezbollahi
toughs. The regime, though, considers Yazdi sufficiently harmless to even arrange
for him to be interviewed by visiting foreign journalists.

The National Party of Iran

Another quasi-oppositional force operating inside Iran is Hez-b-e Melat-e Iran
(the National Party of Iran). Until 1998, the group was headed by Dariush
Foruhar, a liberal democratic crusader associated with Mossadegh, who served as
labor minister in Bazargan's cabinet. Foruhar was a courageous and relatively
charismatic revolutionary who did not conceal his contempt for the regime and
was extremely forthright in his condemnation not only of the regime's policies
but of the regime itself.[13] He was therefore kept under very close surveillance.
"[As] the first test for the revolutionary is his willingness to die for his cause"
(Greene, 1991, p. 84)), Forouhar was given an opportunity to pass this test, when
he (along with his wife) was brutally stabbed to death in his house in Tehran in
November 1998 (see "Forouhar, Wife Stabbed to Death," 1998).
   As was previously noted, the regime, in an unprecedented disclosure prompted
by Khatami, acknowledged that "rouge [right-wing extremists] and irresponsible
elements" from the Intelligence Ministry were responsible for Forouhar's murder.
In the interim, the party has found it difficult to find a suitable replacement for
Foruhar, whose overbearing and domineering personality had been the primary
force behind the party's cohesion. Seeking to weaken and repress the party even

further, however, the Intelligence Ministry, in search of a scapegoat, charged that seven members of the National Party of Iran were in part responsible for student protests in the summer of 1999 ("Aging Nationalists Blamed for Riots," 1999).

Another individual who has recently attacked the regime quite vehemently is retired brigadier general Azizollah Amir Rahimi, who headed the military police immediately after the revolution. General Rahimi has not attempted to create a political party or movement but instead has circulated a series of open letters severely criticizing the regime, its policies, and the ruling elite. In one of his letters, Rahimi states that the rulers of society should be composed of that society's most intelligent, educated, and competent individuals. But the current rulers of Iran, Rahimi maintains, compose the nation's least educated, intelligent, and competent citizens. Maintaining that Iran is teetering on the edge of the precipice, Rahimi states: "[T]he clerics who have ruled the country for years are responsible for this misery. The only way to save the country is through deep changes in the way the country is run. If Rafsanjani is not capable of doing this, he should concede to a national salvation government." Rahimi then calls on the mullahs to willingly relinquish power and allow for free and competitive elections, unrestrained by the vetting procedures of clerical institutions. He also urges the regime to free all political prisoners and reinstate all the military officers purged since the revolution (Wright, 1994). Shortly after the circulation of this letter, Rahimi was imprisoned for several months. He appears to have become far more circumspect after his release.

It can be seen, then, that Iran's opposition forces today are woefully disorganized and bereft of unifying leaders and ideologies. In all likelihood, then, they are incapable of organizing, leading, and sustaining the type of multiclass revolutionary alliance essential for overthrowing the theocratic order. This, however, does not mean that the survival of the Islamic republic is assured. A fragile and shaky regime may be dislodged with a minimal coordinated "push" by the opposition from below. Or even more significant, a fragmented regime can tear itself apart from above, opening the way for internal strife, civil war, and spontaneous popular uprisings. The nature of the regime and the quality of its leaders, therefore, can exert a prominent influence on its demise, survival, or modification. It is to the examination of these factors that we shall now turn.

Notes

1. See also Abrahamian (1982), p. 460.
2. Cited by Kurzman (1992), p. 134.
3. Akhavi (1980) puts the sum total of mosques throughout the country at 9,015. Milani (1994), by contrast, puts the count at 8,439.
4. "In interviews with four clerics in 1974, both moderates and radicals, an Iranian social scientist found 'considerable unanimity of grievance' about secular foreign influence, state control, and 'the entire trend of Iranian society.' . . . the moderates, however, favored

reformist solutions. As late as December 1978, with the revolution in full swing, Ayatollah Kazim Shariatmadari . . . told reporters that overthrow of the Pahlavi dynasty was not necessary. 'What we have in the [1906] constitution is enough, if it is implemented'" (Kurzman, 1992, pp. 142–143).

5. See "Mojahedin Claim Major Actions in West Iran," *Iran Times,* January 2, 1998.

6. See "Regime Denies It Attacks Mojahedin," *Iran Times,* January 2, 1998; "Mojahedin Hit from Two Directions," *Iran Times,* December 26, 1997; "Mojahedin Says Tehran's Shells Miss Three Times," *Iran Times,* January 17, 1997; "Phantoms Bomb Mojahedin in Iraq," *Iran Times,* October 3, 1997; and "Focus—Baghdad Says Iranian Jets Attack Inside," *Reuters,* September 29, 1997; "Mojahedin Says Iran Attacks Again," *Iran Times,* June 11, 1999; "Scuds and Bombs Rain On Mojahedin," *Iran Times,* June 18, 1999.

7. See "Mojahedin Said Giving Big to Politicians," *Iran Times,* September 19, 1997.

8. See "U.S. Denounces Opposition Group," *Facts on File,* 54 (2822), December 31, 1994, p. 100.

9. See "Mojahedin Sign Up 2,000 Legislators," *Iran Times,* November 7, 1997; "Mojahedin May Not Be Hit Hard" *Iran Times,* October 24, 1997; "U.S. Freezes Mojahedin Accounts," *Iran Times,* October 17, 1997; "Rajavi Says U.S. Beholden to Tehran," *Iran Times,* June 28, 1996.

10. See "Yazdi Says Liberals to Run for Presidency," *Iran Times,* November 29, 1996.

11. See "Nuri Refuses to License Liberals," *Iran Times,* February 27, 1998.

12. See "Ebrahim Yazdi Arrested, Jailed at Evin; No Charges," *Iran Times,* December 19, 1997; "Pressure Groups Hobble Khatami," *Iran Times,* January 9, 1998.

13. See "Two Forouhar Followers Disappear," *Iran Times,* June 28, 1996.

6

Comparing the Nature and Leadership Qualities of Prerevolutionary and Postrevolutionary Authoritarian Regimes

The analysis in the previous chapter has shown how the severe weaknesses of the existing oppositional groups tend to inhibit movement toward a coordinated revolutionary uprising against the Islamic Republic. Unlike the prerevolutionary era, the oppositional forces are currently disorganized, fragmented, and without a unifying leader or ideology. These factors appear unlikely to change in the short term. But even if the opposition manages to miraculously transcend its shortcomings and become cohesive, it will still face the daunting task of challenging an oppressive regime that, unlike the previous monarchical order, is well entrenched and highly institutionalized. To assess the prospects for regime change in Iran, therefore, it is illuminating to compare the nature and characteristics of the present-day theocratic and the prerevolutionary neopatrimonial regimes.

Accordingly, this chapter will compare the structural arrangements and institutional underpinnings of the two regimes. As was pointed out in Chapter 2, however, by itself, the structural perspective is deficient because it underestimates the at times paramount qualities of individuals (in both collectivist and personalistic dictatorships) who occupy the state's strategic positions and control its levers of power. The manner in which these individuals act or fail to act, particularly at times of crisis, may exert a determining influence on the outcome of political struggles. Indeed, even during the examination of the organization and coordination of the revolutionary mobilization against the shah's rule, it was necessary to refer on several occasions to the shah's own self-defeating, indecisive, and inconsistent method of dealing with his opponents.

In contrast to the shah, the present regime's survival is not dependent upon the decisiveness of one individual. In fact, much of the regime's top leadership could be removed without seriously jeopardizing the system. Moreover, Iran's rulers have up to now shown that they are capable of overcoming their differences at times of crisis. They have also demonstrated that unlike the shah, they have no compunction against resorting to overwhelming force to crush their common enemies and safeguard their shared interests. As shall presently be made clear, however, since the election of Mohammad Khatami as Iran's president in 1997, intraregime cleavages have become increasingly open and pronounced, raising the likelihood of the regime tearing itself apart. To sharpen our understanding of the Islamic Republic's prospects for survival, this chapter will systematically explore the linkages between individual decisionmakers and formal structures in prerevolutionary and contemporary Iran.

A Personalistic Autocracy

Rather than being institutionalized, power in prerevolutionary Iran was lodged almost entirely in the person of the shah: "To all intents and purposes, the Shah was the regime: monarch and the state had become virtually synonymous" (Parsons, 1984, p. 19). After his restoration to power through a CIA-MI6-backed coup in 1953, the shah travailed to obliterate all independent sources of power (both individuals and institutions) in his endeavor to become the absolute ruler of Iran, and he eventually succeeded. He placed a small band of individuals, composed of his close confidants and cronies, in high-ranking positions and allowed them to exercise power over their subordinates. However, these officials were entirely beholden to him, dispensing patronage and wielding authority at his whim.

Nominally, the country had a constitution, which guaranteed popular sovereignty through an elected parliament, assured the rule of law, and placed severe restrictions on the powers of the monarchy. In actuality, however, the rule of law was virtually nonexistent, and the shah, standing at the apex of the country's power structure, ruled at will: "The Shah was at the center of a series of circles, between which there was little contact except through him—the court, the Imperial Family, the Central Governments, the armed forces, SAVAK, and the police" (Parsons, 1984, p. 19). Many of these institutions were given overlapping functions, and they had to report directly to the shah, who seems to have conceived it to be his mission as well as his right to personally make all the important decisions. As he put it, "[T]o get things done one needs power, and to hold onto power one mustn't ask anyone's permission or advice. One mustn't discuss decisions with anyone" (Halliday, 1982, p. 58).

True to his words, the shah made the creation of any organized political opposition illegal and turned Parliament into a mere rubber stamp. In 1958, the shah ordered the creation of a two-party system by royal decree. The officially sanctioned parties, the Melliyun (Nationalist) and Mardom (People's) parties, headed by two of the shah's confidants, were both subservient to the system and propagated virtually identical promonarchist ideologies (Milani, 1994, p. 67). But the shah, who could not even tolerate the semblance of political competition, effectively established a one-party system in 1963, when the Melliyun was transformed into Iran-e Novin (New Iran), an even more docile political party.

To underscore his modernist and temperate leanings and to portray himself as the defender of the Iranian Constitution, the shah recorded the following remarks in his autobiography in 1961: "If I were a dictator rather than a constitutional monarch, then I might be tempted to sponsor a single party such as Hitler organized . . . I can afford to encourage large-scale party activity free from the straight-jacket of one party rule or the one party state" (Abrahamian, 1982, p. 440). All pretensions about competitive party politics, however, were shattered in March 1975, when the shah arbitrarily decided to abolish the "two-party system," heralding instead the establishment of the very single-party state that he had previously castigated. In inaugurating the single party, the shah maintained that all patriotic Iranians were duty bound to join the party and that those who were reluctant to join must, of necessity, harbor pro-Tudeh, and thus antiregime, sentiments. He offered either to put the "traitors" in jail or to give them free exit visas, so they could leave the country immediately. As we have already seen, the subsequent escapades of the Rastakhiz (Resurgence) party played a pivotal role in further alienating the bazaaris, entrepreneurs, and modern middle class from the Pahlavi regime. In part designed to institutionalize, albeit forcefully, the overly personalistic regime, the party failed miserably to accomplish this task. Instead, the party "proved, as all single-party systems under an authoritarian regime, to be just another extension of the executive" (in this case, the shah) (Graham, 1978, p. 134).

Contrary to the Constitution, the Majles and the cabinet also served as mere appendages, entirely beholden to the shah's whim. Although the Constitution stipulated that the government be responsible to a popularly elected Parliament, in practice the Majles had no say whatsoever in the appointment of ministers and the policies pursued by the government. Declaring (in a private conversation with his minister of court) "Thank God we in Iran have neither the desire nor the need to suffer from democracy" (Alam, 1991, p. 233), the shah had packed the Parliament with his obedient and submissive supporters. As "the people's representatives," the deputies distinguished themselves by trying to outdo one another in showering praise upon the shah and his policy preferences.

Lamenting the shah's refusal to countenance the possibility of even minutely strengthening the nation's powerless institutions, Assadollah Alam, Iran's minister of court (1966–1977), recorded the following dire and revealing passage in his confidential diaries in September 1973:

> Its [the regime's] indifference and, on occasion, its brute aggression towards the people remind me of the way an army of occupation might treat a nation defeated in war. At every level, from parliament down to local and municipal elections, the government denies freedom to the people, imposing its own will and returning its own candidates as if the electorate had absolutely no say in the matter. Having for so long been deaf and blind to the nation's wishes, we should not be surprised that the nation itself regards us with the same degree of bland disinterest. (Alam, 1991, p. 315)

Meanwhile, the sole purpose of the prime minister and the cabinet was to function as instruments for executing the shah's decisions, which were frequently made arbitrarily, without sufficient technical input or prior consultation with specialists and advisers: "Perhaps the most striking feature of the government was its apolitical nature" (Parsons, 1984, p. 30). The shah could appoint and dismiss ministers at will, each of whom, in the words of Alam, "submit[ted] an independent report [generally designed to cultivate the Shah's favor by telling him what he wanted to hear] to HIM [His Imperial Majesty] whose own orders [were] frequently issued without any consultation with our pathetic prime minister" (Alam, 1991, p. 133). In describing his duties to the British ambassador to Iran in the latter half of the 1970s, the Iranian prime minister stated frankly: "[T]he Shah is the chairman of the board and I am the managing director" (Parsons, 1984, p. 31). As the chairman of the board, the shah refused to delegate much authority, preferring instead to render personally all of the significant and many of the insignificant decisions. Even the provincial governors, who were nominally under the authority of the Ministry of the Interior, were appointed by the shah and were required to report directly to him (Foran, 1993, p. 314; Graham, 1978, p. 46).

Just as he personally dominated the governmental institutions, the shah also exerted his exclusive dominion over the institutions that served as the foundations of his regime's power and upon which the survival of his regime crucially depended, the military and security forces. The shah was obsessed with enlarging and expanding the Iranian armed forces as the best means of not only ensuring his regime's survival but also fulfilling his overriding geopolitical ambition of achieving hegemony in the Persian Gulf region. In the early 1970s, two factors combined to help the shah realize his quest for regional superpower status through an unprecedented military buildup. First, in 1971, the Nixon administration authorized the shah to purchase, without prior Defense and State Department approval, unlimited quantities of the most advanced military equipment (short of nuclear weapons) from the United States. Then, in 1973, the staggering fourfold increase in the price of oil placed unexpectedly large resources at the shah's disposal with which to achieve his objectives. The shah moved swiftly to take full advantage of both opportunities. To ensure that the United States would think twice before having a change of heart, the shah also moved to substantially improve Iran's relations with the Soviet Union (Alam, 1991, pp. 13–14; Naraghi, 1994, p. 95; Zonis, 1991, p. 7).

By 1978, Iran possessed the mightiest, best-equipped, and best-trained armed forces in the Persian Gulf region. It had the fifth-largest military force and the fourth-largest air force in the world. With 413,000 men under arms, Iran's military in 1978 was twice as large as the British army. The nation's military budget increased from $293 million in 1963 to $2 billion in 1973, swelling to $7.3 billion in 1977 (Abrahamian, 1982, p. 435, 1989, p. 13; Roberts, 1996, p. 7). In 1978, there were 285,000 soldiers in the army, 28,000 in the navy, and 100,000 in the air force.

In addition, there were 60,000 troops in the gendarmerie (Abrahamian, 1982, p. 435; Roberts, 1996, pp. 7, 8).

In spite of their size and strength, however, the armed forces were entirely beholden to the shah and were incapable of any independent and coordinated action. Fully cognizant that both he (after he fled the country in 1953) and his father had come to power through military coups d'état, the shah had taken all the requisite precautions to make his regime coup proof. His intense distrust of the military had prompted him to compartmentalize and create such unbridgeable rifts within the command-and-control posts of the nation's repressive apparatus that the military as an institution was unable to make any independent decisions.

The shah selected his military commanders on the basis of their loyalty to him alone and prevented them from effectively communicating with each other. The heads of the various branches were each required to report to the shah separately, and they were prohibited from meeting with one another except in his presence. The shah acted as his own chairman of the Chiefs of Staff and personally approved all promotions above the rank of major as well as the takeoff and landing of all military aircraft. To preclude the possibility of a coup, the shah even went so far as to select personal rivals to head the various branches of Iran's armed forces. Subsequently, he did his best to inflame and arouse existing animosities between his military commanders. As he confided to Alam in 1971, "My generals distrust—and lack professional respect for one another . . . I don't think there's a single member of the army prepared to betray us. In any event, they're too much at one another's throats to constitute a threat" (Alam, 1991, pp. 197–198). The shah's military apparatus, then, like the rest of the prerevolutionary governmental machinery, was almost entirely personal and apolitical.

Although the military functioned as the primary foundation of the regime's power, it rarely intervened directly in order to sustain the system. Instead, the shah entrusted his notorious security service, SAVAK, with the task of ensuring that the armed forces would not have to be used in this capacity. Established in 1957 through the assistance of the CIA and the Mossad, SAVAK is estimated to have had over 30,000 full-time employees under the shah (Graham, 1978, p. 144).[1]

> Indiscriminate harassment and brutality rather than sophisticated counter-subversion was SAVAK's style . . . Mass arrests were common and SAVAK was believed to have permeated all important sectors of Iranian national life, government, universities, factories, and Iranian student organizations overseas. (Parsons, 1984, p. 33)

Serving as both an intelligence service and a political police force, SAVAK used methods to deal with dissidence that, though abominable, were not appreciably different from the tactics used in many other Third World countries. Repelled by the shedding of blood and the infliction of torture, the shah seems to have granted SAVAK some leeway in hunting down and persecuting his enemies.

However, though the shah interfered less frequently in the day-to-day activities of SAVAK than he did in other sectors, the organization was nevertheless directly accountable only to him and had to receive his firm backing before undertaking major initiatives. Although only a small fraction of the Iranian populace fell victim to SAVAK's heavy-handed tactics, the organization, ironically assisted by the exaggerations of the shah's implacable opponents, managed to create an aura of omnipotence and omniscience that helped to strike fear in the hearts of people and perpetuate the shah's rule (Milani, 1994, p. 70; Zonis, 1991, p. 293).

An Institutionalized Theocracy

In sharp contrast to the monarchical order, where power was lodged solely in the person of the shah and where institutions were essentially bereft of power, the present regime is dotted with numerous power centers. Unlike the monarchy, the survival of the theocracy is not dependent upon the will and behavior of one individual. To the contrary, the clerics have institutionalized their rule to a remarkable extent through the creation of a multiplicity of organizations, most of which, far from serving as mere window dressing, wield substantial powers. Indeed, it may be argued that the mullahs have gone overboard in their fetish with institution building, as the regime has become highly fragmented. The Islamic Republic has given new meaning to the concept of separation of powers, as the regime is permeated by parallel power structures that compromise efficiency and exacerbate the impact of factionalism.

It should be recalled that according to the Constitution of the Islamic Republic (see the discussion of Khomeini's concept of *velayat-e faqih* in Chapter 2), the regime claims to derive its ultimate basis of authority and legitimacy from God. As the emissary of God on earth, therefore, the *faqih* (supreme leader) is granted extraordinary powers. The present occupier of the institution of *faqih*, Ayatollah Khamenei, has asserted that it is incumbent upon everyone to accord the same degree of respect to the office of *faqih* as that reserved for the Sharia and other Islamic law ("Khamenehi: No Election for Him," 1998). Toward the end of his tenure as the first *valy-e faqih* of the Islamic Republic, Khomeini (who, as the undisputed charismatic leader of the revolution, unlike his successor, did not derive his enormous authority from the institution of *faqih*) went so far as to declare that the *faqih*, if he deems it to be essential, can even order the violation of the Sharia and the Koran in order to assure the survival of the system.

Situated at the apex of the Iranian political structure, the supreme leader serves as the official head of the state, the spiritual guide of the nation, the commander in chief of the armed forces, and the protector of the faith (Amuzegar, 1995, p. 22). According to the 1989 revised Constitution, the leader is empowered to determine all of the general policies of the Islamic Republic and to supervise their implementation. The *faqih* is invested exclusively with the authority to declare war and peace, order general troop mobilization, and call for referenda. The

Constitution also grants the leader the authority to appoint or dismiss many of the nation's key political decisionmakers, including six of the twelve members of the Council of Guardians, head of the judiciary, chief of staff of the armed forces, commanders of the Revolutionary Guards and the military and security forces, director of radio and television networks, heads of the parastate Bonyads (foundations), and members of the Expediency Council. The leader must also sign the decree naming the new president after the president has been popularly elected (Ehteshami, 1995, pp. 48–49; Milani, 1994, p. 222).

Further, the Constitution stipulates that once the office of the leader becomes vacant, the new leader be selected by an eighty-three-member, popularly elected Assembly of Experts. In the event the assembly cannot agree on one person, it has the option of anointing a council of leadership, composed of either three or five individuals. In addition to selecting the leader, the assembly is further empowered to dismiss him (Enayat, 1983, p. 166). The original Constitution of the Islamic Republic, drafted in 1979, had, in accordance with Khomeini's initial formulations, specified:

> During the absence of the Glorious Lord of the Age [the missing Twelfth Imam of the Shi'ite sect], may God grant him relief, he will be represented in the Islamic Republic of Iran as religious leader and imam of the people by an honest, virtuous, well-informed, courageous, efficient administrator and religious jurist, enjoying the confidence of the majority of the people as leader. (Zonis, 1991, p. 86)

However, Khomeini, toward the end of his life, recognizing that all of the living senior religious jurists were by and large inimical toward his doctrines, recanted his earlier pronouncements. In a major declaration a few months before his death in June 1989, Khomeini classified the clergy into two distinct categories, those well-versed in religious and sacred law and those most familiar with contemporary socioeconomic and political affairs: "After two decades of insisting that religious jurists should rule, he . . . now argu[ed] that the political clergy should be the ultimate authority (Abrahamian, 1989, p. 35; Milani, 1994, p. 222). Accordingly, shortly after Khomeini's death, the Constitution was amended, and the clauses stipulating that the *faqih* be a jurist accepted by the majority of the people were duly removed. Khamenei, who at the time was not even an ayatollah, let alone a grand ayatollah, was quickly selected by the Assembly of Experts as the new leader.

Although the members of the Assembly of Experts are elected by the people, they must, prior to standing for elections, be approved by the twelve-member Council of Guardians. Indeed, in addition to assessing the Islamic and constitutional acceptability of all legislation enacted by the Majles, the Council of Guardians is empowered to screen prospective candidates for all popularly elected offices, which include the presidency, Assembly of Experts, and the Majles. Traditionally, the council has not justified its decisions, which are irreproachable and cannot be appealed. Half of the members of the council, however, are themselves directly appointed by the *faqih* from among "qualified" clerics. The other six, selected from a list of lay judges proposed by the head of the judiciary (himself appointed by the leader) are elected by the Majles (whose members have previously been approved by the Council of Guardians).

> In this merry-go-round all major players thus owe their positions to each other in one way or another: the Supreme Leader to the Assembly of Experts; the Assembly of Experts to the Council of Guardians; the Council of Guardians to the Supreme Leader and Majlis; the President of the republic, too, must first be anointed by the Council of Guardians, and, after popular elections, confirmed by the *rahbar* [leader]. (Amuzegar, 1995, p. 26)

As the head of the executive branch of the government, the president also wields significant power. Empowered by the 1989 amended Constitution to select ministers and form a cabinet (whose members each must be approved by the Majles), the president has great leeway in directing the country's economic, political, and foreign and public policies. Although his programs can be thwarted by the legislature, the judiciary, the Council of Guardians, and the *faqih*, which are independent of the executive, the president alone is in charge of implementing the nation's laws. In his capacity as the head of the executive branch, the president ranks only second to the supreme leader in the nation's power structure. In addition, the president serves as the chairman of the eleven-member National Security Council, which constitutes a diverse group of individuals, including clerics, experienced diplomats, and top-ranking officers from the army and Revolutionary Guards. It is the task of the council to forge consensus among the nation's factious ruling elite in regard to matters deemed relevant to the nation's national security (Ashraf, 1994, p. 141; Chubin, 1994, pp. 61–67; Ehteshami, 1995, pp. 51, 60).

The president also controls the selection of mayors, provincial governors, and other provincial functionaries, who are named by his interior minister and approved by the full cabinet ("Half of Governors-Generals Dumped," 1997; "Nuri Faces Majlis Confidence Vote," 1998). The president, though, does not control the city councils, which, although provided for by the 1979 theocratic Constitution, were not convened until 1999 (when in nationwide elections held in February, the candidates endorsed by the Grand Alliance, a coalition of pro-Khatami political groupings, and the Servants of Construction, the political party of pragmatists and technocrats, achieved an overwhelming victory over the conservatives). But the powers of the city councils are in practice rather limited, as they are only authorized to propose mayors. It is up to the interior ministry to appoint the mayors of Iran's twenty-four cities with more than 200,000 inhabitants, with provincial governors general invested with the power to name the mayors of smaller cities ("Local Council's Power May Be Clipped," 1998; "Iranians Vote for Reforms,"

1999). The governors, however, are shadowed by the *imam jomehs* (Friday prayer leaders) ("Children of the Iranian Revolution: A Survey of Iran," 1997). Appointed by the supreme leader, *imam jomehs* are charged with the task of "guiding" the governors, delivering the Friday sermons, and administering the mosques in the cities and towns to which they have been assigned. Indeed, the Islamic Republic has managed to ingeniously utilize the Friday congregational prayers as a means for creating yet another highly integrated and centralized structure. This structure, in addition to extending the dominion of the state over the previously amorphous hierocracy, serves as an intelligence-gathering agency for the regime by requiring the mosques it oversees to keep dossiers on the households in their vicinity (Arjomand, 1988, pp. 163, 168, 173; Abrahamian, 1989, p. 70).

The Islamic Consultative Assembly (Majles) constitutes another formidable institution in the theocracy, whose vitality and relative openness exemplify the structural differences between present and prerevolutionary regimes. Far from functioning as the mere rubber stamp that existed during the shah's reign, the 270-member Islamic Majles (the number of seats in the Majles was increased to 290 in the February 2000 parliamentary elections) has, since its establishment in 1980, "distinguished itself by the openness of its debates and the extensiveness of its legislation" (Arjomand, 1988, p. 165). In general, critical opinions, even those directed toward leaders, are tolerated so long as they do not question or threaten the established order. In addition to being empowered to enact legislation, the Majles must also approve all of the president's cabinet members. After approving the ministers, the Majles is further empowered to oversee and evaluate their conduct and, if it deems necessary, hold impeachment proceedings in order to dismiss them.

With members elected to four-year terms, the composition of each Majles, although manipulated by the Council of Guardians' preelection screening process, has until now had a determining bearing on the policy orientation of each government (Bakhtiari and Harrop, 1996, p. 19). For instance, the third Majles (1988–1992) was dominated by the left-wing radical faction, which at the time primarily favored Khomeini's doctrine of "permanent revolution," advocating direct support of Islamic movements abroad. The radicals also favored strong state intervention in, and control of, the economy. The newly inaugurated government of President Rafsanjani, by contrast, which assumed power in 1989, was dominated by pragmatists primarily concerned with consolidating Iran's revolution through the strengthening of its crippled economy. Exercising their considerable influence in the Majles, the radicals were able to achieve considerable success in thwarting Rafsanjani's efforts at privatization, reduction of subsidies, and ameliorating Iran's relations with the West.

Seeking to further his economic reform agenda, Rafsanjani and his pragmatic faction entered into an alliance with the conservative faction aimed at purging the radicals from the Majles. The ouster of the radicals came about after the parliamentary elections of 1992, when many of them failed to be reelected. Others were "disqualified" from standing for elections by the Council of Guardians. The deci-

sion to bar many radicals from contesting the election seems to have been instigated by the pragmatists and agreed to by the conservatives and the *faqih* (Banuazizi, 1994, p. 4). Rather than helping to advance Rafsanjani's proposals, however,
the social conservatives, who dominated the fourth Majles (1992–1996), proved
even more uncooperative than the radicals. Using the considerable institutional
strength of the Majles, they "frustrated President Rafsanjani's reform agenda by
banning satellite dishes, restoring ruinous subsidies, toughening restrictions on
publishers, and even encouraging vigilante groups to enforce their version of Islamic propriety in dress and speech" (Bakhtiari and Harrop, 1996, p. 19). The 1996
parliamentary elections did not allow any of the factions to achieve outright predominance in the Majles. Of the 270 seats in the Majles, 110 were captured by conservatives and 90 by pragmatists and radicals, who, ironically, now began to cooperate and constituted the core political base of President Khatami. The remaining
70 belonged to independents from the provinces ("238 Hopefuls File for President," 1997; "Khatami Gets Nod," 1997; "'Saint Diana' Leaves Many Questions After 100 Days," 1997). Given the mood of the public, the reformers are likely to cap-
ture most of the seats in the February 2000 parliamentary elections, even though
the conservative-dominated Council of Guardians will undoubtedly strive to restrict the number of eligible reformist candidates. The reformers, however, intend
to register an inordinate number of candidates in order to make it impossible for
the Council of Guardians to prevent a reformist victory. But although the triumph
of the reformers in the coming elections, which appears imminent, will undoubtedly tilt the balance of power in favor of the moderates, it is important to understand that there are divisions within the reformist camp itself. Questions in regard
to the scale, scope, and pace of liberalizing reforms (especially which groups
should be allowed to take part in the political process) are likely to split the reformist camp in the coming years. The more democratically inclined members of
the reformist camp (who are clearly more in tune with the mood of the populace)
have already expressed apprehension about former president Rafsanjani's intention to stand for the 2000 parliamentary elections. They fear that Rafsanjani
(whom they regard as an unprincipled and self-serving opportunist) will once
again become the Speaker of the Majles and utilize his position in order to retard
the pace of reform by compromising with the conservatives. The pragmatic members within the reformist camp, however, have generally applauded Rafsanjani's
intention to once again serve as a Majles member.

In sharp contrast to the monarchy, the judiciary also constitutes a largely independent and powerful institution in the theocratic order. The 1989 amended
Constitution specifies that the judiciary is an independent branch and empowers
judges to arbitrate disputes and administer the laws of the land. Standing at the
apex of the judicial system is the office of the chief justice. Only the supreme
leader has the power to overturn the decisions of the chief justice. As with most
other branches of government, however, dual authority is also exercised in the legal system.

The courts are shadowed by revolutionary courts, where the judges are more likely to
be clerics than in the normal courts, and where an appeal to the supreme court is not
invariably allowed. Any crime considered subversive, or a challenge to the system,
will be tried by the revolutionary courts. ("Children of the Islamic Revolution: A
Survey of Iran," 1997)

Apart from the structures discussed above, the Expediency Council is yet another politically significant institution in the Islamic Republic. Set up by Khomeini in 1988 because a large amount of legislation enacted by the Majles was being
rejected by the Council of Guardians, the Expediency Council is charged with the
task of mediating between the Majles and the Council of Guardians.[2] Yet this is
not all. According to Iran's Constitution, the Council of Expediency, which also
serves as an advisory body to the supreme leader, is further empowered to create
legislation independent of the Majles and, if it deems fit, even contradict the
Sharia and the Constitution. The permanent members of the Council, who currently number twenty-five, including the heads of the three branches of government as well as the six clerical members of the Council of Guardians, are appointed by the supreme leader, who is also charged with determining the
council's agenda. Depending upon the nature of legislation under consideration,
the membership of the council is supposed to expand in order to include the cabinet minister or agency chief most directly concerned with legislation before the
council. The council is now chaired by former president Rafsanjani, and its members include prominent leaders from all three major factions within the Islamic
Republic (Amuzegar, 1995, p. 27; "Khamenehi Gives Raf Brand New Job," 1997).

It can be seen, then, that the theocracy, quite unlike the monarchy, is endowed
with firm institutional foundations. Nevertheless, although the mullahs have ex-
celled in creating governing institutions, they have not been content to base their
regime's survival on such institutions alone. As with the shah before them, Iran's
ruling clerics have established an elaborate repressive apparatus that serves as the
ultimate guarantor of their power. At the same time, they also appear to have inherited the shah's fear and distrust of the armed forces. To preclude the possibility of a coup d'état, they have created a fragmented security apparatus.

Just as the Majles is shadowed by the Council of Guardians, the army (numbering 320,000) is shadowed by Sepah-e Pasdaran (the Revolutionary Guard
Corps, or IRGC, with 120,000 members), the Basiji forces (the volunteer militia,
with 1,300,000 full- and part-time members), both of which are currently geared
primarily toward containing civil unrest ("Children of the Islamic Revolution: A
Survey of Iran," 1997). Each group has its own loyalties and structures. In 1992,
the regime created the Office of Joint Chiefs of Staff in order to bring about
greater integration between Iran's armed forces, since confused lines of command were officially blamed for the country's lamentable performance in the war
against Iraq. However, full integration has purposefully been kept elusive. In his
capacity as the commander in chief, the supreme leader appoints the leaders of

all three components of Iran's motley repressive apparatus, ensuring sufficient division and rivalry between them so as to diminish the likelihood of coordinated action among them. As the commander in chief, the supreme leader is also entrusted with the authority to promote all of the nation's high-ranking officers and NCOs (Rathmell, 1995, p. 450).

The regular army, which, as in the time of the shah's rule, still derives its rank-and-file members through conscription, has been the victim of so many purges since the revolution that its capacity to take part in autonomous institutional behavior has been emasculated. Since it is composed almost entirely of conscripts, the army is not considered to be sufficiently loyal to impose internal security. It is, therefore, directed completely toward external defense. The IRGC, by contrast, created shortly after the revolution (with its own ground, naval, and air branches) to balance the influence of the army, is "considered more reliable . . . and [is] used to block the mobilization of groups and classes" (Parsa, 1989, p. 312).

An adjunct of the Pasdaran (Revolutionary Guards), the Basiji forces are perhaps the most loyal and dependable defendants of the regime. Neither eligible for the army nor the Pasdaran, the Basij corps is mostly composed of those generally considered underage or overage for service in the armed forces. During the Iran-Iraq war, the Basiji forces, some of whom had not even become teenagers yet, distinguished themselves by dutifully marching in front of the regular troops in order to clear mine fields ("Basij Chief Is Replaced," 1998). Since the war, the Basij has on several occasions proved itself capable of harshly crushing demonstrations. As a result, it has been granted the primary task of imposing internal security. There are reportedly up to 1 million part-time Basiji members, who can readily be mobilized at times of crisis. In recognition of the Basij's increasing importance to the regime, its full-time manpower, having tripled since 1991, currently stands at 300,000. In addition, the organization's budget has increased by a factor of four (Rathmell, 1995, p. 450).

As in the previous regime, then, the theocracy's military, or at least a large proportion of it, serves as the ultimate foundation of the system's power. Yet, once again, as in the previous order, it is the Islamic Republic's security and intelligence services that ensure that the military does not have to intervene perpetually in order to sustain the theocratic order. It has already been noted that the Friday prayer leaders as well as the mosques they administer also function as intelligence-gathering organizations in the provinces. The Islamic Republic has thus extended the arms of its intelligence apparatus into hitherto untouched territory. The mosques, however, constitute only one element in the regime's intelligence gathering and countersubversion network. Shortly after the revolution, SAVAK, which had been vehemently attacked by the revolutionaries as the very symbol of Pahlavi despotism, was "refurbished, renamed SAVAMA, and streamlined. Even though it retained some of the Shah era personnel, the institution was relegitimized" (Rubin, 1987, p. 243). During the early years of the revolution, the organization played an instrumental role in detecting and liquidating Mojahedin members and supporters.

Operating under the new name SAVAMA, the institution initially reported to the commander of the Pasdaran, who was himself accountable only to the supreme leader. In 1983, however, the regime established the Ministry of Information, which was to command and coordinate the theocracy's intelligence apparatus. But according to some commentators, in line with the system's policy of promoting dual control, the head of the Pasdaran, to this day has continued to exert a shadow command over the Ministry of Intelligence ("Iran Quarterly Reports," 1997, pp. 24–25). Nevertheless, Iran's intelligence apparatus is now even more awe-inspiring, efficient, and prying than it was under the shah (Arjomand, 1988, pp. 172–173). Brutal methods of dealing with political dissidents still prevail, although their level of severity is in part dependent upon the ascendancy of a given competing faction in the nation's factious political establishment.

Having clarified the nature of Iran's pre and postrevolutionary regimes, this chapter next undertakes comparison of the qualities of the leaders of the two regimes in order to enhance our understanding of the Islamic Republic's prospects for survival. The point of departure, it will be recalled, is that leaders who control the nation's levers of power (by virtue of the way they act or fail to act) can frequently exert a consequential impact on the perpetuation or transformation of the regimes they head.

Comparing Iran's Decisionmakers Then and Now: The Strength of Turbans Versus the Crown

We have seen that the monarchy, bereft of autonomous institutions and overly dependent upon the shah as a ruler, was inherently more fragile and vulnerable to collapse and overthrow than is the Islamic Republic. Even its ultimate pillars of support, the royalist armed and security forces, though highly formidable, could not and would not act without the shah. As we shall presently see, however, the shah, contrary to the image he had tried to project of himself, was a rather insecure, feeble, and faint-hearted ruler with strong fatalistic tendencies, whose proclivities toward indecisiveness, wavering, and vacillation became particularly acute in times of crisis. Indeed, the shah was utterly incompetent in crisis management and had, throughout his rule, established a recurrent "pattern of retreat in the face of adversity or challenge" (Zonis, 1991, p. 98). Ultimately, the shah's inability to commit himself wholeheartedly to the survival of his regime and to respond resolutely to the popular mobilization against his rule resulted in the disintegration of his formidable security forces, thereby allowing the revolutionary coalition to achieve an unexpectedly swift victory.

The present rulers of Iran, by comparison, in addition to being endowed with strong institutional bases, have up to now proved themselves capable of overcoming their occasionally intense factional and political quarrels at times of crisis. We have already seen how, in sharp departure from the shah's modus operandi, the Islamic Republic has "delegated effective authority to governing institutions below the level of the *[faqih]*" (Greene, 1990, p. 172) and is not overly dependent on one individual for its survival. Nevertheless, this apparent source of strength also has the latent potential of easily turning into a liability for the regime if the convictions that have up to now served to bind the nation's ruling clerics together become corroded and compromised. Then the Islamic Republic's numerous centers of power, including the regime's motley repressive apparatus, can come to serve as instruments through which the feuding elite will strive to gain ascendancy in a zero-sum struggle for power, thereby raising the specter of civil war and regime breakdown.

The Shah's Prevarications in the Face of Adversity: A Recurrent Pattern

Mohammad Reza Shah's vulnerabilities and politically debilitating characteristics were perceptively detected by his father, Reza Shah, the founder of the Pahlavi dynasty. A savage dictator who never hesitated to deal swiftly and harshly with his political opponents, Reza Shah is reported to have expressed lingering doubts about the future political prospects of his son as well as the Pahlavi dynasty. Reza Shah apparently based his skepticism on Mohammad Reza's "tenderheartedness" as well as his weak will (Zonis, 1991, p. 106), correctly fearing that such qualities were bound to inhibit his son from adequately asserting his authority and exercising leadership.

But Mohammad Reza Shah was not without physical courage. Indeed, in 1949 "he confronted his would-be assassin on the campus of Tehran University . . . while his bodyguards and military commanders stood paralyzed by fear or amazement" (Zonis, 1991, p. 98). Instead, the shah lacked emotional strength and fortitude. In an interview, he once candidly observed: "[P]hysically I am not afraid, but mentally you're always constantly afraid of something; either by yourself or something that might go wrong with your allies that you're counting on" (Zonis, 1991, p. 98). Whenever the general pattern of events was interrupted by unforeseen or crisis ridden situations, the shah became plagued with obsessive doubts and anxiety about the consequences of his actions. Unlike his father, the shah's temperament was simply not suited to being an effective autocrat. He lacked the ability to render consequential decisions swiftly. Providing a valuable insight into his psyche, in his youth he confided the following revealing desire to his friends: "Had he not been a king . . . he would have liked to be a public servant, earning enough money to indulge his passion for sport. He then went on to make a significant remark, one that runs true to form: He would prefer a job that spared him the burden of decision making" (Alam, 1991, pp. 22–23).

The shah's propensity toward despondency and withdrawal in threatening situations first manifested itself in 1941, when the Allies invaded Iran, forced his father to abdicate, and acquiesced in his accession to the throne as the new king. Young and inexperienced, the shah is purported to have contemplated suicide as a means of extricating himself from the predicament of being an essentially powerless king in an invaded country. Yet encouraged and fortified by the strength of his twin sister, Ashraf, the shah resentfully bore what he regarded as the humiliating burden of being a ceremonial ruler in a vanquished land, while endeavoring to expand his room for maneuver (Amuzegar, 1991, p. 215; Naraghi, 1994, p. 62).

The first truly significant crisis in the shah's rule came about in the early 1950s, when he found himself increasingly outshone and eclipsed by Iran's nationalist prime minister, Mohammad Mossadegh. It should be recalled that the instrumental role Mossadegh played in the nationalization of the Iranian oil industry catapulted him to the position of a national hero for a large proportion of Iranians. As we have seen, Mossadegh's operating principle and favorite maxim was that "the king must reign, not rule." In 1952, one year before he was ousted through a military coup d'état, Mossadegh, protesting the shah's refusal to grant him control over the ministry of war, resigned from his position as prime minister. Following Mossadegh's resignation, massive groups of people gathered in the streets of Tehran demanding that Mossadegh be reinstated. After five days of massive protests, the shah, hesitant to authorize a full-scale crackdown by the army, backed down, reinstated Mossadegh, and granted him full control over the War Ministry. In his last book, written after the revolution while he was dying of lymphatic cancer in exile, the shah asserts that during his confrontation with Mossadegh in 1952, "I refused to order my troops to fire and was *forced* to recall Mossadeqh" (Pahlavi, 1980, p. 118; Zonis, 1991, p. 100).

In August 1953, while the CIA-MI-6-backed coup d'état against Mossadegh was still in preparation, the shah lost his nerve and fled the country, going first to Baghdad and thence to Rome. In the subsequent events which restored him to power, the shah played more the role of an anxious, reluctant, and hesitant bystander than an active participant. The shah, apparently convinced that his rule in Iran had been abolished, decided to pack his bags and leave after Mossadegh refused to accept the shah's order terminating the prime minister's tenure of power. Immediately thereafter, Tehran became tense, with both pro- and anti-Mossadegh forces pouring into the streets. Mossadegh's subsequent order to the armed forces to restore calm allowed the coup instigators, aided generously by dissident clerics, royal elements in the army, prominent bazaar merchants, and a group of paid, knife-wielding thugs, to consummate the coup. The shah's triumphant return following Mossadegh's ouster stood in sharp contrast to his ignominious withdrawal in the face of adversity. Before leaving for Baghdad, the shah had purportedly confided in the American ambassador that "as a constitutional ruler he had decided that he should not resort to force as that would lead to bloodshed, chaos and Soviet infiltration" (Amuzegar, 1991, p. 286; Milani, 1994, p. 41; Roosevelt, 1979; Zonis, 1991, pp. 101–103).

The shah's disdain for bloodshed, as well as his paralysis of will when confronted with a crisis milieu, once again came to the fore during the June 1963 riots instigated by Ayatollah Khomeini (see Chapter 3). In spite of the fact that by this time the shah had largely succeeded in transforming Iran into an absolute monarchy, he again exhibited hesitation and lack of resolve when confronted with Khomeini's challenge. Although he relished his position as the paramount power holder and decisionmaker in the realm (indeed, he could not tolerate even remotely independent personalities and power centers), he found it exceptionally difficult to undertake the steadfast, unequivocal, ruthless, and swift measures that the logic of his preferred mode of governance dictated.

Fortunately for the shah, however, his unquestionably loyal and close adviser and confidant Assadollah Alam, who was serving as the prime minister at the time, was ravaged neither by the shah's paralysis of will nor by his compunctions against resorting to force in order to assert the regime's authority. In fact, Alam's decisiveness, ruthless brutality, and lack of pretentiousness, stood in complete contrast to the shah's personality traits. A close associate once referred to Alam as a person who "can cut your throat with a feather" (Bill, 1988, p. 104). In the very preliminary stages of the 1963 riots, Alam strongly urged the shah to act without delay and respond with overwhelming force. The shah, however, was hesitant and remained opposed to violence. To reassure the shah, Alam, who remained convinced that vacillation and half measures would result in the unraveling of the system, volunteered to initiate the necessary actions to crush the riots and assume full responsibility for the consequences if his efforts failed. The shah, beset by the agony of indecision, was relieved to place his responsibility upon someone else's shoulders. He agreed, asking the commanders of his armed and security forces to abide by the dictates of Alam (Alam, 1991, p. 6; Arjomand, 1988, p. 54; Zonis, 1991, pp. 135–136).

Not mincing words, Alam ordered the commanders to clear the streets by any means necessary, which they did at a great loss of life (several thousand). Several years later, reflecting on the number of people who died in 1963 as a result of his crackdown, Alam recorded the following statements in his confidential memoirs:

> The number was immaterial. I was determined to make a stand since the very survival of our country was at stake. (Alam, 1991, p. 64)

> There was no alternative. Had we backed down, the rioting would have spread to every corner of Iran. (Alam, 1991, p. 279)

As to why he had ordered the troops to fire on the demonstrators, Alam, shortly before his death in 1977, offered the following explanation to the former British ambassador to Iran: "I had to. His Majesty is very soft-hearted and does not like bloodshed" (Parsons, 1984, p. 27).

Thus, when the shah's rule was again under threat in 1963, it was Alam who took it upon himself, in spite of the shah's equivocations, to safeguard it. Without Alam's determined response, it is conceivable, though certainly not determinable, that the world might have witnessed the demise of the Pahlavi monarchy some fifteen years before the 1978–1979 revolution. Left to his own devices, the shah would probably have continued his hesitation, refusing to act with resolution and determination.

Indeed, Alam's reaction to the 1963 protests is reminiscent of how Reza Shah, the founder of the dynasty, responded to disturbances when his rule was under threat. Reza Shah's secularizing reforms, which culminated in his prohibition against the wearing of the Islamic *hejab* (veil) by women in 1935, resulted in massive protests (instigated by the ulama) in the holy city of Mashad, where the Eighth Imam of the Shias is buried. Thousands of people took sanctuary in the Goharshad Mosque adjacent to the shrine of the Eighth Imam. Determined to quell the disturbances forcefully, Reza Shah wasted no time in ordering his troops to shell the mosque with cannon artillery and indiscriminately shoot at the demonstrators (Arjomand, 1988, p. 82). Such behavior, largely in accord with Machiavelli's princely model, is also consonant with how both Hafez al-Assad and Saddam Hussein have dealt more recently with challenges against their rule.

Although the shah's tendency towards vacillation at critical junctures set him apart from his father, Saddam, and Assad, he was nevertheless every bit as keen, if not keener, than these individuals to exercise absolute domination over all instruments of state power. From 1963 to 1977, the shah strengthened his grip on the Iranian regime so firmly that, as we have already seen, the two became virtually synonymous and indistinguishable. He also became the most significant victim of his own gigantic propaganda machine, which appears to have succeeded brilliantly in fanning the flames of his vanity and megalomania. Shunning all independent advisers, he surrounded himself with sycophants who told him only what he wished to hear. Toward the end, only Alam could occasionally muster sufficient courage to challenge the shah's interpretation of reality. Even Alam, however, as he admits in his memoirs, was generally content to act merely as a masterful practitioner of the art of flattery: "We [the prime minister, minister of court, and other dignitaries] all attended lunch and vied with one another in showering compliments on HIM [His Imperial Majesty]" (Alam, 1991, p. 137). Nevertheless, Alam's death from cancer in the fall of 1977 deprived the shah of the only loyal adviser he had who could speak to him frankly.

The shah's rising megalomania during these years (1963–1978), particularly after the fourfold increase in the price of oil in 1973, also served to reinforce his fatalistic tendencies. In 1973, he asserted in an interview:

> I am not entirely alone, because a force others can't perceive accompanies me. My mystical force. Moreover, I receive messages. I have lived with God beside me since I was five years old. (Zonis, 1991, p. 39)

Apparently, the shah believed that he was endowed with divine protection. In a private conservation with Alam, he once made the following exceptionally self-aggrandizing and delusional remark:

> I have learned by experience that a tragic end awaits anyone who dares cross swords with me; Nasser is no more; John and Robert Kennedy died at the hands of assassins; their brother Edward has been disgraced, Khrushchev was toppled, the list is endless. And the same thing goes for my enemies at home; just think of Mossaddeq, or even Qavam. (Alam, 1991, p. 202)

Given his delusions of grandeur as well as his seclusion from reality, the shah may well have been sincere when he told a British journalist in 1974: "Just imagine Iranians . . . demonstrating against their leader after what we have done for the country. It is true hegemony what we have in our country. Everybody is behind their monarch, with their souls, with their hearts" (Abrahamian, 1982, p. 450).[3]

By the time the most precarious crisis in his reign erupted in 1978, the shah was ill-prepared to deal with the mounting mobilization against his rule. He had tried, without success, to allay and mask his innate insecurity by surrounding himself with obsequious servants and engaging in wishful thinking about being divinely guarded. His propensity toward withdrawal and wavering in the face of adversity remained very much intact, as did his lack of bloody resolution. Alam had died, and the shah had himself become afflicted with cancer. Moreover, the United States, his closest and most formidable foreign ally, which had played an instrumental role in restoring him to power in 1953, was now sending him contradictory signals on how to deal with the challenge against his regime. As we shall presently see, the shah's inconsistent, indecisive, conciliatory and at times even noncommittal policies and pronouncements (both immediately before and during the popular uprising against him) helped substantially to facilitate the demise of the monarchy.

The fuse that detonated the explosives of the revolution was lit by the shah's ambivalent and partial policy of liberalization, which he initiated in 1977 primarily to placate the newly installed Carter administration. In his inaugural speech, President Carter, who had criticized Iran's human rights record during his campaign, had made the following declaration: "Our moral sense dictates a clear preference for those societies which share with us an abiding respect for individual human rights" (Bill, 1988, p. 226; Parsa, 1989, p. 171). Exceptionally sensitive toward the West's, particularly America's, attitudes toward his regime, the shah immediately set about to loosen somewhat the bonds of political oppression. During the initial stages of his liberalization campaign, the shah indicated that he had indeed launched his program to please Washington (with the aim of preparing the stage for the eventual accession of his son to the throne serving as a secondary motivation) and is reported to have declared to an associate: "They want liberalization! I'll give them liberalization. I'll loosen the screws until the Americans beg me to tighten them again" (Zonis, 1991, p. 109).

Without an overall strategy, the shah's liberalization "policy" during 1977 entailed well-publicized and carefully selected releases of some 1,000 political prisoners, curtailment of censorship, and improved treatment of dissidents. He allowed the International Red Cross to inspect political prisoners and ordered Parliament to enact legislation prohibiting the detention of prisoners, who could now be represented by civilian attorneys, without trial (Abrahamian, 1989, p. 30; Parsa, 1989, p. 171; Parsons, 1984, p. 49; Zonis, 1991, p. 110). Cautiously optimistic, many prominent, moderately inclined dissidents and intellectuals responded by seeking to engage the shah in a dialogue. Several incisive and highly critical open letters were addressed to the shah seeking to persuade him of the need to truly reform his rule by implementing more fundamental and meaningful liberalization policies along with democratization policies.

After an initial period of silence, during which the moderate opposition, taking advantage of the more relaxed political atmosphere, began to mobilize by holding rallies and politicized poetry-reading nights, SAVAK responded by breaking up some rallies and clobbering and harassing several prominent activists and intellectuals (Katouzian, 1981, p. 342; Zonis, 1991, p. 112). The reduced curtailments on censorship and the rights of political prisoners, however, were not reversed. Such behavior served to convince the shah's opponents, particularly the moderate element, a large fraction of whom were likely to have been co-opted into a more enlightened and broader political structure (Parsons, 1984, p. 53), that the shah's aim was not to reform his regime but to buy time by currying favor with the new pro-human rights Democratic administration in Washington. By failing to initiate meaningful reform when time was still on his side, the shah lost a golden opportunity to divide his opposition and enhance the prospects for the survival of a modified version of his regime.

The shah's anxiety about the Carter administration was temporarily allayed, however, when, in a state dinner given in honor of President Carter's visit to Iran on December 31, 1977, Carter muffled his concern for human rights by pronouncing lavish praise of the shah: "Iran under the great leadership of the Shah is an island of stability in one of the more troubled areas of the world. This is a great tribute to you, Your Majesty, and to your leadership, and to the respect, admiration, and love which your people give to you" (Bill, 1988, p. 233). The shah must have derived additional satisfaction from the fact that Carter, after having derided the sale of sophisticated American weapons to Third World dictatorships during his election campaign, decided, after assuming power, to continue the Nixon and Ford administrations' policy of supplying Iran with unlimited weapons short of the nuclear variety.

Assured of the new president's support, the shah, seeking to discredit dissident clerics (most of whom were supporters of Khomeini), whose sermons had become bolder and more fierce since the initiation of the shah's liberalization policy, authorized the publication of an insulting article on Khomeini in one of the nation's official newspapers in January 1978 (see Chapter 4). As we have seen, the cycle of disturbances and protests over the contents of this article, which, among other things, accused Khomeini of being a British agent and a libertine composer of erotic poetry, afforded Khomeini's disciples the opportunity to take over the mosque networks, catapulted the charismatic and uncompromising Khomeini to the position of unrivaled leader of the anti-shah movement, and prompted the more moderate social and opposition forces to close ranks in favor of ousting the shah.

Without the shah's indecisive, passive, and vacillating leadership, however, the opposition's capacity to overthrow the monarchy would still have been far from assured. Indeed, even as late as a few weeks before his triumphant return to Iran, Khomeini himself is reported to have privately expressed doubts about the ability of the revolutionary coalition to overthrow the shah. On the eve of Khomeini's return in February 1979, Bazargan, who was acting as one of Khomeini's chief representatives in Iran, still believed it was likely that the shah's formidable military apparatus would, at this late stage, intervene to crush the revolutionary upheaval.[4] But the military, as we have seen, could not lift a finger without the shah, whose contradictory directives played a far more instrumental role in enfeebling the regime than did Khomeini's exhortations.

To deal with the mounting opposition and mobilization against his rule, which, since the publication of the diatribe against Khomeini, had spread to the mosques and the bitterly disaffected bazaars and was increasingly being manipulated by Khomeini, the shah appointed Jafar Sharif-Emami to be Iran's prime minister in August 1978. Sharif-Emami, who had served for a long time as the head of the Pahlavi Foundation, was, in the words of the last American ambassador to the shah's court, "regarded as personally corrupt" (Bill, 1988, p. 241; Sullivan, 1981, p. 164). His appointment, therefore, was regarded with contempt and was suspect in the eyes of the increasingly charged and vocal opposition. Had the shah appointed Shapour Bakhtiar, the National Front opposition leader, to whom he turned in desperation in January of 1979, or even Ali Amini (both of whom were willing to serve), he might still have been able to prevent a large fraction of the modern middle class and intellectuals from joining forces with Khomeini (see Chapter 3). Curiously, however, he turned to Sharif-Emami.

According to the shah's wishes, Sharif-Emami's government of reconciliation was charged with the task of further liberalizing the system in order to pacify the opposition. Emami began by freeing additional political prisoners, further relaxing the rules of censorship, abrogating unpopular previous enactments (such as the replacement of the shah's Pahlavi calendar with the traditional Islamic calendar), and closing casinos, which, as the head of the Pahlavi Foundation, he had just recently opened. He vitalized and publicized the debates of the hitherto slavish Majles, which quickly moved to enact legislation providing for rights of the press, academic freedom, and freedom of expression. Much to the consternation of SAVAK and the shah's hard-line generals, on October 17, 1978, the government declared censorship to be over, and guaranteed freedom of the press. In an unprecedented turn of events, pictures of Khomeini, along with sympathetic articles, now began to appear in Iran's major newspapers (Parsons, 1984, pp. 68–69, 82–83). Publicizing interviews with the newly released political prisoners, the newspapers also began to reveal harrowing details about SAVAK's torture chambers (Arjomand, 1988, p. 115).

These concessions, however, only served to further radicalize the opposition and raise people's expectations. The increasingly popular Khomeini continued to insist that the shah must go, and daily demonstrations and strikes, largely coordinated by the mosque network, began to engulf Iran's political landscape. Desperate to quell the uprisings, the shah acceded to the imposition of martial law in the nation's major cities on September 8, 1978, but he refused to roll back his previous reforms. He instructed the government to continue paying the salaries of strikers in the public sector, whose refusal to work (particularly those employed in the sensitive oil and gas industries) was bringing the country's economy to a halt. In fact, he even ordered the government to increase their salaries. Consequently, there was no major disincentive for the strikers not to engage in anti-shah activities (Arjomand, 1988, p. 118). Moreover, the shah declined to grant his generals a free hand in enforcing martial law. The hard-liner General Gholam Ali Oveisi, who had played an instrumental role in suppressing the 1963 uprising, was put in charge of administering martial law in Tehran. Immediately after his appointment, Oveisi ordered his troops to fire on a large number of demonstrators in Jaleh Square in southern Tehran. The opposition was terrified, promptly going into hiding. But the shah's "tenderheartedness," so perceptively detected by his father, now resurfaced with a vengeance. The shah reportedly wept in front of his generals and the cabinet and severely rebuked Oveisi for his transgressions. Henceforth, the "troops were only allowed to fire into the air . . . and commanders in Qazvin, Mashad, Tabriz, and elsewhere who disobeyed Tehran and ordered their men to shoot to kill in self-defence . . . were reprimanded" (Arjomand, 1988, pp. 114–118).[5]

Such contradictory impulses by the shah infuriated his hawkish generals, including the director of SAVAK, General Moghaddam, who reportedly lodged the following complaint against the shah to a representative of the CIA in Tehran: "I declare that the ShanShah has tied our arms and the hands of the armed forces. . . . We are of course astonished as to why the ShanShah follows these policies" (Arjomand, 1988, p. 115). The opposition, however, delighted with the shah's bungled application of martial law, expanded its endeavors to depose the monarchy.

To impel the shah to grant him greater leeway in squelching the revolutionary movement, Oveisi ordered the troops to idly stand by during Tehran's worst riots on November 5, 1978. According to some reports, SAVAK provocateurs also actively took part in the rioting to convince the shah that his inhibited use of the iron fist, along with his insistence on following through with his liberalization policy, were woefully ineffective in containing the demonstrations (Amuzegar, 1991, p. 254; Arjomand, 1988, p. 116). Characteristically, the shah was unable to make up his mind.

Compounding the shah's inherent disposition toward paralysis of will in the face of adversity were the inconsistent signals that he was receiving from the United States, his primary foreign patron. Unable to make up his mind, the shah apparently wanted the United States to render the decision and shoulder the responsibility for his crackdown on the demonstrations[6] (what Alam had agreed to do fifteen years earlier). Whereas President Carter's national security adviser, Zbigniew Brzezinski, pointing to Iran's enormous geopolitical significance, appears to have been well disposed toward shouldering the shah's responsibility for responding to the mass mobilization, the president himself rejected this course of action. Instead, Carter presided over an administration whose various components provided the shah with contradictory advice. In the words of Brzezinski, "[O]ur Ambassador, abetted by State, instead of strengthening the Shah's morale, contributed to his indecision by diluting our [i.e., Brzezinski's] urgings that the Shah act [i.e., crack down]" (Brzezinski, 1983, p. 395).

Seeking to bolster the monarch's confidence, Brzezinski telephoned the shah on November 3, 1978, urging him to terminate his uncertainty and act with determination against the oppositional forces. The following day, however, in a meeting with the American ambassador, the shah requested, but was not granted, confirmation of Brzezinski's recommendation (Arjomand, 1988, p. 116; Amuzegar, 1991, p. 254). Then, on November 6, one day after Tehran's devastating riots, the shah embarked on yet another self-defeating course of action. He dismissed Sharif Emami as prime minister and brought in a military government. But he essentially emasculated the military government from the beginning by restraining its power and forbidding it from effectively applying martial law.

Dejected, his megalomania in tatters, and teetering on the edge of a nervous breakdown, the shah even bungled his announcement of the formation of the military government. Excessively and uncharacteristically apologetic and submissive, the shah's speech served to convince a large fraction of the dissatisfied populace as well as the opposition groups that he had given up the will to fight for his survival. Delivered "from a clear position of weakness, [the shah's address] was an open invitation to the opposition to test the military government's power and determination" (Amuzegar, 19888, p. 255). Going out of his way to placate his increasingly emboldened and intransigent opposition, the shah declared: "I commit myself to make up for past mistakes, to fight corruption and injustices, and to form a national government to carry out free elections . . . I guarantee that after the military government, freedom and the constitution will be reimplemented . . . Your revolutionary message has been heard" (Parsa, 1989, p. 223).

Bypassing the cruel and hawkish General Oveisi, the shah selected an incompetent and frail parlor general, Gholam Reza Azhari, who had never served in combat, to head his military government. A "loyal man who had always avoided politics" (an apt description of Azhari that is attributed to the shah himself), Azhari was now suddenly charged with the task of resolving the most dangerous political turbulence in the shah's thirty-seven-year reign (Amuzegar, 1991, p. 255). Oveisi was meanwhile retained as the chief administrator of the martial law. However, the shah continued to prohibit him from cracking down on demonstrators. "Begin applying the martial law tomorrow," the shah is reported to have told Oveisi after inaugurating a military government, "but I do not want anybody's nose to bleed" (Arjomand, 1988, p. 116). Most significant, the shah also forbade SAVAK from arresting en masse the organizers and coordinators of the revolutionary mobilization, whose names and locations were generally known to the agency. Instead, the shah ordered the release of more political prisoners, including Ayatollahs Motahari and Talegani, who quickly proceeded to organize massive demonstrations against the monarchy. Moreover, to further placate the opposition, the shah allowed Azhari to arrest several former ministers and high-ranking officials, including Amir Abbas Hoveyda, who for thirteen years had obediently served as the shah's prime minister, on charges of corruption.

Rather than inhibiting the activities of the revolutionary forces, then, the shah's absurd insistence on combining a policy of unsystematic pretense to repression with halfhearted attempts at liberalization, facilitated the task of the revolutionaries. Having missed the chance to reform his rule meaningfully when time was still on his side, the shah would have been better advised first to assert his authority and then to initiate reforms (liberalization and democratization). Instead, he reverted to his general pattern of hesitation, vacillation, and submission to fate at times of political strife. Speaking to the British ambassador at the peak of the revolutionary crisis, the shah repeated, almost verbatim, the same line of argument he had advanced in 1953, when he was about to flee the country at a time when his rule was under threat from Mossadegh: "A dictator may survive by slaughtering his people, a king cannot act in such a way" (Parsons, 1984, p. 114).

If by a king he meant a constitutional monarch, then the shah was once again engaging in self-delusion, because the system over which he presided was an ideal-typical textbook example of what Eisenstadt (1978) describes as a neopatrimonial dictatorship. As the primary force that held this system together, the shah's incapacitation and breakdown expedited the disintegration of the Pahlavi state.

The shah's contradictory impulses also served to wreck the cohesion and solidarity of his armed and security forces. The shah forced the soldiers out of their barracks and into the streets so that they could witness the massive outpouring of popular emotions, but lacking the nerve to use the military effectively, he did not grant them permission to crack down. This, in part, explains the relatively small number of casualties that resulted from Iran's massive revolutionary mobilization (between 2,000 and 3,000 from October 1, 1978 to January 15, 1979) (Arjomand, 1988, p. 120). Instead, the soldiers were allowed to fraternize with the revolutionaries and became exposed, for a prolonged period of time, to clerical antimonarchist propaganda. Under such circumstances, therefore, it is rather surprising to learn that up to the shah's departure from Iran on January 16, 1979, the number of desertions on the part of the rank-and-file members of the armed forces amounted to no more than 100–200 soldiers a day (a comparatively insignificant figure, given that overall, there were 413,000 men under arms) (Huyser, 1986, pp. 105, 160).

It is no wonder, then, that even until the very end, Khomeini, Bazargan, and Beheshti continued to agonize over the likelihood of a military crackdown and coups d'état. That is why during the final days of the monarchy, Khomeini substantially expanded his exhortations to the armed forces to shake off the humiliating yoke of the Pahlavi dynasty (Roberts, 1996, pp. 3, 21). But what ultimately brought about the disintegration of Iran's Imperial Armed Forces was not simply the desertion and defection of its soldiers to the ranks of the revolutionaries, although this number expanded dramatically after the shah fled the country (1,000–2,000), causing the already sagging morale of the armed forces to decline even further. It should be recalled that the other significant human component of the army, the Iranian officer corps, was entirely beholden to the shah, whose domination, distrust, and compartmentalization made it impossible for the officers to act without his personal intervention and approval. Throughout the revolutionary upheaval, such unambiguous approval was not forthcoming. Once the shah, in a last-ditch measure of desperation, appointed Shapour Bakhtiar as Iran's prime minister and agreed to abide by Bakhtiar's condition to leave the country, the army could not transfer its allegiance to Bakhtiar. Leaderless, Iran's remaining officers (some, including Oveisi, sensing disaster, had already fled the country), most of whom disliked and distrusted one another, could not even coordinate on how to keep the armed forces intact, let alone instigate a coup d'état.[7]

Overcoming Internal Divisions and Crushing External Challenges: A Recurrent Clerical Pattern?

In prerevolutionary Iran, power was highly concentrated and fused almost entirely in the person of the shah. His paralysis of will and breakdown, therefore, played an instrumental role in the demise of the monarchy. As we have seen, the nature of the present Iranian political system is fundamentally different from the previous order. Rather than being concentrated, political power is now fragmented and separated into different institutions. As in the days of the shah, however, the continued preservation of the system demands that the nation's key decisionmakers who control the regime's levers of power (and their subordinates, who are charged with carrying out their commands) act with decisiveness and clarity in times of crisis. The theocracy's central decisionmakers and power holders must not only overcome internal divisions to put up a common front against external challenges but must also ensure that even if the regime is not being challenged by outside forces, intraregime divisions and struggles for power are themselves kept within limits so that they do not tear the regime apart. Although political institutions designed to resolve differences among the elite can help to facilitate compromise and strengthen cohesion, ultimately it is the individuals who occupy those institutions who must hammer out their differences to keep the system intact. As we shall presently see, although faction-ridden and at times fractious, Iran's collective rulers up to now have repeatedly proven themselves capable of closing ranks to preserve the system. They have also been far more sure-handed and repressive than the shah in dealing with threatening situations. But whether the ruling clergy's adroitness in the art of political manipulation, violence, and compromise will survive the election of Mohammad Khatami remains to be seen.

All of Iran's key decisionmakers today, including the supreme leader, Khamenei, President Khatami, former president and current head of the Expediency Council Rafsanjani, chief of the judiciary Yazdi, and Speaker of the Majles Nategh-Nuri, are Ayatollah Khomeini's close disciples. In the prerevolutionary era, all of them were members of Khomeini's secret cadre in Iran and, in this capacity, played active roles in the anti-shah struggle. All are Shia clerics, who in the course of fulfilling their pedagogical requirements were instructed for varying periods of time by Khomeini. Moreover, all, with the exception of Khatami, were imprisoned and tortured in the prerevolutionary era for engaging in pro-Khomeini activities. Although Khatami himself escaped prison, his late father, Ayatollah Khatami, a close personal friend of Khomeini, who, after the revolution, served as the leader of the Friday congregational prayers and Khomeini's personal representative in Yazd Province, did not. Khamenei and Rafsanjani developed an especially close personal relationship while collaborating in the prerevolutionary struggles against the shah. This relationship was reinforced after the revolution, when for eight consecutive and crucial years while Khomeini was still alive, Rafsanjani served as the Speaker of the Parliament while Khamenei acted as president of the republic. Khamenei studied under President Khatami's father, and the Khatamis and Khameneis were close family friends (Ashraf, 1994, p. 127; Sciolino, 1998a). President Khatami is also related to the Khomeini family by marriage.

Although they share many similar characteristics and backgrounds, Iran's current decisionmakers are nevertheless divided on some significant policy issues. Nategh Nouri, who was Khatami's chief competitor in the 1997 presidential election, and Yazdi are among the primary leaders of the conservative faction. Striving to protect the power and privileges of its bazaari cronies and the corporatist Bonyads, this faction opposes structural economic reforms. Expressing alarm about the cultural invasion by the West and the dangers of permissiveness, Yazdi and Nouri have resisted the lifting of cultural, political, and personal restrictions. Rafsanjani is a clever pragmatist, who is generally amenable to compromise and is willing to embrace hard-line or moderate positions, depending upon the circumstances. In general, however, his aim is to revitalize the Iranian economy through privatization, deregulation, and the reduction of tensions with foreign countries. Although he also appears to favor the reduction of social and cultural restrictions, he is willing to compromise on these issues in order to enhance the prospects for his favorite economic policies. Khatami, by contrast, probably deserves the label of moderate (interestingly, even the head of the Central Intelligence Agency, in testimony before the Senate, recently referred to Khatami as a "moderate" ["CIA Says Iran 'Struggle' Underway," *Iran Times*, February 6, 1998, p. 3]), because he is genuinely interested in institutionalizing the rule of law and promoting greater personal, political, cultural, and economic freedoms. Unlike Rafsanjani, he does not appear willing to easily compromise on any of his policies.

Khamenei has several times changed colors during his political career. In the 1980s, his positions were essentially indistinguishable from those of Rafsanjani. As noted, after he assumed the position of *faqih*, however, his positions and pronouncements gradually acquired a greater conservative hue in order to offset the shortcomings of his meager religious credentials. Most recently, particularly after the landslide victory of Khatami, Khameini appears to be attempting to pick up the mantle of Ayatollah Khomeini, aiming to prevent excluding any major personality or faction from the revolutionary family. Nevertheless, he still appears to be more firmly aligned with the conservatives.

It is important to bear in mind that such divisions and cleavages are not new in the twenty-year history of the Islamic Republic. Indeed, despite sharing a common background, upbringing, and educational experience (sometimes reinforced through intermarriage), Iran's ruling elite has been divided, from the inception of the theocracy, on personal and ideological issues. From the start, distinctively conservative and radical tendencies and approaches to issues of domestic socioeconomic and political development and foreign affairs could be detected in the ranks of Khomeini's clerical followers. Gradually, a more centrist approach also began to manifest itself. So long as Khomeini was alive, no amount of intraregime rivalry could endanger the security and survival of the system, since all personalities readily deferred to Khomeini, whose authority as the undisputed leader of the revolution was unassailable.

Khomeini, meanwhile, who was haunted by the specter of debilitating factionalism among his subordinates, never hesitated to urge unity upon his disciples, threatening "to destroy anyone who [endangered] their collective rule" (Rubin, 1987, p. 247). Just as Reza Shah had agonized over his son's indecisiveness, Khomeini anguished over the consequences of unrestrained factionalism among the ruling clergy. "To seek power, whoever might seek it," he declared, "would lead to one's fall. Satan knows that the best way to manipulate a person is to convince him of his own importance" (Rubin, 1987, p. 247). Khomeini also sought to curtail his own personality cult, directing the media to limit the number of stories about him. Rebuking factional tendencies and leaders who were seeking to exploit his popularity by referring to themselves as the followers of the line of the

Imam, Khomeini declared that "all these presentations [are] deceptions to create disunity. There is no line in Iran except the line of Islam" (Arjomand, 1988, p. 160). Nonetheless, realizing that it was impossible to preclude differences, Khomeini sought to prevent them from becoming overwhelming by encouraging the creation of institutions (Majles, Guardians Council, Expediency Council, National Security Council) within which differences could, within limits, be openly exchanged and compromises hammered out. When all else failed, he never hesitated to render a judgment and impose his authority. To obviate alienating the loyalties of any prominent faction, however, he tended to alternatively support each major faction.

During the infancy of the Islamic system, the Mojahedin's armed uprising, aimed at overthrowing the theocracy, served to unify Khomeini's disparate followers behind the aim of destroying the Mojahedin and preserving the theocratic order. As we have seen, between 1981 and 1982, the regime declared open warfare against the Mojahedin and brutally destroyed the impressive organization as well as its sizable membership, including women and children, within Iran. Unlike the shah, who proved to have feet of clay and refused to direct his formidable coercive apparatus at the appropriate groups in a consistent fashion, the leaders of the Islamic Republic proved capable of mustering the requisite consensus and resolve to crush the uprising.

When the possibility of success in overthrowing the shah seemed highly remote, Khomeini and his disciples had willingly put their lives on the line, enduring the agony of torture and the pain of prison, in order to expedite the demise of the monarchy. After they had succeeded not only in displacing the shah but also in capturing power, they certainly were not about to relinquish power without a fierce struggle. The result was the bloodiest crackdown on dissent in modern Iranian history (Abrahamian, 1989, p. 259). In the process, not only the Mojahedin but also all other organized antiregime organizations were decimated.

After the effective subduing of the organized forces of opposition, the differences between Iran's ruling elite came more clearly to the fore. The radicals in the Majles, seeking to promote the interests of the peasantry and the urban poor, sought to enact legislation providing for a progressive land-reform program, the nationalization of foreign trade, and the expansion of consumer cooperatives. The Council of Guardians, however, dominated by the conservatives, prevented these measures from becoming law (Ashraf, 1994, p. 117). Providing a glimpse into the extent of intraregime schisms, in 1989 a group of prominent radical clerics (including Hojatoleslam Khoiniha, who headed the group of Islamic students responsible for occupying the American embassy and holding its staff hostage, and Hojatoleslam Mohtashami, who had helped to found Hezbollah in southern Lebanon), decided to leave the Association of Combatant Clerics (JRM), the nation's leading clerical fraternal organization. To compete with the JRM, a majority of whose members were conservatives, the leftist clerics established a new radical clerical organization, the Combatant Clerical Association (MRM).

Eventually, the divisions between the radicals and the traditionalists became so profound that in 1987, Khomeini, at the request of Speaker Rafsanjani and President Khamenei, ordered the dissolution of the Islamic Republican Party (IRP), which constituted the only legal political party in Iran.

> In their request, Khamene'i and Hashemi Rafsanjani, surviving founders of the IRP ... pointed out that the party had achieved its purpose of establishing the *velayat-e faqih* and the distinctive institutions of the Islamic Republic of Iran; its activities would henceforth encourage party politics *(tahazzob)* and have a divisive effect on the community. (Arjomand, 1988, p. 169)

Subsequently, in the same year, the cohesion of the theocracy's increasingly divided ruling elite was severely tested. It was alleged that Mehdi Hashemi, a relative of Grand Ayatollah Hossein Ali Montazeri, as well as an important figure in the Revolutionary Guards, had leaked Iran's secret dealings with the United States (what eventually came to be referred to as the Iran-Contra Affair) to a Lebanese newspaper. It was further asserted that Hashemi's leak had been part of an overall grand scheme to overthrow the Islamic regime. These accusations enraged Montazeri, who, in recognition of his status as Khomeini's most senior disciple and confidant, had been designated as Khomeini's successor by the Assembly of Experts in 1985. Shortly thereafter, Montazeri's anger gave way to a sense of vindictive fury when Hashemi, after having been found guilty of sedition by a revolutionary court, was executed. Although Montazeri himself was not implicated in the affair, he was urged to denounce Hashemi and to conduct an intensive purge of his own staff (Milani, 1994, p. 220). Montazeri was not about to budge. In the interim, the execution of Hashemi and the treatment meted out to Montazeri had served to create serious tensions in the ranks of the politicized clerics, since Montazeri was well respected and admired by a large number of the conservatives and centrists.

These tensions became particularly inflamed in February 1989, when Montazeri, on the occasion of the tenth anniversary of the Islamic revolution, wrote a widely publicized open letter to Ayatollah Khomeini in which he lamented the course that the revolution had taken:

> In these ten years, we have shouted slogans which were wrong and which have isolated us in the world and have alienated the people from the regime—there was no necessity for such slogans. . . . I hope there will be a change now that we are entering the second decade . . . I hope the next decade will not be full of slogans but deeds . . . We need a major change in the country's management. ("Iran Quarterly Report," 1997)

Montazeri's letter outraged Khomeini, who now "admitted that he had committed an egregious error in judgment by supporting Montazeri as his successor"

(Milani, 1994, p. 229). Montazeri was promptly dismissed, and all leading personalities and factions of the Islamic Republic solidly closed ranks behind Khomeini in denouncing Montazeri, who, as previously noted, to this day continues to be held under house arrest in Ghom.

As the undisputed leader of the revolution and the republic, Khomeini's word was tantamount to the word of God. His denunciation and rejection of Montazeri, therefore, quickly put an end to all intraregime disputes over the question of Montazeri. At the same time, however, coming at a time when Khomeini's health was rapidly declining and the cleavages among the factions were widening, the removal of Montazeri made the regime vulnerable to instability over the question of succession to the *faqih*.

Following Khomeini's death in June 1989, however, Iran's leaders showed an amazing dexterity in tempering their factional disputes and projecting a unified front. Recognizing that being internally at odds and not putting up a common front might result in the unraveling of the system, leaders and rank-and-file members from all factional stripes wasted no time in making abundantly clear their wholehearted support for the Assembly of Experts' selection of Seyyed Ali Khamenei, who appeared least challenging from the perspective of the major factions, as the new supreme leader. Whatever his private feelings, Ahmad Khomeini, Ayatollah Khomeini's son, in his letter of congratulation to Khamenei, declared: "The Imam [Khomeini] consistently spoke of you as a qualified *mujtahed*, and regarded you as the most qualified leader for the Islamic Republic" (Milani, 1994, p. 223–224). Meanwhile, Rafsanjani, the undisputed leader of the pragmatist faction, seeking to defend Khamenei against those who were questioning the new successor's religious credentials, "maintained that by the time someone becomes a *marja* [source of emulation, i.e., a grand ayatollah], he is usually old and devoid of [the necessary] energy to manage the country." He also asserted that it was the duty of all Muslims to abide by the dictates of the new Supreme Leader (Milani, 1994, pp. 222, 224).

The ability of Iran's ruling clerics to engineer a smooth transition of power following Khomeini's death is all the more impressive in light of the nation's recent tumultuous history. Of the six kings who ruled Iran during the approximately 150 years prior to Khomeini's accession to power, four, including Mohammad Reza Shah and his father as well as Ahmad Shah and Mohammad Ali Shah from the Qajar dynasty, were deposed and died in exile. One was assassinated, and only one died of natural causes while serving as king, paving the way for a peaceful transition of power to his heir.

Up to now in the post-Khomeini era, Iran's rulers have continued the pattern (set during Khomeini's supervision of the Islamic system) of not allowing internal divisions to hamstring them in contending with external challenges to their collective rule. As previously noted, from 1990 to 1995 seven major spontaneous urban uprisings, generally involving urban squatters and shantytown dwellers, rocked Iran. The regime's response to all such disturbances, supported unanimously by all of the competing factions and personalities, was consistently swift, overwhelming, and ruthless repression. In sharp contrast to the shah, the Islamic system has not responded to disturbances with trepidation and half measures. Instead, it has created and made effective use of special antiriot forces, which are adept at rapidly suppressing uprisings in order to prevent them from spreading. To ensure its survival, the regime has not shied away from meting out summary executions, either. Indeed, according to one estimation, "in the twenty years of the rule of mullahs, 120,000 Iranians have been sentenced to death after quasi-legal proceedings—some forty times the number of those executed during the entire reign of the late Shah" (Akins, 1998).

However, the mullahs have also continued their tendency toward internal struggles and quarrels. Indeed, with the passing of Khomeini such schisms have become ever more bitter, though they have still been kept within bounds. We already have seen how the conservatives and the pragmatists conspired to prevent the radicals from achieving ascendancy in the Parliament in 1992. We also saw how this alliance incrementally unraveled in the course of the subsequent four years, when the conservatives utilized their domination over the Majles and the Council of Guardians in order to block or curtail the pragmatists' social and economic agenda.

During his tenure as president, however, Rafsanjani skillfully, patiently, and tactfully handled the assault of the conservatives by taking their considerations into account, demonstrating willingness to compromise with them on key issues and endeavoring to refrain from offending their sensibilities. Khamenei, meanwhile, seeking to bolster his position among the ulama, generally favored the demands of the conservative faction. At the same time, to assure everyone that there were no fundamental rifts between himself and Rafsanjani, from time to time Khamenei went out of his way to shower the Rafsanjani administration with lavish praise and approbation. "In the entire history of Iran," Khamenei declared at a time when there was widespread speculation that the two men had become estranged, "we have never had such a good collection of ministers." As for Rafsanjani, Khamenei pronounced him to be "a religious, learned man, struggling in the path of God, with complete competence regarding the affairs of the country, [and he is] experienced. All this goes without saying" ("Khamenehi Adores Prez and Full Cabinet," 1996). As a result, factional divisions did not become overly hostile, pronounced, or debilitating. But also as a result, the attempts of Rafsanjani and his followers to realize their objectives were frequently watered down or abandoned, despite their policy preferences generally being *more* in tune with the mood of the populace.

To enhance the prospects of achieving their visions, Rafsanjani's supporters created an entirely new reformist political organization in 1996, which they modestly named the Servants of Construction. Their aim was to use the organization as a political machine to compete with the conservative-dominated JRM, to bring about an end to the conservative domination of the Majles in the 1996 parliamentary elections, and eventually to transform their grouping into a full-fledged political party. Switching tactics, they also entered into a tacit political alliance with the radicals, most of whom, after their defeat in 1992, had withdrawn from the political scene, had developed a new respect for political tolerance, and had modified their advocacy of etatist economic policies. Nevertheless, probably at the urging of Rafsanjani, "in a bid to play down its differences with the opposition [conservative] faction, the moderates . . . inserted on their own list the names of ten [JRM] candidates," including Nategh Nouri (the conservative Speaker of Majles)" (Daniszewski, 1996a; "Rival Factions Within Leadership Contest Iran Elections," 1996). The differences between the factions, however, were now visibly apparent and were becoming increasingly open.

Such differences became even more glaring during the 1997 presidential campaign. In 1996, the conservatives had utilized their control over the Council of Guardians to vet the candidacy of several pragmatist and radical candidates. As a result, they continued to retain the largest number of seats in the Majles, although they lost their absolute majority. To improve their position in the country's power structure, the pragmatists and the radicals once again joined forces and threw their weight behind the presidential candidacy of Mohammad Khatami. Khatami was a former minister of culture and professor of philosophy who had distinguished himself by his tolerant interpretation of Islamic principles as well as his attempt to reconcile what he regarded as the most salutary components of modern Western culture with Islam. Under pressure from conservative deputies, who had accused him of being excessively lax and permissive, Khatami had resigned from his post at the Ministry of Culture in 1992. Somewhat unusual among Shia clerics, Khatami, apart from proper Islamic credentials, holds university degrees in philosophy and education. Significantly, he has devoted many of his scholarly publications and much of his teaching career to expounding and propagating historic and contemporary attempts at reconciling Islam with modernity.

The differences between Khatami and his archrival for the presidency, Nategh Nouri, were great. Khatami advocated the opening up of the system, encouraging the development of a vibrant civil society, institutionalizing the rule of law to prevent arbitrary rule, and expanding the realm of permissible social, political, and personal activities ("Khatami's 12-Point Platform Long on Individual Rights," 1997; "Khatami: Economy Needs Urgent Care," 1997; "Khatami Takes Daring Liberal Line in First Campaign Speech," 1977). Nouri, by contrast, emphasized the need to combat the cultural invasion of the West and the need to create a more Islamically pure society. Never before in the history of the Islamic Republic or, for that matter, the monarchy, had the public been offered a more clear-cut choice. Although highly circumscribed (the Council of Guardians rejected the candidacy of 234 out of the 238 aspiring candidates) the election was a genuine contest, and it managed to rouse the nation's populace.

There is no doubt that a significant proportion of the ruling elite, including the supreme leader (implicitly) and the members of the powerful conservative faction (explicitly), favored Nouri's candidacy. Indeed, not only was Nouri much more prominently featured on radio and television (controlled by the conservatives), but both the Council of Guardians and a group of leading theologians associated with Khamenei in the holy city of Ghom made their support for Nouri abundantly clear. Some conservatives endeavored to cast doubt on Khatami's commitment to the system by portraying him as a dangerous "liberal." The former commander of the Revolutionary Guards, Mohsen Rezai, who occupied this sensitive position for sixteen years before being switched to another post by Khamenei in 1997, is reported to have announced that the Revolutionary Guards "would not allow 'liberals' to rule in Iran" ("Iran Quarterly Reports," 1997; "Rezai Wanted Out 3 Years Ago," 1997). Others, notably Hezbollahi zealots, went so far as to disrupt Khatami's campaign rallies ("Brawl Breaks Up Khatami Campaign Speech in Mashad," 1997). However, Khatami, whom many Iranians had scarcely heard of prior to the start of the campaign, was able to achieve his stunning victory in large measure because of the conservative establishment's support for his archrival Nouri. Khatami's ability to garner 20.7 million (70 percent) of the 29.7 million ballots cast (with 90 percent of eligible voters [those above the age of fifteen] going to the polls) is a clear indication of the extent of popular dissatisfaction, especially among the country's youthful population, with the status quo.

The Impact of Khatami's Election: From Open Confrontations and Widening Schisms to Unrestrained and Debilitating Factionalism?

Attempting to close the divisions that had opened up during the election campaign, all of the Islamic Republic's key political figures from competing factions took part in a demonstration of national unity on the occasion of the eighth anniversary of Ayatollah Khomeini's death on June 6, 1997. During this gathering, the supreme leader Khamenei went out of his way to argue that the immense voter turnout was, in fact, a resounding approval of the Islamic Republic rather than an expression of discontent (as the "enemies of Islam" had maintained). Sitting side by side, all leaders, including the newly elected Khatami, brandished their revolutionary credentials, seeking to demonstrate that in spite of their disagreements on policy, they were united on preserving the legacy of Khomeini and destroying the enemies of the system ("Shrine Focus for Unity Pledges," 1997).

Subsequent events have demonstrated, however, that the show of unity was deceptive since the "preservation of the legacy of Khomeini," a vague and nebulous objective, has itself come to be interpreted differently by the reformers (composed of a vast proportion of the pragmatists and former radicals, most of whom have now come to embrace varying shades of political and economic moderation) and the conservatives (themselves increasingly divided among those who are willing to resort to violence in order to block moderate reforms and those who, although generally opposed to reform, abhor violence and fear that it might lead to the dissolution of the system).

Speaking in defense of violent acts designed to safeguard an "Islamic" society, Ayatollah Mohammad Taqi Mesbah Yazdi, a hard-liner who occasionally leads the Tehran Friday prayers, has declared: "Tolerance and compromise are presented as positive values while violence is portrayed only in negative terms . . . The taboo that says every act of violence is ipso facto bad must be broken . . . the enemies of Islam must feel the harsh and violent hand of Islam" ("Clerics Brawl over Utility of Violence," 1999). Khatami and his reformist allies, in the meantime, have consistently denounced violence as inimical to the rule of law and the proper functioning of civil society, which they endeavor to create. Shortly after the suppression of student riots in the summer of 1999, Khatami addressed a group of his supporters and declared: "Violence in any shape or form is abhorrent and deplorable, as our eminent leader said in his recent remarks . . . The supporters of violence are committing a mistake no matter what their rationale. In fact, their guilt is compounded when they use violence on the basis of religious sanctions (quoted in "Khatami Says It's Time to Get Rid of Street Toughs," 1999).

Khatami's intelligence minister, Hojatoleslam Ali Yunesi (who is himself a rather conservative cleric and replaced Dori Najafabadi, because Khamenei wanted the ministry to remain under conservative control after it was revealed that "rouge" elements from within the ministry were responsible for the killing of writers and dissidents) has even pledged to suppress and prosecute Hezbollahi thugs and vigilantes, who justify the use of violence against anyone they deem to be insufficiently devoted to the revolution. In the words of Yunesi, "Most of the members of this minority group are motivated by religious values, but they are extreme, harsh and self-willed people headed for destruction" ("Yunesi Pledges Crackdown on Street Toughs for 1st Time," 1999). Some in the reformist camp are seeking to exploit the divisions among the conservatives by forging an alliance with the "rational" segment of this group. The outcome of this project is unclear and remains in doubt.

However, unlike Rafsanjani, who was willing to accommodate the conservatives, Khatami, with the support (even if acquired through default and the absence of other viable alternatives) of the overwhelming majority of the electorate behind him, appears less willing to compromise on his principles. At the same time, though, he has proved himself to be a cautious politician, devoted to preserving the Islamic system and avoiding head-on clashes with his political opponents, preferring instead to pursue his reforms incrementally through legal and peaceful means. To avoid hopelessly offending the sensibilities of the conservatives and to guard against making himself vulnerable to the charge of endeavoring to undermine the system, Khatami has thus far refused to appoint any Islamist "radical" reformers (those who intend to accelerate the pace of reform and allow even some secularists to enter the political process not only as participants but also as contestants) to top-level decisionmaking positions. But the conservatives, alarmed about the ideological and, perhaps more important, the social and political ramifications of Khatami's reforms (the reasonable concern that they may come to lose their enormous power, privileges, and status in a pluralistic, more popularly based political order), have sought to derail the realization of Khatami's platform. But few as yet have dared to attack Khatami personally. Instead, they have concentrated on undermining his deputies and taking indirect swipes at his policies.

Nor is this all. In the relatively more open atmosphere that Khatami has managed to create since his assumption of power in August 1997, the at times fierce intraregime schisms have come to be increasingly aired and heralded. In a speech to a closed and confidential meeting of Pasdaran officers in May 1998, the contents of which were apparently recorded and leaked to the pro-Khatami press, the commander of the Pasdaran, Brigadier General Yahya Rahim Safavi, is reported to have told the officers that the time was ripe for cracking down on dissent. In his remarks, Safavi is reported to have singled out two of Khatami's ministers, Ataollah Mohajerani, the minister of culture and Islamic guidance, and Hojatoleslam Abdullah Nouri, who at the time was serving as Khatami's minister of the interior, for special rebuke. Mohajerani is disliked by the conservatives for having relaxed the rules of censorship and for allowing the publication of "liberal" newspapers, while Nouri is despised for having authorized rallies by proreform groups.

Safavi is reputed to have said:

> [L]iberals have entered the foray with cultural artillery. They have taken over our universities, and our youth are now shouting slogans against despotism . . . We are seeking to root out anti-revolutionaries wherever they are. We have to cut the throats of some and cut off the tongues of others. Our language is the sword. We will expose these cowards . . . Newspapers are published these days that are threatening our national security. They contain the same material as American newspapers. ("Pasdar Commander Is Furious over Press Leak of His Speech," 1998)

While asserting that Safavi's remarks had been distorted, Safavi's office put out a statement that also ominously warned about "poisonous pens that misuse the new atmosphere of tolerance to inculcate their sick and contaminated ideas . . . to abandon this unseemly trend that seeks to deflect public opinion from the plots and hostile intentions of Iran's sworn enemies and create tension and division within the ranks of the people" ("Pasdar Commander Is Furious over Press Leak of His Speech," 1998).

It can be inferred that Safavi's remarks were leaked by proreform officers present at the confidential Pasdaran meeting who were seeking to embarrass and expose Safavi. Thus, even though the Pasdaran is headed by a staunch conservative and undoubtedly houses numerous conservatives within its officer corps and rank and file, it cannot be assumed to be beholden to them. Indeed, Khatami's margin of victory is so enormous that the Revolutionary Guards, in spite of having been urged by their leadership to support the candidacy of Nategh Nouri, must have overwhelmingly voted for Khatami. And what is true of the Guards can apply, with equal force, to members of the regular army and, perhaps with less certainty, to the Basij. It cannot be taken for granted, therefore, that if the current intraelite divisions degenerate into irreconcilable schisms, the conservatives will automatically emerge triumphant because of their control of the coercive apparatus. Rather, the armed forces, reflecting the divisions among the elite, are themselves likely to split, paving the way for open confrontation and warfare within and between the nation's motley repressive apparatus. Although the outcome of this struggle cannot be predicted, we can venture to guess that the more popular forces are more likely to prevail.

One of the most serious tensions thus far between the ruling factions erupted in April 1998, when Iran's conservative-dominated judiciary, under the leadership of Ayatollah Mohammad Yazdi (a particularly fierce and uncompromising partisan) ordered the arrest of Tehran's pragmatist and staunchly pro-Khatami mayor, Gholam Hossein Karbaschi. The mayor, who was appointed by Rafsanjani and managed Iran's capital of 10 million people for almost nine years, was charged with financial corruption, including influence peddling, receiving bribes, embezzling approximately $5 million, and misappropriating public funds to finance political campaigns (Sciolino, 1998b). Although Karbaschi's guilt had not as yet been substantiated, his arrest was justified by the judiciary on the basis of a law that permits the detention of suspected individuals up to thirty days prior to trial. Indeed, from the beginning, most conservatives—spearheaded by Yazdi, who devoted most of his Friday sermons to discussing the injustices committed by Tehran's municipality—asserted (without demonstrating) Karbaschi's guilt.

Karbaschi's reformist allies, however, vehemently asserted the mayor's innocence, claiming that the arrest had been politically motivated. Indeed, several months prior to his arrest, when first faced with investigations of wrongdoing, Karbaschi himself had complained that the "investigations were political harassment by conservatives"[8] ("Sweating Mayors Write Resignations," 1997). Following Karbaschi's arrest, Faezeh Hashemi, who is the daughter of former president Rafsanjani, a leading reformist, and a Majles deputy from Tehran, declared, "This affair [the mayor's arrest] has a political color to it . . . Karbaschi's arrest is a blow to democracy and to political and cultural reform." Similarly, the entire cabinet of President Khatami expressed "sorrow and regret" over the arrest, "of the successful and ambitious mayor" (Jehl, 1998), and asserted that "the charges [against the mayor] did not conform to reality" ("Karbaschi Jailed for Corruption," 1998).

To underscore their claim that the persecution of Karbaschi was a politically motivated effort by the conservatives to thwart Khatami's reforms, the reformers pointed to the fact that Karbaschi had been a founding member of the Servants of Construction and had played an instrumental role in promoting Khatami's presidential campaign. It was also pointed out that Karbaschi's widely popular measures to beautify Tehran had been financed by imposing hefty taxes on many powerful bazaaris to whom the conservatives were beholden.

Tensions soared as top leaders of the Islamic Republic openly broke with one another over the question of Karbaschi's arrest. In interviews with the media, Yazdi, chairman of the judiciary, launched an attack on those who claimed that the prosecution of the mayor was driven by political ulterior motives. In a public and pointed repudiation of Yazdi, Rafsanjani declared that the mayor had been a "victim of character assassination." He went on to say that "we should not allow differences of style and factionalism to damage the prestige and integrity of capable and competent people." Whereas Rafsanjani had avoided attacking Yazdi by name, Abdullah Nouri, the minister of interior, in an unprecedented event in the history of the Islamic Republic, publicly stated, "I hope in the future that Mr. Yazdi will respect the position that he holds." Nouri also went on to launch an indirect attack on the conservative-dominated Council of Guardians for arbitrarily excluding many of the reformist candidates who had expressed interest in standing for the Majles by-elections ("Nuri Attacks Yazdi by Name for Misconduct in Office," 1998). Underlying the close collaboration of the erstwhile radicals and pragmatists, the former radical Speaker of the Majles, Mehdi Karubi, also came to the defense of the embattled mayor ("Yazdi May Jail Reporter for Asking," 1998).

As the detention of Karbaschi continued, the polarization of the ruling elite became more pronounced. In a Friday congregational prayer sermon, Rafsanjani lamented the "unlawful way the Judiciary had handled the case [of Karbaschi]." He also called the incident "an historical injustice . . . [that] is one of the bitter moments of our recent history." Rafsanjani's speech was interrupted, however, by a group of hecklers who chanted that "the plunderer of public treasury must be executed." Undeterred, Rafsanjani asked rhetorically: "[W]ho is to absolve the many people, including the Youth, who have become cynical about the Revolution because of the notion that there is widespread corruption in the country?" He then went on to make the astounding argument that it would be tragic for the Islamic Republic to commit the mistake of the shah by imprisoning presumed political opponents ("Rafsanjani Heckled During Friday Sermons," 1998). Of course, he neglected to mention that this is precisely what the Islamic Republic has been doing since its inception, except now it was happening to one of Rafsanjani's own political allies.

Given the charged political atmosphere, it did not take long for the sharp rifts among the nation's ruling elite to spill onto the streets. Emboldened by the election victory of Khatami, at least 4,000 Tehran University students took part in a demonstration calling for Karbaschi's release, even though the Khatami administration had asked the students not to engage in demonstrations. Moreover, as the students left the university campus and ventured into the city, the demonstration "attracted ordinary citizen marchers like a magnet." According to reporters present on the scene, the demonstration was finally broken up through the intervention of baton-wielding police, who, according to some reports, also used tear gas ("First Unauthorized Demonstration Backs Mayor," 1998; Wright, 1998).

Seeking to quell what had turned into an increasingly raucous crisis, Khamenei is reported to have asked the nation's key players, including Khatami,

Rafsanjani, Yazdi, and Nategh Nouri, to find a mutually acceptable, face-saving solution. Apparently, the leaders were unable to do so, largely due to Yazdi's intransigence. Finally, responding to a letter written to him by Khatami, the supreme leader ordered Yazdi to release Karbaschi, pending a public trial. Seeking to demonstrate his "unquestionable obedience to the instructions issued by the eminent leader," Yazdi promptly obliged. In so doing, he argued that his action had "thwarted foreign enemies and their agents inside the country who wanted to exploit the case to harm the interests of Iran and its system of government" ("Mayor Freed at Request of Khamenehi," 1998).

In his letter to Khamenei, the text of which was released to the Iranian media, Khatami asserted:

> I believe that the continuation of the current situation is not in the interests of the system or society . . . Our policy, endorsed by yourself, is to have a system of law and to maintain social, economic, and judicial security in the country . . . I further believe, in this case, that the continued detention of the mayor of Tehran can only serve to complicate matters, disrupt the process of state management, and pave the way for improper confrontations and ill-judged statements by people of different persuasions, leading, eventually, to the *unraveling of all forces* . . . Therefore, I beg to your eminence that the mayor of Tehran be released. (emphasis added) ("Letters on Karbaschi Case," 1998).

Khamenei's clear siding with the reformists in this particular instance was undoubtedly a significant blow to the conservative forces. It showed that Khamenei, despite his hitherto conservative leanings, is clearly cognizant of the greater popular appeal of the reformers and is willing to act as the final arbiter, even if it means going against the interests of his allies, in order to promote stability. But the struggle for power is far from over, and its outcome is far from clear. Karbaschi was subsequently found guilty of embezzlement by a conservative jurist, who served as both a prosecutor and a judge, and was sentenced to five years in prison, sixty lashes, and a monetary fine. He was also banned from government employment for twenty years. Due to his contributions to the revolution, however, his lashing sentence was suspended. Despite requests from Khatami, Rafsanjani, and other prominent reformers, the conservative-dominated appeals courts refused to commute or overturn Karbaschi's sentence. What is more, Khamenei, now seeking to emulate Khomeini's modus operandi of alternatively siding with different factions so that none will feel excluded or alienated, has refused to pardon Karbaschi. In response to a letter signed by 146 of the Majles' 235 deputies, implicitly asking the supreme leader to pardon Karbaschi, Khamenei declared: "Defending our leaders has its place and I approve of that. But I don't want it to turn into judicial immunity for failure to respect the law . . . It would be best if the honorable deputies and other officials did not rail public opinion, which is the goal of our enemies" (Karbaschi Gets 5 Years Behind Bars," 1998). In prison, however, Karbaschi reportedly receives perks and privileges, such as catered meals, access to two mobile phones, and permission not to wear the prison uniform, which are denied to other prisoners ("Mayor Goes First Class in Evin Cell," 1999).

As events unfold, the conservatives have certainly not given up trying to thwart the reformer's policies. In the summer of 1998, Abdullah Nouri, the minister of interior, narrowly failed to win a vote of confidence in an impeachment proceeding convened at the behest of conservative deputies in the Majles. Nouri's primary offenses were that he had "issued permits for meetings that resulted in violence [and had been] giving provocative speeches and interviews." Nouri had allowed advocates of reform, including those who are seeking to change the electoral laws so as to prevent the Council of Guardians from arbitrarily rejecting candidates, to take part in demonstrations. Although several of these demonstrations had resulted in injuries, the violence had not been instigated by the demonstrators but by the Hezbollahi thugs who had attacked the peaceful marchers. The reference to provocative utterances concerns Nouri's staunch expressions of support for Karbaschi while the latter was detained for eleven days ("Nouri Faces Majlis Confidence Vote," 1998).

Spearheading the right-wing onslaught against Nouri, Majles deputy Mohammad Reza Bahonar "warned that Nouri was leading Iran toward divisions as severe as those in Yugoslavia. Opening Iran to 'suspicious groups' will have an unstable result so that 'no stone will stay on top of the others'" (Peterson, 1998, p. 7). In the clashes between hard-liners and reformers during the course of some of the demonstrations licensed by Nouri, the Hezbollahis are reported to have chanted "Death to opponents of *velayat-e faqih*," while the reformists had countered, "Death to monopoly of power" ("Embassy Rally Turns into Battle," 1997). Although the conservatives took care not to mention Khatami or his overall policies during the impeachment proceedings against Nouri, it was apparent that their assault was directed against Khatami's reform agenda. After all, Khatami had earlier gone out of his way to defend Nouri as "one of the most competent ministers whose absence would harm both the government and the nation" (Peterson, 1998, p. 7). He had also declared that "it may be possible to silence all voices for a while. However, these silent voices will eventually emerge in the form of an explosion" ("Suppression Will Cause 'Explosion,'" 1998). Undaunted by the legislative assault, Khatami immediately selected Nouri to be vice president for development and social affairs, a position that does not require the approval of the Majles.

Khatami, meanwhile, appointed another moderate, Abdol-Vahed Musavi Lari, as Nouri's replacement. Nouri subsequently resigned from this position in order to take part in the February 1999 municipal elections as a candidate for Tehran. Once again demonstrating their extreme dissatisfaction with the conservatives, Tehran's electorate voted for Nouri by enormous margins, turning him into by far the largest vote receiver in the elections. Lari, who is much more low key and far less confrontational than Nouri, was promptly approved by the Majles. More significantly, Nouri's dismissal served to enhance the bonds between the supreme leader and Khatami. Not trusting Nouri, Khamenei, who is the commander in chief of Iran's armed and security forces, had refused to allow Nouri to exert authority over the nation's police force (Amuzegar, 1998, p. 79; "Lari Is Named to Command Police," 1998). Lari's appointment, however, caused Khamenei to sign over nominal control over the nation's law enforcement agencies to the interior minister, granting Lari a power that had previously been routinely bestowed upon all other previous interior ministers (except Nouri). This move, in turn, served to augment the power and bolster the position of Khatami and the reformist camp vis-à-vis their political opponents.

Indeed, fully cognizant that the still-popular Khatami represents the theocracy's best hope of making itself more palatable to the disgruntled masses, especially the alienated and frustrated youth, Khamenei has not hesitated to throw his support behind Khatami at other critical junctures. In the summer of 1999, at the height of the most serious and widespread demonstrations in the history of the Islamic Republic since the Mojahedin had sought to overthrow the theocracy in 1981 (which was infiltrated by right-wing provocateurs and degenerated into street riots, as noted in Chapter 3), twenty-four of the leading commanders of the Revolutionary Guards wrote Khatami a letter in which they declared that their patience with the president's reform program was coming to a halt. They also threatened, albeit implicitly, to instigate a coup d'état against the president unless Khatami cracked down on the demonstrations. In their letter, the commanders complained:

> Our hands are tied [as we] watch the wilting of the flower [revolution]. Enemies are entering the fray in droves . . . we can see the footprints of the enemy . . . We can hear its drunken crackle. You must understand this today because tomorrow will be too late . . . How long must we observe this with tears? How long must we suffer in silence? . . . *We cannot accept that nothing is done* (my italics) ("Coup Letter Is Repudiated by Pasdar Chief," 1999).

It is now clear that it was Khamenei who, in exchange for the president's agreement to close ranks behind the aim of suppressing the demonstrations, reigned in the Pasdar commanders. Khamenei also apparently persuaded his protégé, the commander of the Pasdaran, General Yahya Safavi, who had conspicuously not signed the letter and only a year previously had declared his intention to slit the throat of "liberals," to repudiate the letter written by his subordinates. Four days after the publication of the confidential letter by three conservative dailies, Safavi declared: "The Pasdaran have always been a supporter of President Khatami and would not tolerate the acts of those who [have] sought to diminish the role and stature of the presidency . . . We [the Pasdaran] will support the president with all our might and will not tolerate any insult against him" (quoted in "Coup Letter Is Repudiated by Pasdar Chief," 1999).

Following the squelching of the demonstrations (which was successfully and bloodlessly accomplished by the police and club-wielding Basiji, without the intervention of the Revolutionary Guards) and, significantly, after Khatami had reiterated his commitment to pursuing his reform agenda and declared his government's intention to crack down on street toughs, Khamenei stated publicly: "I support the respected president and the job he is doing 100 percent" (quoted in "Iran's Holy Alliance," 1999). Khamenei also praised Khatami's response to the protests, asserting that "His [Khatami's] handling of events was completely proper . . . There are no differences among the leadership." In addition, seeking to temper nasty factional struggles, Khamenei selected Ayatollah Mahmud Hashemi-Shahrudi to replace Mohammad Yazdi, whose second five-year term as chairman of the judicial branch of government expired in August 1999. Although a conservative, Hashemi is respected by many leading moderates and is purported to be a far less partisan and confrontational figure than Yazdi ("Hashemi Is Going to Replace Yazdi," 1999). It should be recalled that Khamenei even assisted Khatami in exposing several rather high-ranking proponents of violence and murder in the ministry of intelligence. He also assented to the detention and trial of seven top-ranking security officials for their involvement in the ransacking of a Tehran University student hostel, which sparked the student demonstrations. According to one of Khamenei's close aides, the president regularly consults with the supreme leader, and the two have developed a special relationship, which has possibly diminished Khamenei's dependence on hard-liners. Khatami himself has sought to exploit his close working relationship with Khamenei, declaring, "My government is trying to fulfill the views of the leader" ("Iran's Holy Alliance," 1999).

There are, however, limits to the extent to which Khamenei has sought to protect Khatami and promote the cause of the reformist camp. Khamenei has consistently been careful not to alienate the affections of the mainstream conservative faction. He has also sought to preserve his own power and has been on guard against jeopardizing the concept of *velayat-e faqih*. He has appointed conservative clerics to significant posts, particularly in the judiciary, and has refused to interfere with their partisan decisions. Above all, he has refused to curtail the power of the Council of Guardians or to transform its nature as a bastion of conservatism. Upon his retirement from his position as the chairman of the judiciary, for instance, Yazdi was immediately appointed by Khamenei to become a member of the Council of Guardians.

Prior to the 1998 election for the selection of the members of the Assembly of Experts, whose members are elected every ten years and are empowered to select (and if they deem it essential, remove) the supreme leader, the Council of Guardians vetted the vast preponderance of prospective reformist candidates. In November 1999, in a move that in all likelihood was designed to prevent Abdullah Nouri from running for the position of Majles Speaker in the aftermath of the February 2000 parliamentary elections, the special clerical court found Nouri guilty of spreading lies, sowing confusion, and opposing Islam. The special court, which is controlled by the conservatives and was established by the decree of Ayatollah Khomeini in order to bring recalcitrant members of the clergy into line, sentenced Nouri to five years in prison. The court operates outside the judicial branch of government and is answerable only to the supreme leader. The charges against Nouri stemmed from articles that had been published in the daily *Khordad*, whose license was held by Nouri. These articles had questioned the wisdom of forcing the *hejab* (veil) on women, had argued in favor of the rehabilitation of Ayatollah Montazeri and reestablishing relations with the United States, and had referred to the Liberation Movement and the National Front as "honorable" organizations. During the trial, Nouri won the hearts of many disgruntled Iranians by refusing to recognize the legality and legitimacy of the clerical court (for which there are no provisions in the Constitution), defending the articles in *Khordad*, and arguing forcefully that no one (including the supreme leader) is above the law. Khamenei and a large proportion of the conservative establishment, however, were apparently not amused ("Jury to Nuri: Guilty," 1999; "Nuri Rushed Off to 5 Years in Prison," 1999; "Fire-Breathing Nuri Tells Court Where It Can Go," 1999; Burns, 1999).

However, as noted, insofar as the reformists are concerned, there have also been some silver linings on the horizon. In a compromise probably prompted by Khamenei, designed to avert another potentially threatening street uprising, leading conservatives and reformists have reached consensus on how the Council of Guardians should screen candidates for the 2000 Majles elections. The Expediency Council, which derives its members from the leaders of the various factions, has decided that the Council of Guardians, departing from precedent, must now provide rejected candidates with a written justification, explaining the rationale behind their disqualification. Rejected candidates will also be permitted to appeal the council's decision, but the appeal will be directed back to the council itself. Although insignificant, the compromise, which is unlikely to have been reached without Khamenei's approval, indicates that despite his rhetoric and extremist pronouncements, Khamenei is not the archconservative he is frequently made out to be. Indeed, it appears that Khamenei, if he deems it to be essential and expedient, can even begin the process of diminishing his reliance upon the conservative camp.

It remains to be seen whether Khamenei will tilt toward the position of the reformists after the inauguration of the newly enlarged 6th Majles in May 2000. With the conservatives having been dealt yet another humiliating defeat by Iran's disgruntled, youthful, and politically conscious electorate, the reformist coalition (whose largest group is headed by Mohammad Reza Khatami, President Khatami's younger brother, who is a physician by training) is undoubtedly going to dominate the new parliament. The reformists, who are themselves a heterogeneous lot composed of 18 different tendencies, clearly agree on the overarching aim of institutionalizing a more liberal interpretation of the constitution in order to open the system socially, politically, and culturally and improve Iran's relations with the outside world. But they are likely to splinter over the scale and scope of liberalizing political and economic reforms.

The former radical clerics, who have now joined the reformist camp, are primarily interested in reconciling Islam with modernity and pluralism. But there is a question as to the extent to which they are willing to secularize and open up the system. Furthermore, although most of them have modified their statist ideology, the radical clerical association still contains individuals who favor an étatist approach to economic development. The centrist Servants of Construction, by contrast, are primarily interested in reinvigorating the Iranian economy through the initiation of privatization and deregulation measures. Meanwhile, the Islamic Iran Participation Front, which is headed by President Khatami's brother and constitutes the largest reformist block, is most keen on expeditiously institutionalizing freedoms and democratizing the system. But there are divisions within the block itself on allowing secular forces to contest elections and the desirability and scale of economic liberalization.

Regardless of their divisions, however, having captured control of Iran's parliament, the reformists will be held more directly responsible by the nation's impatient population, who will expect the reformers to generate an upturn in the economy and take concrete steps toward lifting social and private restrictions and democratize the polity. In the short term, Khamenei and the weakened, yet still powerful, conservatives will probably tone down their rhetoric and assume a wait and see posture. But they are likely to be on the lookout to detect and exploit the divisions, which are bound to arise in the reformist camp. Many of today's reformists are destined to become the conservatives of tomorrow.

In the long run, however, the ruling elite cannot remain oblivious to the fundamental demographic and cultural shifts and trends within the nation's civil society. The children of the revolution will ultimately devour the revolution, and the leaders who are more in tune with the mood of the populace are more likely to prevail. The question, of course, is whether this transformation will take place through reform or revolution.

Notes

1. Abrahamian (1982) maintains that SAVAK had over 5,300 full-time members.

2. Initiating the Expediency Council on February 6, 1988, Ayatollah Khomeini declared: "[I]n case the Islamic Assembly [Majles] and the Surveillance Council [Council of Guardians] fail to reach an agreement in matters concerning the *shari'a* and laws, a chamber . . . for the safeguarding of the regime's supreme interest must be created . . . All honorable members must bear in mind that the safeguarding of the Islamic regime's supreme interest is a vital necessity, the neglect of which would toll the knell of our dear Islam . . . The regime and the population's supreme interest in of utmost importance; its neglect would endanger Islam of the disinherited for an indefinite period of time, leaving the victory to the American Islam of the powerful and arrogant" (quoted in Niknam, 1999, p. 19).

3. Quoted from an interview with the *Guardian*, January 19, 1974.

4. On Khomeini's doubts, see Bakhash (1984), p. 45. On Bazargan, see Brzezinski (1983), p. 395.

5. See also Zonis (1991), pp. 92–93. According to Zonis, during the early stages of the revolution, the governor of the province of Khorasan, Colonel Abdul Azim Vallian (prohibited from acting on his own initiative), had called to seek the shah's instructions on how to deal with demonstrations in his province. After a long delay, he was given the following vague and contradictory orders by the shah. In the words of Vallian, "He [the shah] told me to let the demonstrations go on but to control and contain them. But under no circumstances was I to let the troops shoot at the crowds" (quoted in Zonis [1991], p. 93).

6. This assertion is consonant with the conclusions drawn by Carter's national security adviser, Zbigniew Brzezinski. See Brzezinski (1983), pp. 371–375.

7. In this regard, one of the experiences of the American air force general Robert E. (Dutch) Huyser, who was sent by President Carter to Iran during the final days of the shah's rule, is particularly illuminating. The objective of his mission to Iran was to "encourage the Iranian military to support Bakhtiar's civilian government's plan for possible direct military action to bolster the civilian regime, [and] support a military takeover by Iranian forces if public order collapsed" (Sick [1987], p. 163). However, commencing work on January 18, with the full might of Iran's armed forces at his command, Huyser was not even able to realize the much more humble objective of unloading the contents of a U.S. oil tanker when he departed Iran on February 3, 1979 (Huyser [1986], pp. 146, 194, 205, 222; see also Arjomand [1988], p. 126).

8. The daily newspaper *Hamshahri*, which is published by Tehran's municipality, was launched by Karbaschi shortly before the 1997 presidential election. Prior to the campaign, the newspaper took a leading role in promoting Khatami, who at the time was considered a long-shot candidate. The conservatives never forgave Karbaschi for his promotion of Khatami. Nor did they forgive him for the fact that during his tenure as mayor, "the municipality effectively entered Tehran's commodity distribution network by establishing nearly 50 produce markets throughout the city and by building two department store chains, organized as joint stock companies with publicly issued shares. These projects were viewed as political challenges to the traditional merchant capital of the bazaar" (quoted in Ehsani, 1999a, p. 24).

7

Conclusion:
The Problem of Revolution Revisited

Up to now, history has been unkind to those who have tried to predict the course of Iran's political trajectory. When the Allies invaded Iran in 1941 and forced Reza Shah to abdicate in favor of his son, few thought that the young and inexperienced Mohammad Reza had more than a minuscule chance of retaining power. Yet his reign lasted thirty-seven years, and even as late as six months prior to his demise, the vast majority of analysts, including those employed by the CIA, were unanimous in maintaining that the shah's rule was secure. Following the overthrow of the shah, many of these same commentators, engaging in ex post facto analysis, published books in which they explained why, given the monarchy's fragile popular base and the neopatrimonial nature of the shah's rule, the destruction of the Pahlavi dynasty was virtually preordained. After the revolution, few thought that Khomeini and his followers, even if they were interested in governing Iran, would prevail in the postrevolutionary power struggle. Once a theocracy was established, however, most analysts projected that the clerical order would not survive the death of its charismatic founder. Writing in 1985, Mohsen Milani, who subsequently became one of the foremost scholars of the Iranian revolution, summed up the prevailing consensus among the scholarly community: "Upon Khomeini's death, a period of intense rivalry and a bloody power struggle among competing centers of power will begin. It is precisely at this conjuncture that the opposition can play a determining role" (Milani, 1985, p. 486).

Seeking partially to accomplish what far more qualified individuals have failed to achieve, I am fully cognizant that the conclusions of this study can prove to be just as inappropriate as the propositions of those who have previously sought "to extrapolate some plausible trends on the basis of current configurations" (Bernard and Khalilzad, 1984, p. xiii). Nevertheless, however rash and audacious my intention may be, I now proceed to assess the prospects for regime change in Iran. My only consolation is that the conclusions that are about to be proffered are based on an in-depth, theoretically informed, comparative analysis of present-day and prerevolutionary Iran. Moreover, I am not seeking to provide a precise prediction, which is impossible, but rather to narrow the range of possibilities by examining some of the factors that make regime changes more likely, not inevitable.

It has been the contention of this study that the revolutionary obliteration of an existing regime generally results from the convergence of two sets of interrelated variables: the regime's internal defects and vulnerabilities and the coordinated actions of the social groups and individuals opposed to it. In this analysis of the varieties of revolution, two "ideal-typical" forms of revolutionary change (collapses and overthrows) have been identified. In the past, some regimes have fallen with minimal coordinated, prolonged, and purposive popular endeavor (collapse). Others, however, although fragile, would not have been destroyed without the concerted pressures and demands placed upon them from within civil society (overthrow). As we have seen, the 1979 Iranian revolution belongs to the latter case. Based on the analyses presented in the previous chapters, prospects for the overthrow of the Islamic Republic are currently low. However, the chances for the obliteration or modification of the prevailing order, because of debilitating factional rivalries and confrontations, are moderate.

The analyses in the previous chapters have shown that although an increasing number of Iranians have become alienated from the theocratic order, the disjunction between the Islamic Republic and Iranian society is not as great as it was in the prerevolutionary era. Unlike the previous regime, the theocracy enjoys a solid base of devoted adherents who can readily be mobilized in support of the regime. Intragroup divisions have split the Iranian class structure, producing a social environment less conducive to a revolutionary transfer of power. From the perspective of their survival, Iran's politicized clerics have acted far more wisely than the shah by not dissolving their links with all of the significant components of the nation's civil society. Although not politically accountable, many of the regime's governmental institutions and officials are now to some extent responsive to different constituencies within Iranian society. Unlike the shah's regime, the theocracy is not bereft of politically significant social underpinnings.

Nevertheless, although the present regime is endowed with firmer social roots than the previous one, it is certainly not supported and accepted by the majority of the population. As we have seen, the economy is in a shambles, and most people's standards of living are lamentable. Social, political, and private restrictions are despised by a large fraction of the populace (especially the young), and the glaring disparity between the pious pronouncements of the ruling clerics and the prevailing, rampant venality is a constant source of irritation.

The Islamic Republic, particularly in the post-Khomeini era, has exacerbated the divisions within the Shia establishment. Iran's unpoliticized ulama, who constitute a majority of the clerical class, are now for the most part dissatisfied with the prevailing political order. The cleavages separating them from the theocratic state, however, are not for the most part as pronounced as the rift was between the entire hierocracy and the enveloping secular state in prerevolutionary Iran. The oppositional ulama today are mostly reformist in outlook, and none of them is endowed with Khomeini's charismatic and popular appeal. Moreover, the fact that a segment of the hierocracy itself now controls the state apparatus serves to divide the ulama and thereby reduces their capacity for collective action. The political predominance of the ruling clergy also enables them to establish their dominion over the nation's mosques, something the shah was unable (or unwilling) to do. It must be recalled that without access to the mosque networks, the ulama would not have been able to orchestrate their spectacular mobilization during the revolutionary process.

The Islamic Republic today also has the backing of a wider segment of the bazaari community than the monarchy did in prerevolutionary Iran. Although many bazaaris are dissatisfied with the prevailing order, they are not as disaffected as they were under the shah. Unlike the shah, the theocracy has not intentionally endeavored to sever all links with the bazaar. Although highly unequal, various sectors of the bazaar are all endowed with a line of access to the regime. In prerevolutionary Iran, the bazaars were able to mobilize against the shah by utilizing the mosque network and taking full advantage of the reduced governmental repression resulting from the shah's liberalization policy. Today, however, the regime monopolizes the mosques (and even the reformists associated with Khatami) and is steadfastly vigilant against antirevolutionary activities. Divided and more effectively repressed, bazaaris today are less susceptible to the formation of cross-cutting alliances.

In addition, although the urban poor are generally dissatisfied with their plight, as with the bazaaris and the ulama, intraproletariat divisions between those who support and those who are disenchanted with the regime are much greater today than they were before the revolution. Deplorable living conditions may occasionally prompt portions of the urban poor to engage in spontaneous acts of rebellion, but such uncoordinated outbursts have been suppressed in the past and are likely to be controlled in the future. Given the present regime's effective monopoly and control over the nation's mosques and religious networks, it has now become exceptionally difficult for any opposition group to incite and coordinate the activities of that segment of the urban poor that is not connected with the regime.

In comparison to the ulama, the bazaaris, and the destitute, the proportion of intellectuals, those in the modern sector of the middle class, and entrepreneurs with any meaningful linkages to the theocracy is quite small. Being economically squeezed, politically constrained, and culturally alienated in many respects, these groups today find themselves in even more precarious positions than before the revolution. Whatever they might have expected to gain from the revolution has not materialized.

As the biggest losers of the revolution, they have become estranged from the clerical order, with their sense of disenchantment aggravated by the regime's paternalistic and meddlesome demeanor. From the perspective of these groups, however, the present regime does have an advantage over the previous one. Particularly after the emergence of Khatami, the regime's multiplicity of factions has begun to represent increasingly substantive choices to the electorate. The middle class, the intellectuals, and the business community favor Khatami because they regard the policies he espouses as the best possible alternative available to them under the current system. "Khatami is a mullah, but he is an enlightened and relatively tolerant mullah," is how most middle-class residents of Tehran describe Khatami. But precisely because of the existence of other powerful factions ("intolerant and ignorant mullahs"), Khatami's chances of fulfilling his campaign promises are far from being assured. Paradoxically, then, members of the middle and upper classes are now both alienated and hopeful. Their sense of alienation will undoubtedly be magnified if Khatami's reform measures are impeded. But if Khatami succeeds, in part or in full (which appears more likely, given the mood of the politically awakened populace and the fact that throughout history, more liberally inclined and popular groups have eventually prevailed over their extremist and doctrinaire adversaries), will Iran's disaffected social classes become satisfied, or will reform, as Alexis de Tocqueville argued, merely serve to whet their appetites for still more fundamental transformations?

Thus, though the present regime is endowed with firmer social foundations than the previous order, it certainly does not enjoy the active and unquestionable support and acceptance of the overwhelming preponderance of the populace. Indeed, anecdotal evidence and inferential logic suggest that a majority of the people are dissatisfied with their lot and discontented with the regime. But though there is large-scale public dissatisfaction, there is no active, organized, and consolidated opposition. If Iran's opposition forces had been more competent, they could have taken advantage of the power struggle in the ranks of the ruling clerics in order to expedite the demise of the theocracy. As we have seen, however, today the forces that are opposed to the theocracy remain hopelessly fragmented, organizationally weak, and bereft of any charismatic leaders or unifying ideologies. In all likelihood, they are incapable of orchestrating the coordinated action (which has also become more difficult because of intragroup divisions) necessary to dislodge the regime.

Effective, coordinated action entails, above all, the formation of a broadly based revolutionary coalition of the opposition groups that represent the society's major classes. It must be borne in mind that the shah's rule lasted thirty-seven years, primarily because he was able to keep the opposition forces from becoming united and largely decimated their organizational capacity. The shah was deposed when his diverse opponents, many of whom had no interest in establishing an Islamic theocracy in Iran, submitted to the charismatic leadership of Ayatollah Khomeini in order to overthrow the monarchy.

During the revolutionary process, the role and personality of Khomeini in holding the revolution's disparate supporters together became all the more important because the movement's ideological appeals were highly incoherent and diffuse (Greene, 1991, pp. 52–53). The ideology that justified the Iranian revolution was succinctly summarized by Khomeini when he repeatedly stated, referring to the shah, "This man must leave." It was thus left to Khomeini to stubbornly and courageously reassure his followers that the hour of deliverance was at hand and that they should not waver from the path of revolution.

Today's Iranian opposition forces are similarly composed of a variety of groups with a multiplicity of divergent ideologies. But none of the opposition leaders today can even remotely approximate Khomeini in terms of charismatic and popular appeal. There is also a fundamental question as to the extent to which the existing opposition groups represent Iran's major social classes. Moreover, the opposition has lost control of the mosque networks, which remain under the exclusive domain of the regime.

The theocratic regime's total control over Iran's religious institutions is extremely significant in terms of the regime's survival. It should be recalled that in prerevolutionary Iran, the mosque constituted the only significant institution in civil society that had been allowed to remain autonomous from the encroachment of the highly centralized state, which at the time was virtually synonymous with the shah. During the revolutionary process, it was the Shia hierocracy that was most instrumental in inciting, organizing, and directing the masses in anti-shah demonstrations.

Now, however, a proportion of the hierocracy itself dominates the state, and this domination provides the regime with certain benefits. First, the regime now effectively controls all institutions of civil society, including the mosques. Second, instead of the exclusive leadership of the shah, the hierocracy provides the regime with a more collective leadership. Although the collective leadership of the mullahs, with their pervasive factionalism, has inhibited the formulation of coherent foreign and economic policies, it has, at the same time, provided them with an advantage. The shah's regime became particularly fragile and vulnerable to revolution when he broke down emotionally and became increasingly weak and indecisive. In prerevolutionary Iran, as in other neopatrimonial regimes that have undergone revolutions, the paramount leader alone served as the glue that bonded the system together. Consequently, as we have seen, the shah's tendency, when left to his own devices, toward equivocation and withdrawal when his rule was threatened and the situation called for swift, decisive, and unambiguous measures played an important part in costing him the peacock throne.

The collective leadership of the mullahs, however, if they continue to temper their factional differences in times of crisis and if their coercive apparatus continues to remain loyal, makes the survival of their regime less dependent upon the decisiveness of one or a few individuals. Indeed, given the existence of powerful and functioning institutions, much of the top leadership of the Islamic Republic can be decimated without seriously jeopardizing the system.

Moreover, unlike the shah, Iran's clerical rulers, in spite of their numerous other flaws, are not vulnerable to the charge of being beholden to foreign powers. The shah's rule was undermined in part because of his close association and perceived subservience to Western powers, particularly the United States. More significant, the shah's unwillingness to respond decisively to the mass mobilization against his rule was motivated, in some measure, by his obsession with projecting a favorable impression of himself to the foreign press. The shah's position was also compromised because of the confusion of policymakers in the Carter administration, who sent him contradictory signals on how to respond to Iran's revolutionary upheaval. The present regime, by contrast, has been unconcerned about the opinions of U.S. officials and journalists. Moreover, it has had absolutely no compunction about resorting to overwhelming force and even state-sponsored vigilantism when its survival has demanded that it should act energetically.

Thus, not only is the Islamic Republic structurally stronger than the monarchy, but up to now, it has also been endowed with far more decisive and politically adroit leadership. Given the frailties of the opposition and the divisions in the class structure, so long as this leadership continues to settle its factional differences, it will be able to retain power by effectively preventing the populace from mobilizing to overthrow it. As we have seen, however, since the election of Mohammad Khatami as Iran's president in 1997, intraregime rivalries within the theocracy have become increasingly pronounced and open. Such divisions, if they continue unabated, can lead to debilitating factional schisms, enhancing the likelihood of the regime tearing itself apart.

Will the cleavages dividing the ruling clerics give way to all-out confrontations? Up to now, most of the key decisionmakers have continued to downplay their differences in order to preserve the system. Both the reformers and conservatives have also continued to defer to the positions of Khamenei. Khamenei, meanwhile, as the final arbiter of power, has apparently realized that with the masses solidly behind Khatami's agenda (even if through default), he can no longer afford to bolster the position of conservatives alone. Nevertheless, he still appears unwilling to isolate or abandon the conservatives and the Hezbollahis, whom some regard as the backbone of the revolution. But while the key leaders have shown that they can still forge (albeit with much more difficulty than they used to) a modicum of consensus and common ground, their followers are now much more apt to engage in all-out, all-or-nothing attacks. The potential for the preservation and peaceful modification of the prevailing system, therefore, is now largely dependent upon whether key players will continue to seek consensus, whether they will continue to defer to Khamenei, whether Khamenei will adroitly exercise the art of political manipulation, and whether the faction leaders will lose control of their followers.

Providing straightforward answers to the above questions will go a long way toward clarifying the outcome of what was undoubtedly one of the world's most populist, voluntarist, and unexpected revolutions. Regrettably, however, such answers are beyond the reach of this, or perhaps any other, study, underscoring the central point that (despite the undeniably significant influence of objective structures and variables) we cannot discount the at times paramount impact of subjective factors. Predicting how exactly these forces will act and react to each other's (as well as to external) actions and reactions is not possible. Politics continues to be at least as much art as it is science, ensuring that precise forecasting will continue to elude us. The best we can hope for is to narrow the range of potential possibilities. It is appropriate, therefore, to conclude with the wise quotation from Alexis de Tocqueville that introduced this inquiry: "The human mind may succeed in tracing a wide circle, as it were, which includes the future; but within that circle chance rules, and eludes all our foresight. In every picture of the future there is a dim spot which the eye of understanding cannot penetrate" (de Tocqueville, quoted in Zetterbaum, 1967, pp. 9–10).

If this study has helped to clarify and diminish the size of the dim spot surrounding the prospects for revolutionary change in Iran, then my efforts have not been in vain.

References

Abdo, G. 1999a. "Tehran Hardliners Take Revenge." *Guardian*, August 5.

_____. 1999b. "From Revolution to Revelations: Iran Struggles for Reforms." *Middle East Reports* 29 (2) (Summer):7–9.

Abrahamian, E. 1980. "Structural Causes of the Iranian Revolution." *Middle East Research and Information Project (MERIP) Reports* 87 (May):21–26.

_____. 1982. *Iran Between Two Revolutions*. Princeton: Princeton University Press.

_____. 1989. *The Iranian Mojahedin*. New Haven: Yale University Press.

_____. 1993. *Khomeinism: Essays on the Islamic Republic*. Berkeley: University of California Press.

Adelkah, F. 1995. "A Boom in the Marketplace of Ideas." *Le Monde Diplomatique*, trans. *World Press Review* (April):15.

"Ag Minister Says Farming Is Failing All Over Iran." 1998. *Iran Times*, January 2.

"Aging Nationalists Blamed for Riots." 1999. *Iran Times*, July 23.

"AI: Iran Suppresses Clergy." 1997. *Iran Times*, June 6.

"Ailing Still." 1999. *Economist*, August 14.

Akhavi, S. 1980. *Religion and Politics in Contemporary Iran: Clergy-State Relations in the Pahlavi Period*. Albany: State University of New York Press.

Akins, J. 1998. "Seeing Iran Through Rose-Colored Glasses." *Los Angeles Times*, June 15.

Alam, A. 1991. *The Shah and I: The Confidential Diary of Iran's Royal Court*. London and New York: Tauris.

Albee, E., A. Ginsberg, and J. Irving. 1994. "Writer's Death in Iran Calls for an Inquiry." Letter to the editor. *New York Times*, December 4.

Amirahmadi, H. 1992. "Economic Costs of the War and the Reconstruction in Iran." In C. Bina and H. Zangeneh, eds., *Modern Capitalism and Islamic Ideology in Iran*. New York: St. Martin's Press.

_____. 1999. "Adopt a Longer-Term Perspective on Iran." In Amirahmadi Hooshang, ed., *Revisiting US-Iran Relations*. Princeton: American Iranian Council.

Amuzegar, J. 1991. *The Dynamics of the Iranian Revolution*. Albany: State University of New York Press.

_____. 1995. "Islamic Fundamentalism in Action: The Case of Iran." *Middle East Policy* 4 (1 and 2) (September):22–33.

_____. 1998. "Khatami's Iran: One Year Later." *Middle East Policy* 6 (2) (October):76–93.

"An Economy in Disarray." 1994. *Middle East* 29 (December):29.

"An Iranian Martin Luther Preaches Islamic Reforms." 1995. *Christian Science Monitor*, April 20.

Andoni, L. 1995. "Iran's Islamic Rule Under Fire by Revolutionaries." *Christian Science Monitor*, April 20.

"Ansar: Violence Good—and You Better Like It." 1996. *Iran Times*, July 12.

Appiah, K. Anthony. 1999. "Writing Dangerously in Iran." *New York Times,* January 9.

Arendt, H. 1979. *On Revolution.* New Haven: Yale University Press.

Arjomand, S. A. 1986. "Iran's Islamic Revolution in Comparative Perspective." *World Politics* 38 (3) (April):383–414.

_____. 1988. *The Turban for the Crown.* New York: Oxford University Press.

Ashraf, A. 1994. "Charisma, Theocracy, and Men of Power in Postrevolutionary Iran." In M. Weiner and A. Banuazizi, *The Politics of Social Transformation in Afghanistan, Iran, and Pakistan.* Syracuse, N.Y.: Syracuse University Press.

Aya, R. 1984. "Popular Intervention in Revolutionary Situations." In C. Bright and S. Harding, eds., *Statemaking and Social Movements: Essays in History and Theory.* Ann Arbor: University of Michigan Press.

Azneh, Y. 1994. "Qazvin Riots Raise Questions About Iran's Mullahs." *Reuters,* August 7.

"Backlash of Intolerance Stirring Fear in Iran." 1996. *New York Times,* September 20.

Bakhash, S. 1984. *The Reign of the Ayatollahs.* New York: Basic Books.

Bakhtiari, B., and W. S. Harrop. 1996. "Battle for Control in Iran." *Christian Science Monitor,* March 6.

Banuazizi, A. 1994. "Iran's Revolutionary Impasse: Political Factionalism and Societal Resistance. *Middle East Report* 24 (6) (November–December):2–8.

Barraclough, C. 1995. "Rise of the Technocrats Challenges the Powers of Iran's Muslim Clerics." *Christian Science Monitor,* December 8.

Bashiriyeh, H. 1984. *State and Revolution in Iran, 1962–1982.* New York: St. Martin's Press.

"Basij Chief Is Replaced." 1998. *Iran Times,* March 20.

Bayat (still need to add source). 1994.

BBC Summary of World Broadcasts. 1995. July 17.

Behdad, S. 1995. "The Post-Revolutionary Economic Crisis." In *Iran After the Revolution: Crisis of an Islamic State.* London: I. B. Tauris.

Berejikian, J. 1992). "Revolutionary Collective Action and the Agent-Structure Problem. *American Political Science Review* 86 (3) (September):647–657.

Bernard, C., and Z. Khalilzad. 1984. *The Government of God: Iran's Islamic Republic.* New York: Columbia University Press.

Bill, J. 1988. *The Eagle and the Lion: The Tragedy of American-Iranian Relations.* New Haven: Yale University Press.

Bloom, A. 1987. *The Closing of the American Mind.* New York: Simon and Schuster.

Boroujerdi, M. 1996. *Iranian Intellectuals and the West: The Tormented Triumph of Nativism.* Syracuse: Syracuse University Press.

Borkenau, F. 1937. "State and Revolution in the Paris Commune, the Russian Civil War, and the Spanish Civil War." *Sociological Review 29* (January):74–75.

"Brawl Breaks Up Khatami Campaign Speech in Mashad." 1997. *Iran Times,* April 25.

Brinton, C. 1965. *The Anatomy of Revolution.* New York: Vintage.

Brzezinski, Z. 1983. *Power and Principle: Memoirs of the National Security Adviser.* New York: Farrar, Straus, Giroux.

Burns, John F. 1999. "Cleric's Trial Becomes Flash Point of Iran's Political Fate." *New York Times,* October 31.

"Businessmen Pay Pittances for Tax." 1997. *Iran Times,* June 20.

"Call out for New College Purges." 1996. *Iran Times,* June 21.

Calvert, P. 1990. *Revolution and Counter-Revolution.* Minneapolis: University of Minnesota Press.

Carnegie, M. 1999. "Iran's Conservatives Tighten Control on Government." *Agence France Presse,* July 22.

"Carpet Bazaar Goes on Strike." 1996. *Iran Times,* August 2.

Chehabi, H. E. 1990. *Iranian Politics and Religious Modernism: The Liberation Movement of Iran Under the Shah and Khomeini.* Ithaca: Cornell University Press.

"Children of the Islamic Revolution: A Survey of Iran." 1997. *Economist,* January 18.

Chirot, D. 1992. "What Happened in Eastern Europe in 1989?" In J. N. Wasserstorm and E. J. Perry, eds., *Popular Protest and Political Culture in Modern China: Learning from 1989.* Boulder: Westview Press.

Chittendin, A. 1979. "Bankers Say Shah's Fortune Is Well Above a Billion. *New York Times,* January 10.

Chubin, S. 1994. *Iran's National Security Policy: Capabilities, Intentions, and Impact.* Washington, D.C.: The Carnegie Endowment for International Peace.

"CIA Says Iran 'Struggle' Underway." 1998. *Iran Times,* February 6.

"Clergy Calls for Purifying Westernized Professors." 1996. *Xinhua News Agency,* January 5.

"Clerics Brawl over Utility of Violence." 1999. *Iran Times,* September 10.

Colburn, F. D. 1994. *The Vogue of Revolution in Poor Countries.* Princeton: Princeton University Press.

"Cops Hustle Women Busting Dress Code." 1997. *Iran Times,* December 5.

Cordesman, A. H. 1994. *Iran and Iraq: The Threat from the Northern Gulf.* Boulder: Westview Press.

Cottam, R. 1990. "Inside Revolutionary Iran." In R. K. Ramazani, ed., *Iran's Revolution: The Search for Consensus.* Indianapolis: Indiana University Press.

"Country Report: Iran." 1995. *Economist Intelligence Unit,* 3d quarter.

"Country Report: Iran." 1996. *Economist Intelligence Unit,* 2d quarter.

"Coup Letter Is Repudiated by Pasdar Chief." 1999. *Iran Times,* July 30.

Dabashi, H. 1993. *Theology of Discontent: The Ideological Foundations of the Islamic Revolution in Iran.* New York: New York University Press.

Daniszewski, J. 1996a. "Iran's Elections Carry Big Implications." *Los Angeles Times,* March 7.

_____. 1996b. "Iranian Youths Frustrated by Religious Constraints." *Dallas Morning News,* March 31.

Davies, J. C. 1962. "Toward a Theory of Revolution." *American Sociological Review* 27 (1):5–19.

de Tocqueville, A. 1955. *The Old Regime and the French Revolution.* Translated by S. Gilbert. New York: Doubleday Anchor.

Dekmejian, R. H. 1987. "Charismatic Leadership in Messianic and Revolutionary Movements." In R. J. Antoun and M. E. Hegland, eds., *Religious Resurgence: Contemporary Cases in Islam, Christianity, and Judaism.* New York: Syracuse University Press.

_____. 1995. *Islam in Revolution: Fundamentalism in the Arab World.* 2d ed. New York: Syracuse University Press.

"Deputy Minister Quits over New Censorship." 1996. *Iran Times,* February 23.

Dickey, C. 1999. "Tehran's Intellectuals Won't Keep Quiet." *Newsweek,* February 22.

"Director of Iranian Paper Which Sparked Riots Says Closure 'Illegal.'" 1999. *Agence France Presse,* July 22.

Dix, R. H. 1984. "Why Revolutions Succeed and Fail." *Polity* 16:423–446.

Dogan, M., and D. Pelassy. 1990. *How to Compare Nations: Strategies in Comparative Politics.* Chatham, N.J.: Chatham House Publishers.

"Don't Count on Us, Ayatollah." 1994. *Economist*, August 27.

"Downsizing." 1996. *Iran Times*, June 28.

Dunn, J. 1972. *Modern Revolutions*. London: Cambridge University Press.

Earle, J. 1996. "Rafsanjani Aims to Revive the Economy." *Jane's Intelligence Review* 8 (6) (June).

Eckstein, H. 1972. "On the Etiology of Internal Wars." In I. K. Feierabend, R. Feierabend, and T. R. Gurr, eds., *Anger, Violence, and Politics: Theories and Research*. Englewood Cliffs, N.J.: Prentice Hall.

Eckstein, H. 1992. "The Idea of Political Development: From Dignity to Efficiency." In H. Eckstein, ed., *Regarding Politics: Essays on Political Theory, Stability, and Change*. Berkeley: University of California Press.

"Economist Says Iran Worst Place to Invest Any Money." 1999. *Iran Times*, April 23.

Ehsani, K. 1999a. "Municipal Matters: The Urbanization of Consciousness and Political Change in Tehran." *Middle East Report* 29 (3) (Fall):22–27.

_____. 1999b. "The Temptation of Democracy: A Conversation with Morad Saghafi." *Middle East Report* 29 (3) (Fall):47–51.

_____. 1994. "Tilt But Don't Spill: Iran's Development and Reconstruction Dilemma." *Middle East Report* 24 (6) (November–December):16–21.

Ehteshami, A. 1995. *After Khomeini*. London: Routledge.

Eisenstadt, S. N. 1978. *Revolution and the Transformation of Societies: A Comparative Study of Civilizations*. New York: Free Press.

_____. 1992. "The Breakdown of Communist Regimes and the Vicissitudes of Modernity." *Daedalus* 121 (2) (Spring):21–41.

"Embassy Rally Turns into Battle." 1997. *Iran Times*, November 7.

Enayat, H. 1983. "Iran: Khumayni's Concept of the Guardianship of the Jurisconsult." In J. P. Piscatoni, ed., *Islam in the Political Process*. New York: Cambridge University Press.

"Endorsements Matter." 1999. *Iran Times*, March 5.

Evans, K. 1996. "Youthful Urges Faze Mullahs." *Guardian*, March 6.

"Even Clerics Question Regime." 1996. *Iran Times*, December 13.

Fairbanks, S. C. 1997. "A New Era for Iran." *Middle East Policy* 5 (3) (September):51–57.

"Faith in Numbers." 1994. *Index on Censorship* 2 (2) (November–December):63–65.

Farhi, F. 1990. *States and Urban-Based Revolutions: Iran and Nicaragua*. Urbana: University of Illinois Press.

Faruqi, A. 1999. "Iran's Top Military Leaders Warn Khatami," *Associated Press*, July 20.

"Few Jobs for College Grads." 1996. *Iran Times*, April 26.

"Fire-Breathing Nouri Tells Court Where It Can Go." 1999. *Iran Times*, November 5.

"First Female Criminal Court Judge Named Since 1979." 1998. *Iran Times*, July 3.

"First Unauthorized Demonstration Backs Mayor." 1998. *Iran Times*, April 17.

Fischer, M.M.J. 1980. *Iran: From Religious Dispute to Revolution*. Cambridge: Harvard University Press.

Fisk, R. 1995. "Tehran Relaxes to the Sounds of Brahms and BBC; Iran Glimmers of Liberalism." *Independent*, May 28.

Foran, J. 1993. *Fragile Resistance: Social Transformation in Iran from 1500 to the Revolution*. Boulder: Westview Press.

_____. 1994a. "A Century of Revolution: Comparative, Historical, and Theoretical Perspectives on Social Movements in Iran." In *A Century of Revolution: Social Movements in Iran*. Minneapolis: University of Minnesota Press.

_____. 1994b. "Introduction on the Study of Social Movements in Iran." In *A Century of Revolution: Social Movements in Iran*. Minneapolis: University of Minnesota Press.

_____. 1994c. "The Iranian Revolution of 1977–79: A Challenge for Social Theory." In *A Century of Revolution: Social Movements in Iran*. Minneapolis: University of Minnesota Press.

_____. 1995. "State, Culture, and Society in Recent Works on Revolution." In N. Keddie, ed., *Debating Revolutions*. New York: New York University Press.

"Forouhar, Wife Stabbed to Death." 1998. *Iran Times,* November 27.

"Fury Mounts as Majles Nips Holiday." 1999. *Iran Times*, September 3.

Gage, N. 1978. "Iran: The Making of a Revolution." *New York Times Magazine,* December 17.

"General Rezai's Son Defects to the U.S." 1998. *Iran Times,* July 10.

Gerth, H. H., and C. W. Mills. 1981. *From Max Weber*. New York: Oxford University Press.

Ghazi, K. 1995. "From Friday Prayers to Video Nights." *New York Times*, February 18.

Ghoneishi, A., and D. Zahedi. 1997. "Prospects for Regime Change in Iran." *Middle East Policy* 5 (1) (January):85–101.

"God Rules, Not the People: Yazdi." 1999. *Iran Times*, April 16.

Goldstone, J. A. 1980. "Theories of Revolution: The Third Generation." *World Politics* 32 (2) (April):425–453.

_____. 1995a. "Analyzing Revolutions and Rebellions: A Reply to Critics." In N. R. Keddie, ed., *Debating Revolutions*. New York: New York University Press.

_____. 1995b. "Predicting Revolutions: Why We Could (and Should) Have Foreseen the Revolutions of 1989–1991 in the U.S.S.R. and Eastern Europe." In N. R. Keddie, ed., *Debating Revolutions*. New York: New York University Press.

Goldstone, J. A., ed. 1994. "Introduction: The Comparative and Historical Study of Revolutions." In *Revolutions*. Florida: Harcourt Brace.

Goldstone, J. A., T. R. Gurr, and F. Moshiri, eds. 1991. *Revolutions of the Late Twentieth Century*. Boulder: Westview Press.

Goodwin, J., and T. Skocpol. 1989. "Explaining Revolutions in the Contemporary Third World." *Politics and Society* 1 (4) (December):489–509.

"Gov't Must Obey Law for a Change." 1997. *Iran Times,* June 13.

Graham, R. 1978. *Iran: The Illusion of Power*. London: Croom Helm.

Green, J. D. 1982. *Revolution in Iran: The Politics of Counter-Mobilization*. New York: Praeger.

Greene, T. H. 1990. *Comparative Revolutionary Movements: Search for Theory and Justice*. Englewood Cliffs, N.J.: Prentice Hall.

Greenstein, F. I. 1971. "The Study of Personality and Politics: Overall Considerations." In F. I. Greenstein and M. Lerner, eds., *A Source Book for the Study of Personality and Politics*. Chicago: Markham Publishing.

Gurr, T. R. 1970. *Why Men Rebel*. Princeton: Princeton University Press.

Haeri, S. 1994. "A Fate Worse Than Saudi." *Index on Censorship* 23 (4–5) (September–October):49–51.

Haghayeghi, M. 1993. "Politics and Ideology in the Islamic Republic of Iran." *Middle Eastern Studies* 29 (1) (January):36–52.

Hagopian, M. N. 1975. *The Phenomenon of Revolution*. New York: Dodd, Mead.

"Half of Governors-Generals Dumped." 1997. *Iran Times*, October 24.

Halliday, F. 1979. *Iran: Dictatorship and Development*. Harmondsworth, N.Y.: Penguin.

_____. 1994. "An Elusive Normalization: Western Europe and the Iranian Revolution." *Middle East Journal* 48 (2) (Spring):309–326.

_____. 1998. "Mohammad and Mill: What Does Mohammad Khatami Think?" *New Republic* 219 (14) (October):30–35.

"Hashemi Is Going to Replace Yazdi." 1999. *Iran Times*, July 2.

Herbst, H. 1996. "Review of Tim. J. Tuckes, *Opposition in South Africa: The Leadership of Z. K. Matthews, Nelson Mandela and Stephen Biko* (CT: Praeger Publishers, 1995)." *Political Science Quarterly* 3 (1) (Spring):196–197.

"Hezbollahi Gang Goes on Rampage." 1997. *Iran Times*, November 21.

Hofstadter, R. 1963. *Anti-Intellectualism in American Life*. New York: Knopf.

"Home Construction Is Booming in Iran." 1996. *Iran Times*, May 17.

Hoodfar, H. 1994. "Devices and Desires: Population Policy and Gender Roles in the Islamic Republic." *Middle East Report* (September–October):11–17.

Hook, S. 1965. *The Hero in History: A Study in Limitation and Possibility*. Boston: Beacon Press.

Hourani, A. 1991. *A History of the Arab Peoples*. Cambridge: Harvard University Press.

Hunter, S. 1992. *Iran After Khomeini*. New York: Praeger.

_____. 1998. "Is Iranian Perestroika Possible Without Fundamental Change?" *Washington Quarterly* 21 (40) (Autumn):23–42.

Huntington, S. P. 1968. *Political Order in Changing Societies*. New Haven: Yale University Press.

Huyser, R. E. 1986. *Mission to Tehran*. New York: Harper and Row.

"Imports Continue Their Downward Spiral." 1996. *Iran Times* May 10.

"Inflation Fuels Discontent Against Iran's Government." 1994. *New York Times*, November 20.

"Insider's Perspective." 1997. *Iran Times*, June 6.

"Internet, Satellite TV Threaten Chastity." 1999. *Iran Times*, April 23.

"Iran's Holy Alliance." 1999. *Economist*, August 21.

"Iran's Pro-Reform Press Warns Crackdown Could Spark More Unrest." 1999. *Agence France Presse*, July 22.

"Iran's Richest Are Still Richer Than Most Rich." 1996. *Iran Times*, March 1.

"Iran's Whiff of Liberalism." 1998. *Economist*, May 9.

"Iran Comes Clean." 1999. *Economist*, January 9.

"Iran Has 266,000 Child Laborers." 1996. *Xinhua News Agency*, January 6.

"Iran Hurts Economy More Than U.S. Efforts." 1996. *Iran Times*, December 20.

"Iran Ignores Own Offer to Open Prisons to View." 1995. *Iran Times*, December 22.

"Iran More Statist Than Old Commies." 1997. *Iran Times*, December 5.

"Iran Quarterly Reports." 1997. *Future Alliances International* 1 (1) (November):24–25.

"Iran Ranked 9th Most Venal Government." 1997. *Iran Times*, November 7.

"Iran Seeks More Taxes from Bazaar Merchants." 1998. *Iran Times*, October 16.

"Iran Won't Let Sonoush Leave." 1997. *Iran Times*, July 18.

"Iran: Conservatives Seen Gaining Upper Hand, But for How Long?" 1999. *Mideast Mirror* 13 (135), July 16.

"Iran: Country Profile." 1996–1997. *Economist Intelligence Unit*.

"Iran: Country Report." 1995. 2d quarter. *Economist Intelligence Unit*.

"Iran: Reforming Win." 1999. *Economist*, March 6.

"Iran: Time Matures." 1999. *Economist*, May 15.

"Iranian Opposition Leaders Arrested over Riots." 1999. *Agence France Presse*, July 26.

"Iranian Press Least Free." 1996. *Iran Times*, May 10.

"Iranians Vote for Reforms." 1999. *Iran Times*, March 5.

"Is Clerical Court Over-Reaching?" 1999. *Iran Times*, March 12.

"Islam's Balancing Act." 1999. *Economist*, April 17.

Jehl, D. 1996. "Iran's Economic Plight Casts a Pall on Today's Vote." *New York Times*, March 8.

_____. 1997. "Critic in Iran May Face Treason Trial." *New York Times*, December 16.

_____. 1998. "Tehran Mayor Arrest Seen as Political Move by Hardliners." *New York Times*, April 8.

_____. 1999a. "Despite Police Dismissals, Iran Protest Is the Angriest Yet." *New York Times*, July 12.

_____. 1999b. "Uphill Job in Iran: Keeping '79 Fever Alive." *New York Times*, February 5.

Jenkins, J. C., and C. Perrow. 1977. "Insurgency of the Powerless: Farm Workers Movements (1946–1972)." *American Sociological Review* 42 (2) (April):249–268.

Johnson, C. 1966. *Revolutionary Change*. Boston: Little, Brown.

"Jury to Nuri: Guilty." 1999. *Iran Times*, November 19.

"Kadivar Is Sentenced to 18 Months." 1999. *Iran Times*, April 30.

"Kadivar Says He's Ready to Go Attack in Court." 1999. *Iran Times*, April 16.

"Kadivar Tried: Critic or Criminal." 1999. *Iran Times*, April 23.

Kamrava, M. 1990. *Revolution in Iran: The Roots of Turmoil*. London: Routledge.

"Karbaschi Behind Bars." 1999. *Iran Times*, May 14.

"Karbaschi Gets 5 Years Behind Bars." 1998. *Iran Times*, July 31.

"Karbaschi Jailed for Corruption." 1998. *Iran Times*, April 10.

Karimi-Hakak, A. 1994. "A Storyteller and His Times: Aliakbar Sa'idi-Sirjani of Iran." *World Literature Today* 64 (3), (Summer):516–522.

Karshenas, M., and M. H. Pesaran. 1995. "Economic Reform and the Reconstruction of the Iranian Economy." *Middle East Journal* 49 (1) (Winter):89–111.

Katouzian, H. 1981. *The Political Economy of Modern Iran: Despotism and Pseudo-Modernism*. London: Macmillan; New York: New York University Press.

Katzenell, J. 1999. "Iran Callers Flood Israeli Radio." *Associated Press*, July 14.

Kazemi, F. 1980. *Poverty and Revolution in Iran*. New York: New York University Press.

Keddie, N. 1981. *Roots of Revolution*. New Haven: Yale University Press.

Keddie, N., ed. 1995a. "Can Revolutions Be Predicted; Can Their Causes Be Understood?" In *Debating Revolutions*. New York: New York University Press.

_____. 1995b. Introduction to *Debating Revolutions*. New York: New York University Press.

_____. 1995c. "Response to Goldstone." In *Debating Revolutions*. New York: New York University Press.

Keddie, N. R. 1995d. *Iran and the Muslim World: Resistance and Revolution*. New York: New York University Press.

"Khamenehi Adores Prez and Full Cabinet." 1996. *Iran Times*, June 28.

"Khamenehi Gives Raf Brand New Job." 1997. *Iran Times*, March 18.

"Khamenehi: Halt Protests." 1997. *Iran Times*, December 5.

"Khamenehi: No Election for Him." 1998. *Iran Times*, February 13.

"Khamenehi: Yankees Can't Scare Iranians." 1997. *Iran Times*, February 7.

"Khatami's 12-Point Platform Long on Individual Rights." 1997. *Iran Times*, April 11.

"Khatami Gets Nod." 1997. *Iran Times*, January 31.

"Khatami Says It's Time to Get Rid of Street Toughs." 1999. *Iran Times*, August 6.

"Khatami Takes Daring Liberal Line in First Campaign Speech." 1977. *Iran Times*, February 7.

"Khatami: Chicken Cure for Ill Economy." 1997. *Iran Times*, November 28.

"Khatami: Economy Needs Urgent Care." 1997l. *Iran Times*, August 22.

Kian-Thiébaut, Azadeh. 1999. "Political and Social Transformations in Post-Islamist Iran." *Middle East Report* 29 (3) (Fall):12–16.

Kimmel, M. S. 1990. *Revolution: A Sociological Interpretation*. Philadelphia: Temple University Press.

Kirkpatrick, J. 1979. "Dictatorship and Double Standards." *Commentary* 68 (November):34–45.

Kurzman, C. 1992. *Structure and Agency in the Iranian Revolution of 1979*. Ph.D. diss., Department of Sociology, University of California, Berkeley.

_____. 1996. "Structural Opportunity and Perceived Opportunity in Social-Movement Theory: The Iranian Revolution of 1979." *American Sociological Review* 61 (February):153–170.

Laipson, E., G. Sick, and R. Cottam. 1995. "Symposium: U.S. Policy Toward Iran: From Containment to Relentless Pursuit?" *Middle East Policy* 4 (1 and 2) (September):1–21.

Lancaster, J. 1999. "Calm in Tehran Masks a Longing for Freedom." *Washington Post*, July 16.

Laqueur, W. 1994. *The Dream That Failed: Reflections on the Soviet Union*. New York: Oxford University Press.

"Lari Is Named to Command Police." 1998. *Iran Times*, August 7.

"Leader Says No to Proposal to Set Up Private Colleges." 1996. *Iran Times*, May 24.

"Letters on Karbaschi Case." 1998. *Iran Times*, April 24.

Lijphart, A. 1988. "The Comparative Method." In L. J. Cantoni and A. H. Ziegler Jr., eds., *Comparative Politics in the Post-Behavioral Era*. Boulder: Lynne Rienner Publishers.

Linchbach, M. 1989. "An Evaluation of 'Does Economic Inequality Breed Political Conflict' Studies." *World Politics* 41 (July):431–470.

Linz, J. 1975. "Totalitarian and Authoritarian Regimes." In F. I. Greenstein and N. W. Polsby, eds., *Handbook of Political Science, vol. 2: Macropolitical Theory*. Reading, Penna.: Addison-Wesley.

"Local Council's Power May Be Clipped." 1998. *Iran Times*, December 25.

Looney, R. E. 1981. *Economic Origins of the Iranian Revolution*. New York: Pergamon Press.

"Lost in the Bazaar." 1995. *Economist*, January 31.

MacFarquhar, N. 1996. "Backlash of Intolerance Stirring Fear in Iran." *New York Times*, September 20.

MacLeod, S. 1998. "Our Veils, Ourselves." *Time*, July 27.

Mahdavy, H. 1970. "The Patterns and Problems of Economic Development in Rentier States: The Case of Iran." In M. A. Cook, ed., *Studies in the Economic History of the Middle East*. New York: Oxford University Press.

"Majlis Hears Rug Merchants." 1997. *Iran Times*, January 21.

"Makhmalbaf Skips Gabbeh Opening." 1997. *Iran Times*, June 27.

Marlowe, L. 1995. "Revolutionary Disintegration: The New Embargo May Hurt, But the Greatest Danger to the Mullahs Is from Their Own People." *Time*, June 26.

"Maroufi, Golshiri Awarded Human Rights Watch Grants." 1997. *Iran Times*, July 11.

Marx, K. 1978. "The Eighteenth Brumaire of Louis Bonaparte." In R. C. Tucker, ed., *The Marx-Engels Reader*. New York: W. W. Norton.

"Mass Arrests of Clerics Reported." 1995. *Iran Times*, December 12.

"Mayor Freed at Request of Khamenehi." 1998. *Iran Times*, April 24.

"Mayor Goes First Class in Evin Cell." 1999. *Iran Times*, May 28.

McDaniel, T. 1991. *Autocracy, Modernization, and Revolution in Russia and Iran*. Princeton: Princeton University Press.

"Mending Fences." 1999. *Iran Times*, July 9.

Merat, Z. 1999a. "Pushing Back the Limits of the Possible: The Press in Iran." *Middle East Report* 29 (3) (Fall):32–35.

_____. 1999b. "The Conservatives Have Misjudged: A Conversation with Ahmad Bourghani." *Middle East Journal* 29 (3) (Fall):36–38.

Middle East Economic Digest. 1995. May 5.

Milani, M. 1985. *The Making of the Iranian Revolution*. Ph.D. diss., Department of Political Science, University of Southern California.

_____. 1992. "The Transformation of the Velayat-e-Faqih Institution: From Khomeini to Khamenei." *Moslem World* 82 (3–4) (July–October).

_____. 1994. *The Making of Iran's Islamic Revolution: From Monarchy to Islamic Republic*. 2d ed. Boulder: Westview Press.

Miller, J. 1996. *God Has Ninety-Nine Names*. New York: Simon and Schuster.

Moadel, M. 1993. *Class, Politics, and Ideology in the Iranian Revolution*. New York: Columbia University Press.

"Mojahedin Claim Major Actions in West Iran." 1998. *Iran Times*, January 2.

"Mojahedin Murder General." 1999. *Iran Times*, April 16.

"Mojahedin Says Iran Attacks Again." 1999. *Iran Times*, June 18.

"Mojahedin Slay Ex-Warden." 1998. *Iran Times*, August 28.

Moshiri, F. 1991. "Revolutionary Conflict Theory." In A. Goldstone, T. R. Gurr, and F. Moshiri, eds., *Revolutions of the Late Twentieth Century*. Boulder: Westview Press.

Mossavar-Rahmani, B. 1999. "Challenges Facing Iran's Oil Industry: The U.S. Factor." In H. Amirahmadi, ed., *Revisiting U.S.-Iran Relations*. Princeton: American Iranian Council.

"Most Prisoners Just Disappear." 1996. *Iran Times*, June 28.

Mottahedeh, R. P. 1998. "In Iran Power Is Broadly Defined." *New York Times*, January 9.

Mousavi, N. 1992. "The Obscure Limits of Freedom." *Index on Censorship* 21 (3):18.

Nafisi, A. 1999. "The Veiled Threat—The Iranian Theocracy's Fear of Females." *New Republic*, February 22.

Naraghi, E. 1994. *From Palace to Prison: Inside the Iranian Revolution*. Translated from the French by N. Mobasser. Chicago: Ivan R. Dee.

"Newsmen Vote for New, Free Unions." 1997. *Iran Times*, October 10.

Niknam, A. 1999. "The Islamization of Law in Iran: A Time of Disenchantment." *Middle East Report* 29 (3) (Fall):17–21.

"No Novel Published in Year." 1996. *Iran Times*, October 4.

"Now Villagers Are Found Using Forbidden TV Dish." 1995. *Iran Times*, December 22.

"Nuri Attacks Yazdi by Name for Misconduct in Office." 1998. *Iran Times*, March 13.

"Nuri Faces Majlis Confidence Vote." 1998. *Iran Times*, June 19.

"Nuri Rushed Off to 5 Years in Prison." 1999. *Iran Times*, December 3.

Pahlavi, M. R. 1988. *Answer to History*. New York: Stein and Day.

Palmer, R., and J. Colton. 1995. *A History of the Modern World*. New York: Alfred A. Knopf.

Parsa, M. 1989. *The Social Origins of the Iranian Revolution*. Brunswick, N.J.: Rutgers University Press.

Parsons, A. 1984. *The Pride and the Fall: Iran, 1974–1979*. London: Jonathan Cope.

"Pasdar Commander Is Furious over Press Leak of His Speech." 1998. *Iran Times*, May 8.

"PEN Says Writer Murdered." 1996. *Iran Times*, December 13.

Peterson, S. 1996. "Iran's Revolution Competes with Holy CNN." *Christian Science Monitor*, September 24.

_____. 1998. "Victory over U.S. Plays into Iran's Big Debate." *Christian Science Monitor*, June 23.

Pope, W. 1986. *Alexis de Tocqueville: His Social and Political Theory*. Beverly Hills, Calif.: Sage.

Popper, K. R. 1968. *The Logic of Scientific Discovery*. New York: Harper and Row.

"Poverty Still Causing Prostitution." 1995. *Iran Times*, October 27.

"Privatization Plan a Midget." 1998. *Iran Times*, January 30.

Przeworski, L. A. 1991. *Democracy and the Market: Political and Economic Reforms in Eastern Europe and Latin America*. New York: Cambridge University Press.

"Purge Has Eyes on Foreign Educated." 1996. *Iran Times*, June 28.

"Rafsanjani Heckled During Friday Sermons." 1998. *Iran Times*, April 24.

Ramazani, R. K. 1989. Editorial. "The Islamic Republic of Iran: The First Ten Years." *Middle East Journal* 43 (2) (Spring):165–167.

Rathmell, A. 1995. "Khamenei Strengthens His Grip." *Jane's Intelligence Review* 7 (9) (October 10).

"Reformists Score Points as Iran Marks Two Decades of Revolution." *Middle East Mirror* 13 (29), February 12.

"Regime Eases Currency Rules." 1996. *Iran Times*, June 21.

"Regime Seeks to Cow Reformers." 1997. *Iran Times*, November 28.

Rejai, M. 1977. *The Comparative Study of Revolutionary Strategy*. New York: McKay.

"Rezai Wanted Out 3 Years Ago." 1997. *Iran Times*, September 19.

"Rial Resumes Deadly Slide." 1999. *Iran Times*, June 4.

"Rival Factions Within Leadership Contest Iran Elections." 1996. *Agence France Presse*, March 5.

Roberts, M. J. 1996. *Khomeini's Incorporation of the Iranian Military*. Washington, D.C.: Institute for National Strategic Studies.

"Rohani Dies in Qom at 78." 1997. *Iran Times*, August 1.

Roosevelt, K. 1979. *Counter-Coup: The Struggle for Control of Iran*. New York: McGraw Hill.

Rouquié, A. 1987. *The Military and the State in Latin America*. Translated by P. E. Sigmund. Berkeley: University of California Press.

Roy, O. 1994. *The Failure of Political Islam*. Translated by C. Volk. Cambridge: Harvard University Press.

Rubin, B. 1987. *Modern Dictators*. New York: McGraw-Hill.

Russell, D.E.H. 1974. *Rebellion, Revolution, and Armed Force*. New York: Academic Press.

Rustow, D. W. 1970. "The Study of Leadership." In *Philosophers and Kings: Studies in Leadership*. New York: George Braziller.

Sacker, S. 1993. "Letter from Tehran." *New Statesman and Society* 6 (259), July 2.

Said, E. 1994. *Representations of the Intellectual*. New York: Pantheon Books.

Saikal, A. 1980. *The Rise and Fall of the Shah*. Princeton: Princeton University Press.

"'Saint Diana' Leaves Many Questions After 100 Days." 1997. *Iran Times*, November 14.

Sanger, D. E. 1995. "Fear, Inflation and Graft Feed Disillusion Among Iranians." *New York Times*, May 30.

Scalapino, R. 1989. *The Politics of Development: Perspectives on Twentieth-Century Asia*. Cambridge: Harvard University Press.

Sciolino, E. 1998a. "Mullah Who Charmed Iranians Cannot Change Status Quo." *New York Times*, February 1.

_____. 1998b. "Reform Is on Trial in Case of Tehran Mayor." *New York Times*, July 1.

_____. 1998c. "The Post Khomeini Generation." *New York Times*, November 1.

_____. 1999. "Iran Protests Spread to 18 Cities; Police Crack Down at University." *New York Times*, July 13.

Selbin, E. 1993. *Modern Latin American Revolutions*. Boulder: Westview Press.

"7,000 TU Students Protest Regime Control." 1995. *Iran Times*, October 27.

Sewell, W. H. 1994. "Ideologies and Social Revolutions: Reflections on the French Case." In T. Skocpol, ed., *Social Revolutions in the Modern World*. New York: Cambridge University Press.

"Shirazi Entourage Has Police Run-In." 1996. *Iran Times*, July 5.

Shirley, E. G. 1993. "Not Fanatics, and Not Friends." *Atlantic Monthly* (December):105–112.

_____. 1995. "Is Iran's Present Algeria's Future?" *Foreign Affairs* 74 (3) (May–June):36.

"Shrine Focus for Unity Pledges." 1997. *Iran Times*, June 13.

Siavoshi, S. 1995. "Regime Legitimacy and High School Text Books." In *Iran After the Revolution: Crisis of an Islamic State*. London: I. B. Tauris.

Sick, G. 1987. *All Fall Down: America's Tragic Encounter with Iran*. Harrisburg, Va.: Penguin Books.

"6,600 Poor Are Wed Massively." 1997. *Iran Times*, August 1.

Skinner, Q. 1992. "Machiavelli." *Great Political Thinkers*. New York: Oxford University Press.

Skocpol, T. 1979. *States and Social Revolutions*. Cambridge: Cambridge University Press.

_____. 1994a. "Cultural Idioms and Political Ideology in the Revolutionary Reconstruction of State Power: A Rejoinder to Sewell." In *Social Revolutions in the Modern World*. New York: Cambridge University Press.

_____. 1994b. "Explaining Social Revolutions: First and Further Thoughts." In *Social Revolutions in the Modern World*. New York: Cambridge University Press.

_____. 1994c. "Reflections on Recent Scholarship About Social Revolutions and How to Study Them." In *Social Revolutions in the Modern World*. New York: Cambridge University Press.

_____. 1994d. "Rentier State and Shi'a Islam in the Iranian Revolution." In *Social Revolutions in the Modern World*. New York: Cambridge University Press.

Skocpol, T., and M. Somers. 1980. "The Uses of Comparative History in Macrosocial Inquiry." *Comparative Studies in Society and History* 22 (2) (April):174–197.

Smelser, N. J. 1963. *Theory of Collective Behavior*. New York: Free Press of Glencoe.

Snyder, R. 1992. "Explaining Transitions from Neopatrimonial Dictatorships." *Comparative Politics* 24 (4) (July):379–397.

Soroush, A. 1993. *Fourbehtar Az Ideologi [More powerful than ideology]*. Tehran: Serat.

"Soroush Is Beaten After Lecturing." 1999. *Iran Times*, August 4.

"Soroush Talks 'Roots and Fruits.'" 1997. *Iran Times*, April 4.

"Soroush: Clerics Not God or Prophet; Can Be Criticized." 1997. *Iran Times*, December 26.

"Speeches Point Way to the Future." 1997. *Iran Times*, May 23.

"Stocks Down 6%, Rial Down 32% During 1998." 1999. *Iran Times*, January 15.

Sullivan, W. H. 1981. *Mission to Iran*. New York: W. W. Norton.

"Suppression Will Cause 'Explosion.'" 1998. *Iran Times*, May 1.

"Sweating Mayors Write Resignations." 1977. *Iran Times*, September 26.

"Taxing News." 1997. *Iran Times*, January 24.

Taylor, S. 1984. *Social Science and Revolutions*. London: Macmillan.

"Tehran May Become More Aggressive." 1996. *Iran Times*, March 1.

Teimourian, H. 1994. "Iran's 15 years of Islam." *World Today* (50) (40) (April):67–70.

_____. 1996. "Facing Up to Iran." *Jane's Intelligence Review* 8 (3) (March 15):126.

"The Connection: An Exclusive Look at How Iran Hunts Down Its Opponents Abroad." 1994. *Time*, March 21.

"The Islamic Republic of Iran Turns 20." 1999. *Mideast Mirror*, February 11.

"The Meaning of Freedom." 1999. *Economist*, July 31.

"Those Behind Cried Forward." 1998. *Economist*, May 30.

"3,232 Candidates Qualify to Run for Next Week's Parliamentary Elections in Iran." 1996. *Mideast Mirror*, February 29.

"Tied Economy, Tied President." 1994. *Economist*, July 16.

Tilly, C. 1978. *From Mobilization to Revolution*. Reading, Mass.: Addison-Wesley.

_____. 1992. "Review of Jack A. Goldstone, Tedd Robert Gurr, and Farrok Moshiri, eds., *Revolutions of the Late Twentieth Century* (Boulder: Westview Press, 1992) and Tim McDaniel, *Autocracy, Modernization, and Revolution in Russia and Iran* (Princeton: Princeton University Press, 1991)." *American Political Science Review* 86 (4):1084.

_____. 1993. *European Revolutions, 1492–1992*. Oxford: Blackwell Publishers.

_____. 1995. "The Bourgeois Gentilshommes of Revolutionary Theory." In N. Keddie, ed., *Debating Revolutions*. New York: New York University Press.

Torabi, B. 1995. "Iran Braces for Riots by the Poor a Week After Uprising." *Deutche Presse-Agentur*, April 11.

Trotsky, L. 1961. *The History of the Russian Revolution*. Translated by Max Eastman. New York: Monad Press.

Tucker, R. C. 1970. "The Theory of Charismatic Leadership." In D. A. Rustow, ed., *Philosophers and Kings: Studies in Leadership*. New York: George Braziller.

_____. 1980. *Politics as Leadership*. Columbia: University of Missouri Press.

"238 Hopefuls File for President." 1997. *Iran Times*, May 2.

"UN Again Raps Iran over Rights." 1998. *Iran Times*, November 27.

"UN Panel Knocks Iran Human Rights." 1995. *Iran Times*, December 22.

"UN Rights Report: Iran Needs to Learn Tolerance." 1998. *Iran Times*, October 30.

"UN Says Executions in Iran Now Are Doubling Annually." 1997. *Iran Times*, November 14.

"U.S. Sees No Human Rights Improvement." 1997. *Iran Times*, February 7.

"Wake Me at Five." 1996. *Iran Times*, November 29.

Waldman, P. 1994. "Anti-Iran Guerrillas Lose Disciples But Gain Friends." *Wall Street Journal*, October 4.

_____. 1995. "Iranian Revolution Takes Another Turn, But Where Is It Going?" *Wall Street Journal*, May 11.

Walt, S. M. 1992. "Revolution and War." *World Politics* 44 (3) (April):321–368.

Wasserstrom, J. N. 1995. "Bringing Culture Back In and Other Caveats." In N. Keddie, ed., *Debating Revolutions*. New York: New York University Press.

Wasserstrom, J. N., and E. J. Perry, eds. *Popular Protest and Political Culture in Modern China: Learning from 1989*. Boulder: Westview Press.

"Where Are They Now?" 1996. *Time*, June 10.

"Why Isn't Khamenei Doing More to Avert an Explosion in Iran?" 1999. *Mideast Mirror*, March 23.

Wickham-Crowley, T. P. 1991. *Exploring Revolution: Essays on Latin American Insurgency and Revolutionary Theory*. New York: M. E. Sharpe.

"World Bank Leader Says Iran Economy Precarious." 1995. *Iran Times*, October 27.

Wright, R. 1994. "Mullas Losing Grip in Iran." *Los Angeles Times*, December 13.

_____. 1995. "Silencing Ideas: The Crisis Within Iran's Theocracy." *Los Angeles Times*, December 31.

_____. 1996. "Dateline Tehran: A Revolution Implodes." *Foreign Policy* 103 (Summer):161–174.

_____. 1998. "Key Democrat Urges Strong Moves to Open Ties with Iran." *Los Angeles Times*, April 16.

"Writer's Body Found with Stab Wounds." 1997. *Iran Times*, April 11.

"Yazdi May Jail Reporter for Asking." 1998. *Iran Times*, March 6.

"Young Still Await Khatami Changes." 1998. *Iran Times*, January 30.

"Yunesi Pledges Crackdown on Street Toughs for 1st Time." 1999. *Los Angeles Times*, September 3.

Zabih, S. 1979. *Iran's Revolutionary Upheaval*. San Francisco: Alchemy Books.

Zahedi, D. 1997–1998. "What to Do About Iran?" *Harvard Middle Eastern and Islamic Review* 4 (1–2):108–121.

Zahedi, D., and A. Ghoneishi. 1996. "Iran's Security Concerns in the Persian Gulf." *Naval War College Review* 49 (3) (Summer):73–95.

Zetterbaum, M. 1967. *Tocqueville and the Problem of Democracy*. Stanford: Stanford University Press.

Zimmerman, E. 1983. *Political Violence, Crises, and Revolutions*. Cambridge: Schenkman Publishing.

Zonis, M. 1991. *Majestic Failure*. Chicago: University of Chicago Press.

_____. 1993. "Exaggerating Islam." Letter to the editor. *Foreign Affairs* (Spring):190–1.

Index